Library of Congress
Cataloging-in-Publication Data:

Star wars. English.
Star wars : the action figure archive/
edited by Stephen J. Sansweet with Josh Ling.

p. cm.

Originally published under the same title in Japanese
by Neko, Tokyo, Japan, 1997.

ISBN 0-8118-2279-6 (pbk.)

1. Star Wars figures.
2. Action figures (Toys)
I. Sansweet, Stephen J., 1945– .
II. Ling, Josh.
III. Star wars (Motion picture)
IV. Title.

NK4894.3.S73S7213 1999

791.43'75—dc21   98-26349
                        CIP

Printed in Hong Kong.

Text edited by Stephen J. Sansweet
        with Josh Ling
Original Japanese edition published
        by Neko Publishing Co., Ltd.
Written by Eimei Takeda and Seiji Takahashi
Original American edition by Chronicle Books
Coordinated by Lucy Autrey Wilson
Edited by Allan Kausch (Lucasfilm)
        and Sarah Malarkey (Chronicle Books)
Cover photography by John William Lund
Designed by Public, San Francisco

Distributed in Canada by Raincoast Books
8680 Cambie Street
Vancouver, British Columbia V6P 6M9

10 9 8 7 6 5 4 3

Chronicle Books
85 Second Street
San Francisco, California 94105

www.chroniclebooks.com

STAR WARS

THE ACTION FIGURE ARCHIVE

Edited by Stephen J. Sansweet

with Josh Ling

CHRONICLE BOOKS

SAN FRANCISCO

about this book

By the mid-1980s, *Star Wars* fandom was at an all-time low. The sale of *Star Wars* collectibles also had hit a slump, with very little new merchandise of any kind available. My good friend Eimei Takeda, whom I met in 1985, remembers going to toy and model shows in Japan and introducing himself as a *Star Wars* expert. He almost always got the same reaction. "*Star Wars*? My kids had *all* those toys." Or, "Remember the little figures? I had them all!" That instant nostalgia, while we didn't realize it then, would help lead to the phenomenal success of the *Star Wars Trilogy Special Edition* a dozen years later and the great anticipation for the long-awaited prequels. Because of the incredible merchandising success of the original *Star Wars* films in the late 1970s and early 1980s, many people associate the collectibles—especially the ubiquitous Kenner 3 ³/₄-inch action figures—with the films. In fact, Eimei and I, who started our friendship by trading the toys, are firmly convinced that kids playing with some of the quarter of a billion action figures that were produced over eight years are one of the reasons for the continued strength of the *Star Wars* phenomenon. In recent years, I've become more involved in collecting *Star Wars* memorabilia, started writing books about it, and even worked with some of the Lucasfilm licensees, and Eimei has, too. In fact, his personal business card reads "*Star Wars* Servant," since he was once a public servant (as a public high school teacher). A few years ago Eimei and fellow enthusiast and sculptor Seiji Takahashi compiled a magnificent volume, the *Star Wars Chronicles,* a deluxe photo book that takes readers through every aspect of the *Star Wars* universe, both on-screen and behind the scenes. In 1994, as they were working on that book, Seiji visited the Tokyo Toy Fair and saw early prototypes for a brand-new yet very familiar toy line. The rumors, he saw, were true. The hugely successful *Star Wars* action figure toy line from Kenner—now a unit of the giant Hasbro Inc.—was going to be revived with a new assortment of characters from the classic films, sculpted with a detail and accuracy that would bring the twenty-year-old toys into the 1990s.

In 1997, a Japanese publisher asked Eimei and Seiji to take the same approach as they did with the breakthrough *Star Wars Chronicles* and apply it to action figures and related toys from George Lucas' dazzling trilogy. Since the toys were modeled after the characters and vehicles found in the *Star Wars* films, they wanted to provide a book that could show the detail of the toys and how closely they were modeled after the actual film costumes and hardware.

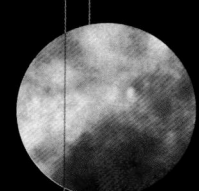

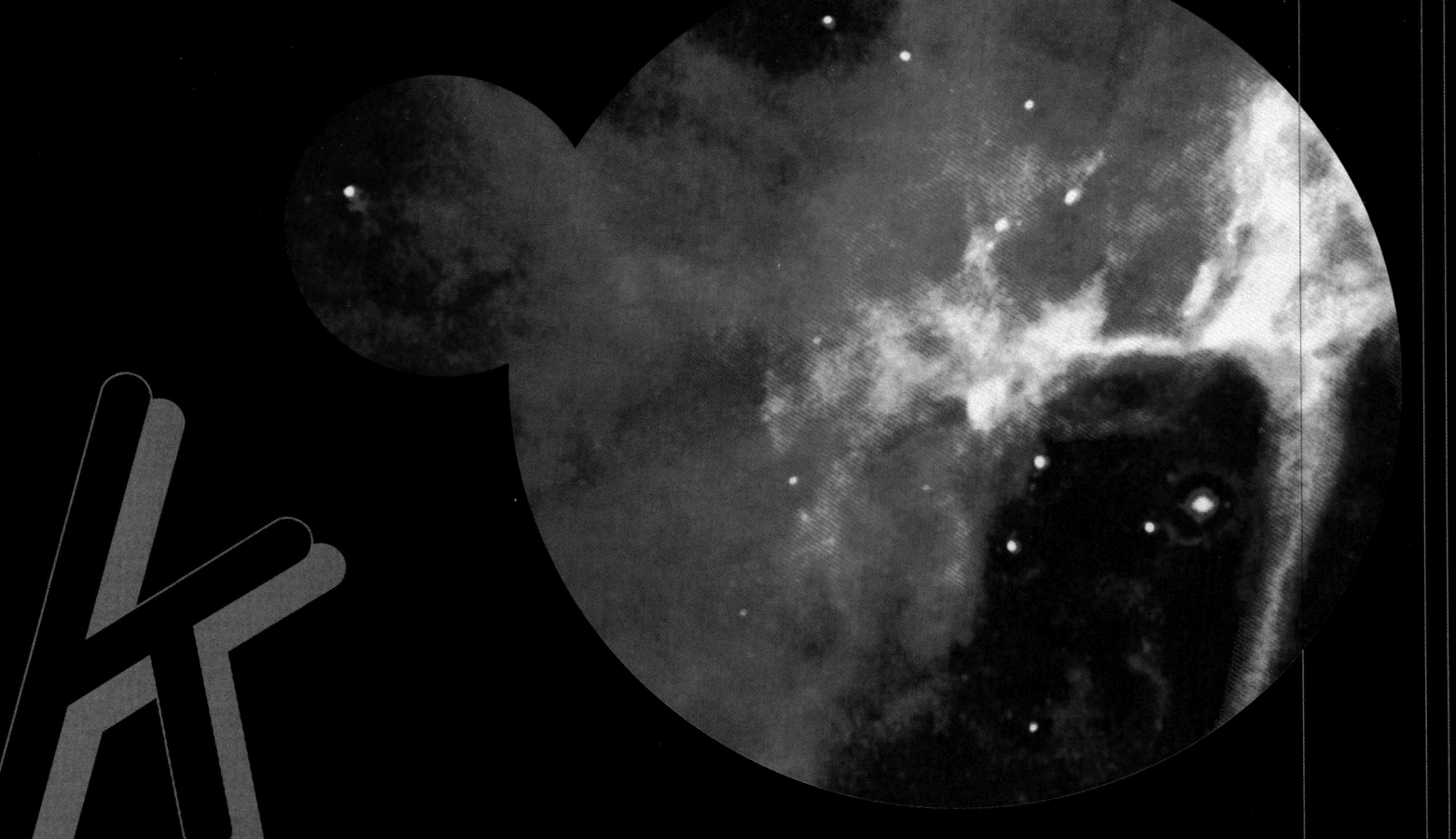

They also believed it was important to include the newly minted figures as well as the vintage ones. Many collectors of the new action figure line weren't around for the original theatrical release of the *Star Wars* trilogy, yet they are among the biggest fans, and they have started to take an interest in the vintage toys dating back some twenty years. Likewise, many of the fans who were collectors in the 1970s and 1980s are now returning to the hobby and buying the current toys. This book, then, is an attempt to satisfy fans both new and old.   I'll admit that I was initially dubious. In 1996, Eimei and Seiji made several field trips to my house in Los Angeles to do some initial photography and research, and I would find them in the morning fast asleep on the floor in one of the toy rooms, action figures and vehicles sprawled all over the place. Finally, Eimei and a representative from Neko Publishing had a chance to present their idea to Lucasfilm, and all systems were go. And quickly! Eimei and Seiji spent days poring through the outtake files at the Lucasfilm photo archive. Meanwhile four photographers, one in Los Angeles and three in Tokyo, began taking photos of the toys and their packaging.

With the help of some top U.S. collectors and my archival assistant, Josh Ling, the book quickly took shape. Because of prior business arrangements, Neko had scheduled the "mook"—a peculiarly Japanese cross between a magazine and a book—for publication in December 1997, giving the authors, photographers, designers, and printers just a few months to put together a very complicated project. Lucasfilm editor Allan Kausch, photo assistant Cara Evangelista, and I speeded up the process on this side of the Pacific. That the authors succeeded is evident in these pages, which Josh and I have adapted for English-speaking readers.   Chronicle Books, which published the American edition of Eimei and Seiji's first *Star Wars* book, expressed interest in what had come to be called *Star Wars: The Action Figure Archive.* After some initial delays with the English-language edition, we all decided that it was important to add a new section that would update the book with the latest Hasbro/Kenner creations. For that our thanks go to the great folks at the company, especially Linda Baker in Public Relations. At Chronicle, much appreciation to a great team: Sarah Malarkey, Julia Flagg, and Mikyla Bruder.

Feast your eyes, then, on a book with a double dose of wonderment: first, the unparalleled universe that George Lucas created, and second, the miniature version from the Kenner and Hasbro designers, engineers, and marketers, the one that let the world's children actually become part of that galaxy far, far away.

Stephen J. Sansweet

contents

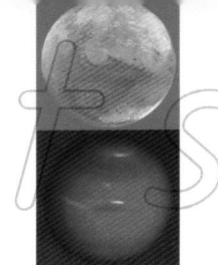

A *guide* TO THE GUIDE

Here are some tips to help readers understand how the information in this book is organized.

Character Name/Release Period
Character's name and when the figure was released.

Cards and Packages
Details on card or box packaging as well as variations. Major packaging changes in the current line take place each year to "freshen" the look.

Quick Reference
Describes character's role in the trilogy and special features of the figure.

Weapons and Accessories
Each weapon and accessory is shown, some with the actual film prop to compare details.

Photo from the Film

Icons
Identify on what cards the figures were packaged through December 1997.

ICON KEY

Red/Orange Card—
the first wave of new figures, through the end of 1996, called orange in text.

Green Card—
the 1997 figures.

Variation—
a major one—in figure, accessory, or card.

Last card number through December 1997
The first version of each card is numbered .00; that number is changed when there is a change to the card, ranging from a correction in spelling to photo substitution.

Foil stickers,
added to cards to celebrate the 20th Anniversary of *Star Wars*.

Photo card,
without the foil sticker applied. Photos were under all of the foil stickers except for the *Shadows of the Empire* segment.

Luke Skywalker

Luke Skywalker (Deluxe)

Luke Skywalker in Stormtrooper Disguise

Luke Skywalker in Stormtrooper Disguise (Death Star Escape)

Luke Skywalker in Ceremonial Outfit

Luke Skywalker in Hoth Gear

Luke Skywalker in X-wing Fighter Pilot Gear

Princess Leia Organa (Speeder Bike)

Han Solo

Han Solo (Deluxe)

Han Solo (with Jabba the Hutt)

Han Solo in Stormtrooper Disguise

Han Solo in Stormtrooper Disguise (Death Star Escape)

Han Solo in Hoth Gear

Bespin Han Solo

Luke Skywalker

Luke Skywalker (Imperial Stormtrooper Outfit)

Luke Skywalker X-wing Pilot

Luke Skywalker (Hoth Battle Gear)

Luke Skywalker (Bespin Fatigues)

Luke Skywalker (Jedi Knight)

Luke Skywalker (Battle Poncho)

Han Solo in Carbonite Chamber

Han Solo (Trench Coat)

Chewbacca

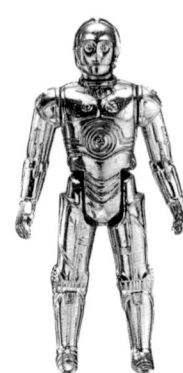
C-3PO

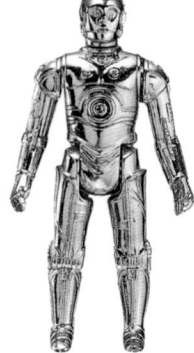
C-3PO with Removable Limbs

R2-D2

R2-D2 with Sensorscope

Luke Skywalker
in Dagobah
Fatigues

Luke Skywalker in
Imperial Guard
Disguise

Jedi Knight Luke
Skywalker

Luke Skywalker
(Speeder Bike)

Jedi Knight
Luke Skywalker
(Power F/X)

Princess Leia
Organa

Leia in
Boushh Disguise

Princess Leia
Organa as
Jabba's Prisoner

Han Solo
in Carbonite
Block

Han Solo
in Endor Gear

Chewbacca

Chewbacca
(Death Star Escape)

Chewbacca
in Bounty Hunter
Disguise

C-3PO (Japan)

C-3PO (USA)

R2-D2

Princess
Leia Organa

Princess Leia
(Hoth Outfit)

Princess Leia
(Bespin Gown)

Princess Leia
(Boushh Disguise)

Princess Leia
(Combat Poncho)

Han Solo

Han Solo
(Hoth Outfit)

Han Solo
(Bespin Outfit)

R2-D2 with
Pop-Up Lightsaber

Ben (Obi-Wan)
Kenobi

Yoda

Lando Calrissian

Lando Calrissian
(General Pilot)

Lando Calrissian
(Skiff Guard
Disguise)

General
Madine

R2-D2 (Power F/X)   Ben (Obi-Wan) Kenobi   Ben (Obi-Wan) Kenobi (Cantina Showdown)   Ben (Obi-Wan) Kenobi (Power F/X)   Spirit of Obi-Wan   Yoda   Lando Calrissian

2-1B Medic Droid   Darth Vader   Darth Vader (Power F/X)   Darth Vader (Vs. Xizor)   Emperor Palpatine   Emperor Palpatine (Power F/X)   Grand Moff Tarkin

Admiral Ackbar   Nien Nunb   Rebel Soldier (Hoth Battle Gear)   Rebel Commander   Rebel Commando   Prune Face

Imperial Dignitary   Emperor's Royal Guard   Imperial Commander   Death Squad Commander (Star Destroyer Commander)   AT-AT Commander   AT-ST Driver   Stormtrooper   Imperial Stormtrooper (Hoth Battle Gear)

Lando Calrissian as Skiff Guard

Admiral Ackbar

Nien Nunb

Wedge Antilles

Hoth Rebel Soldier

Hoth Rebel Soldier (Deluxe)

A-wing Pilot

Rebel Fleet Trooper

Emperor's Royal Guard

AT-AT Commander

Stormtrooper

Stormtrooper (Deluxe)

TIE Fighter Pilot

Death Star Gunner

Sandtrooper

Sandtrooper (with Dewback)

A-wing Pilot

B-wing Pilot

Anakin Skywalker

2-1B

FX-7 Medical Droid

Darth Vader

The Emperor

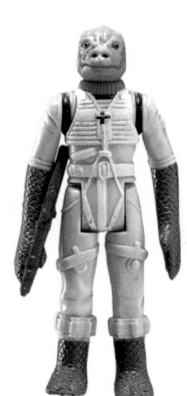

Imperial Gunner

AT-AT Driver

Imperial TIE Fighter Pilot

Biker Scout

Boba Fett

Bossk (Bounty Hunter)

IG-88 (Bounty Hunter)

4-LOM

Snowtrooper

Snowtrooper
(Deluxe)

Scout Trooper

AT-ST Driver

AT-AT Driver

Boba Fett

Boba Fett
(Vs. IG-88)

Jawa
(with Ronto)

Momaw Nadon
(Hammerhead)

Greedo

Ponda Baba

Ponda Baba
(Cantina Showdown)

Garindan
(Long Snoot)

Cantina Band
Member
with Bandfill

Zuckuss

Dengar

Jawa

Sand People
(Tusken Raider)

Hammerhead

Snaggletooth (Red)

Snaggletooth
(Blue)

Gamorrean Guard

Nikto

Klaatu (Skiff
Guard Outfit)

Rancor
Keeper

Barada

Amanaman

Boba Fett (Deluxe)

IG-88 (Vs. Boba Fett)

Bossk

Dengar

4-LOM

Tusken Raider

Jawas

Cantina Band Member with Ommni Box

Cantina Band Member with Fanfar

Cantina Band Member with Kloo Horn

Cantina Band Member with Fizzz

Saelt Marae (Yak Face)

Bib Fortuna

Weequay Skiff Guard

Greedo

Walrus Man

Ree-Yees

Weequay

Bib Fortuna

Squid Head

Klaatu

Yak Face

Sy Snootles

Max Rebo

Droopy McCool

Bespin Security Guard (White)

Bespin Security Guard (Black)

Ughnaught

HASBRO/KENNER FIGURES

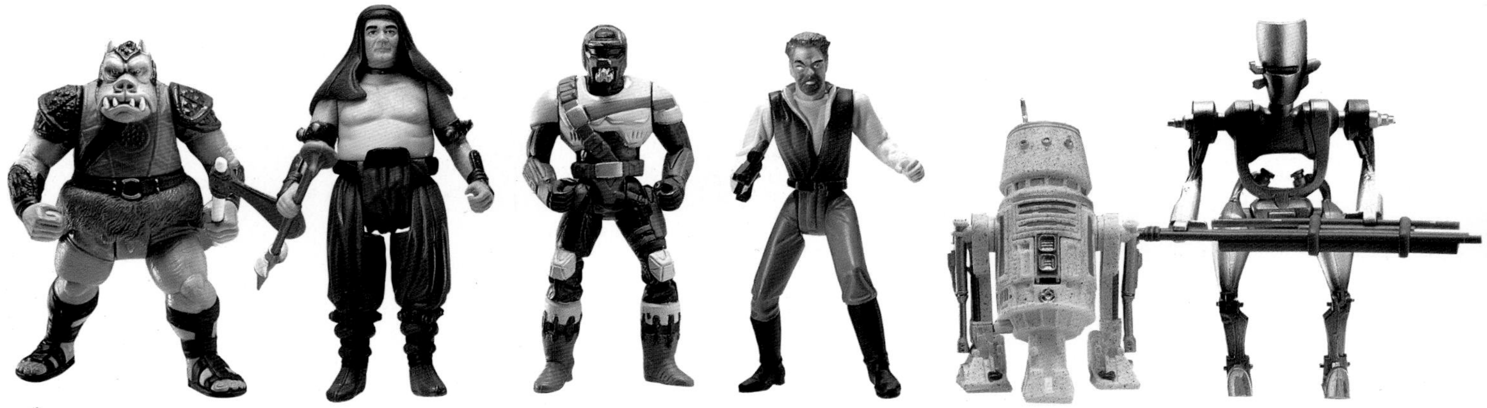

Gamorrean Guard

Malakili (Rancor Keeper)

Swoop Rider

Dr. Evazan

R5-D4

ASP-7

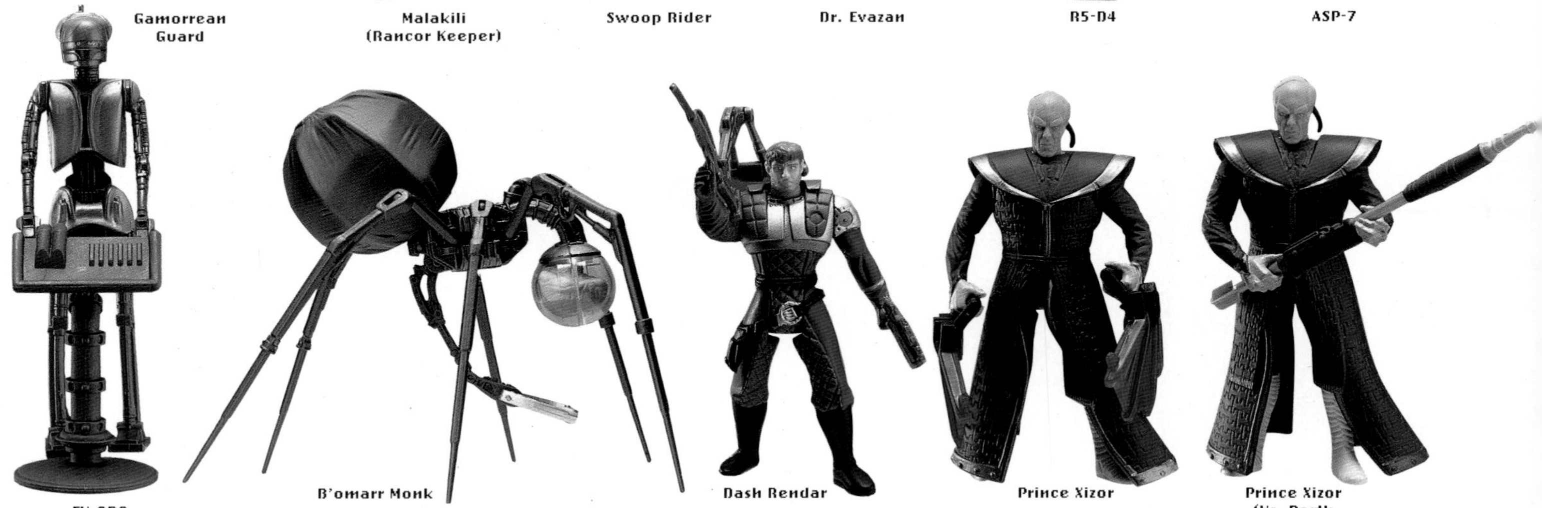

EV-9D9

B'omarr Monk

Dash Rendar

Prince Xizor

Prince Xizor (Vs. Darth Vader)

KENNER FIGURES

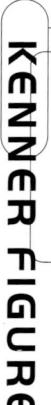

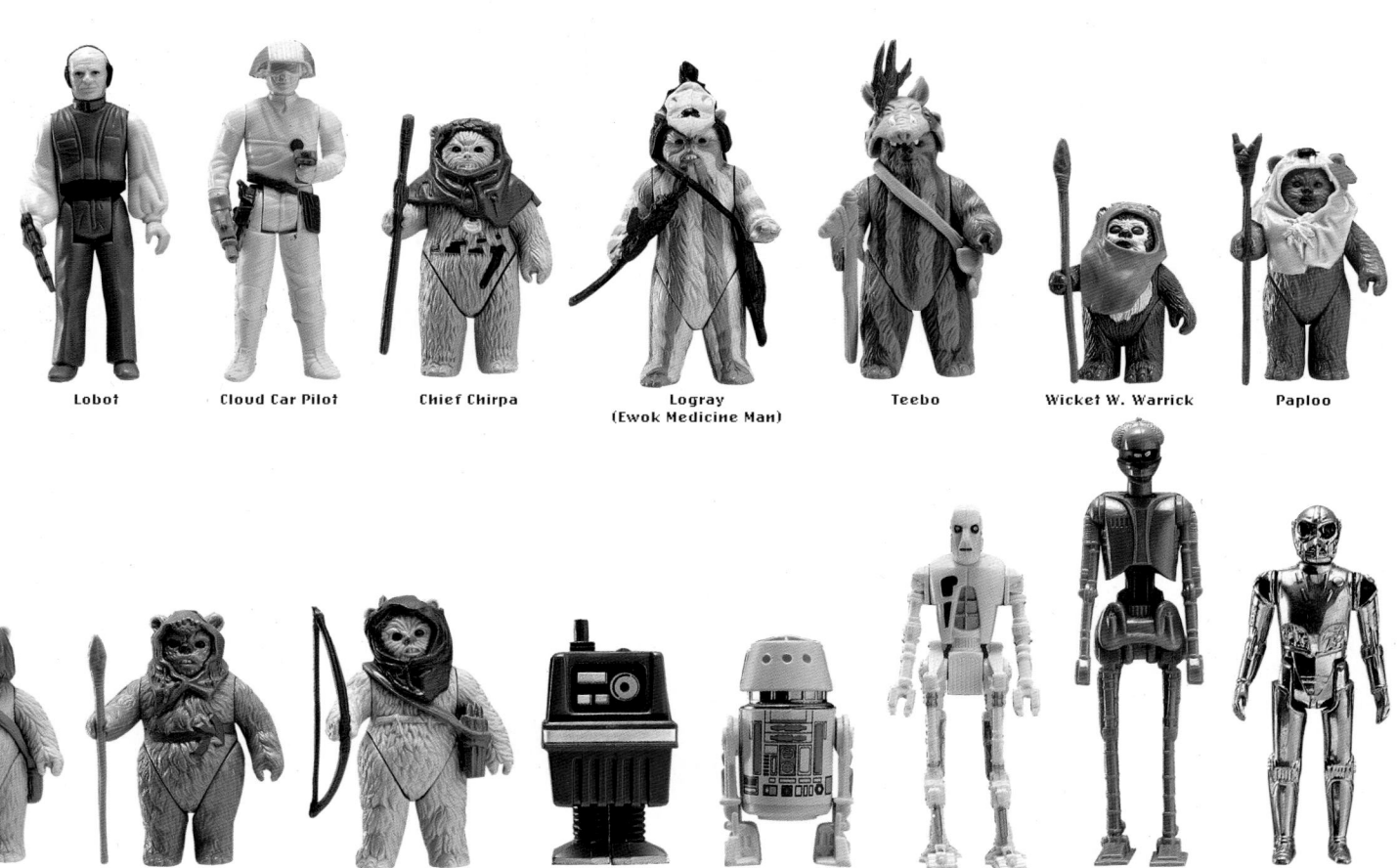

Lobot

Cloud Car Pilot

Chief Chirpa

Logray (Ewok Medicine Man)

Teebo

Wicket W. Warrick

Paploo

Lumat

Romba

Warok

Power Droid

R5-D4

8D8

EV-9D9

Death Star Droid

star wars

1995-97

Hasbro/Kenner Toys

The year 1995 marked the much-anticipated return of *Star Wars* action figures and related toys. It had been twelve years since the release of *Return of the Jedi*, and nothing new was announced about a theatrical rerelease of the trilogy, much less new films, but the *Star Wars* line became one of the hottest of the year. These weren't reissues of the old figures, as some had speculated, but rather all new designs with new packaging. Young children who had never seen the films on the big screen were buying the figures as eagerly as if the films had been playing at their neighborhood multiplex.

"Biggs is right. I'm never going to get out of here!"

LUKE SKYWALKER

Luke has always dreamed of leaving the desert wasteland of Tatooine. Living with his aunt and uncle, young Skywalker becomes the new owner of the droids C-3PO and R2-D2, who is carrying information that can strike a major blow at the Empire. The droids lead Luke to the Jedi Knight Obi-Wan Kenobi, even as an Imperial search team traces the droids to Luke's home. Luke returns to find his Aunt Beru and Uncle Owen have been killed, and with nothing left to hold him back, he decides to leave the planet and help Obi-Wan deliver the droids' vital information to the Rebellion.

Star Wars

This figure was released only on an orange card.

Star Wars

The new Luke Skywalker is sculpted with a much more muscular body—many said a bit too muscular—and painted with more detail than his 1978 release.

WEAPONS

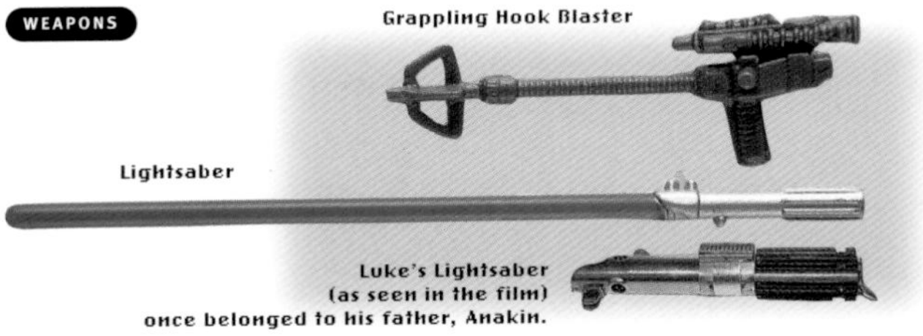

Grappling Hook Blaster

Lightsaber

Luke's Lightsaber (as seen in the film) once belonged to his father, Anakin.

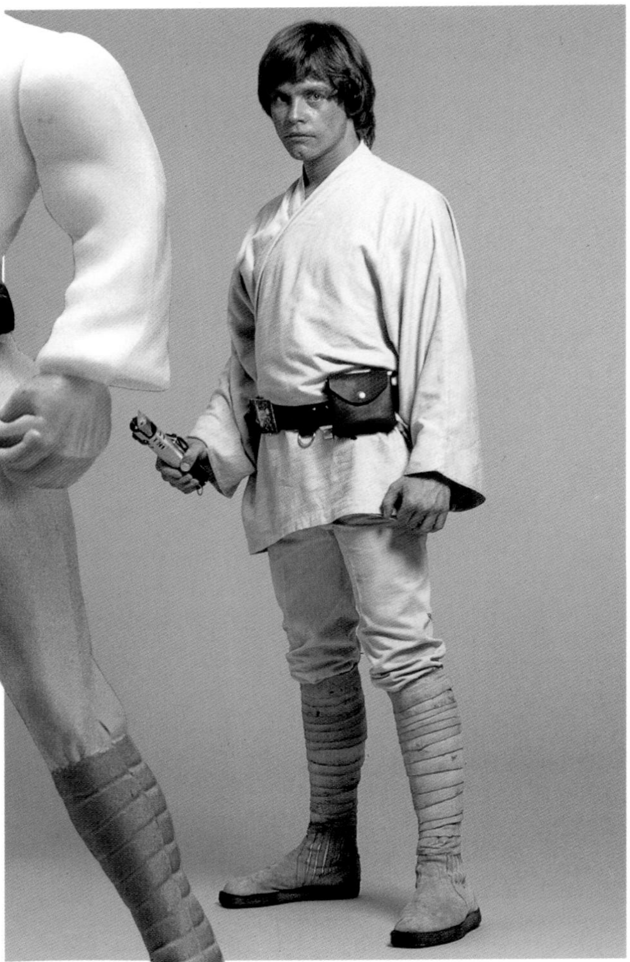

Lightsabers:
THE WEAPONS OF THE TRUE JEDI

"Your father's lightsaber.
This is the weapon of a Jedi Knight.
Not as clumsy or random as a blaster.
An elegant weapon from a more civilized day."
—Obi-Wan Kenobi

The concept of a "laser sword" was developed very early in the production process. Early paintings by concept artist Ralph McQuarrie show even stormtrooper-like characters wielding lightsabers, but as the script developed, they became weapons reserved for Jedi.

Immediately following the release of *Star Wars*, glowing sabers became an instant phenomenon in other films, children's cartoons, and toy manufacturing. There were several in the original Kenner line, and two nifty electronic lightsabers made by Hasbro/Kenner were released in 1996. The design was accurate and featured a glowing, extending blade and movie sound effects.

In 1995, with the initial release of the new Hasbro/Kenner *Star Wars* action figure line, figures of Ben, Luke, and Darth Vader came with realistic-looking lightsabers with transparent blades. The blades of the earliest lightsaber accessories were a bit too long and had a tendency to droop at the end. The length was shortened in subsequent assortments.

Star Wars

Star Wars

"She's fast enough for you, old man . . ."

HAN SOLO

Captain of the *Millennium Falcon*.

Star Wars

Han + SoloFlex = Han Solo. Solo on Steroids, as some wags called the figure, was as pumped up as the Luke Skywalker figure.

CARD VARIATIONS

ORANGE PHOTO CARD .oo.

GREEN CARD WITH FOIL STICKER .01.

GREEN CARD WITHOUT FOIL STICKER .01.

Star Wars

Luke and Ben arrive at the Mos Eisley cantina looking for the best star pilot to transport them and the droids safely to Alderaan. At a small table they meet Han Solo, who insists that his ship is the fastest in the galaxy. Luke is dubious, but Han's piloting skills are truly one of a kind.

Star Wars

The pants worn by Harrison Ford are actually blue jeans with embroidered red striping.

WEAPONS

Blaster Pistol

Han's pistol from the film

Heavy Assault Rifle

CHEWBACCA

Chewbacca is mighty, and he owes Han Solo his life, but he spooks much too easily.

Ben Kenobi first meets Chewbacca the Wookiee at the Mos Eisley cantina while looking for a charter to Alderaan. Chewie is the first mate on the freighter *Millennium Falcon,* and he is loyal to his captain, Han Solo.

Although Chewbacca is the tallest main character in the *Star Wars* saga, the action figure is about the same height as Darth Vader.

Star Wars

CARD VARIATIONS

ORANGE PHOTO CARD .oo.

GREEN CARD WITH STICKER .01.

Some of the early Chewbacca figures have his bandolier painted with a glossy finish.

Star Wars

WEAPONS

Bowcaster

Chewie's Bowcaster from the film

Heavy Blaster Rifle

DARTH VADER

"Join me.
We can end this destructive conflict
and bring order to the galaxy!"

Emissary of the Emperor, Lord Vader watches Tarkin's moves on the original Death Star. After the planet-sized weapon is destroyed, Vader becomes the supreme commander of the Imperial Navy. He employs the dark side of the Force to help both himself and the Empire, using it to choke the life out of his opponents if necessary.

WEAPONS   Lightsaber   Vader's Lightsaber from the film

A deleted scene from *Return of the Jedi*.

Star Wars

Star Wars

Like the original costumed actor, the action figure is dressed completely in black, although detail and realism are added by painting the armor pieces glossy while leaving the cape with a more matte finish. The new version of Darth Vader is also much more muscular than the original Kenner action figure.

CARD VARIATIONS

1 ORANGE CARD WITH LONG SABER .oo.
2 ORANGE CARD WITH SHORT SABER .oo.
3 GREEN CARD WITH FOIL STICKER .o1.
4 GREEN CARD WITHOUT FOIL STICKER .o2.

 .02

The Vader action figure originally included with the Darth Vader Vs. Prince Xizor two-pack was available individually on a green card with minor sculpting variations. The orange carded version has three saber/bubble combinations.

STORMTROOPER

Not afraid to die for the Empire.

Wearing white Imperial armor, the Empire's countless stormtroopers are spread throughout the galaxy to enforce the Emperor's control. The Rebellion is nothing more than "local trouble" to this Imperial force.

The mouth on the action figure helmet (left) shows it was modeled after the *Star Wars* prop (center) not *Jedi* (right).

Star Wars

CARD VARIATIONS

ORANGE CARD .oo.
ORANGE CARD WITH FOIL STICKER .oo.
GREEN CARD .o1.

Star Wars

The new action figure is sculpted in a more dynamic and action-oriented pose. This stormtrooper is ready for battle, not just standing at attention.

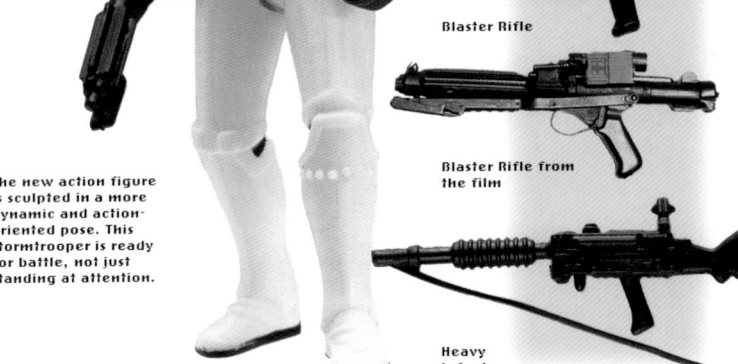
WEAPONS

Blaster Rifle

Blaster Rifle from the film

Heavy Infantry Cannon

The Empire Strikes Back

WAVE 1 · 7.95

R2-D2

Short-tempered but heroic, Artoo has helped the Rebel Alliance many times.

Programmed by Princess Leia with a special message for Obi-Wan Kenobi, the astromech droid R2-D2 escapes from the captured Blockade Runner and flees to the desert planet Tatooine.

CARD VARIATIONS

ORANGE CARD .00.

GREEN CARD WITH FOIL STICKER .01.

GREEN CARD WITHOUT FOIL STICKER .01.

R2 has a retractable third leg and a glowing red eye.

Star Wars

.01

WEAPONS

Lightsaber

Ben's Lightsaber from Star Wars

WAVE 1 · 7.95

BEN (OBI-WAN) KENOBI

"Oh, he's not dead . . . not yet. . . . He's me!"

Luke thinks old Ben Kenobi is a strange hermit who lives out in the Dune Sea. Little does he suspect that Ben is really a Jedi Knight who once trained Luke's father. Ben sacrifices himself so that the Rebellion can survive. Even though his body is gone, the spirit of Obi-Wan is still with Luke to guide him to the light side of the Force.

Star Wars

The old Kenner Obi-Wan action figure had a simple vinyl cape; the new Ben wears a sculpted soft plastic robe.

The Empire Strikes Back

CARD VARIATIONS

ORANGE CARD WITH LONG SABER .00.

ORANGE CARD WITH SHORT SABER .01.

GREEN CARD .02.

.02

With the change of the orange card from .00 to .01 came the change of the photo on the card back, .01 (top right) and .00 (bottom right).

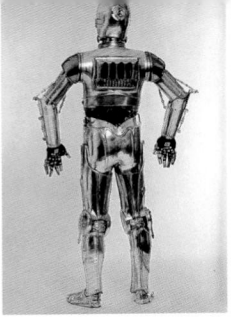

"We're doomed!"
C-3PO

Poor Threepio! He gets into lots of trouble, some because of his companion Artoo-Detoo. But C-3PO finally has his moment of glory on the throne of an Ewok village in *Return of the Jedi*. George Lucas first saw the character as a sort of used car dealer from Brooklyn. But he discovered that actor Anthony Daniels' portrayal inside the costume worked best with Daniels' own voice as sort of a fussy British butler.

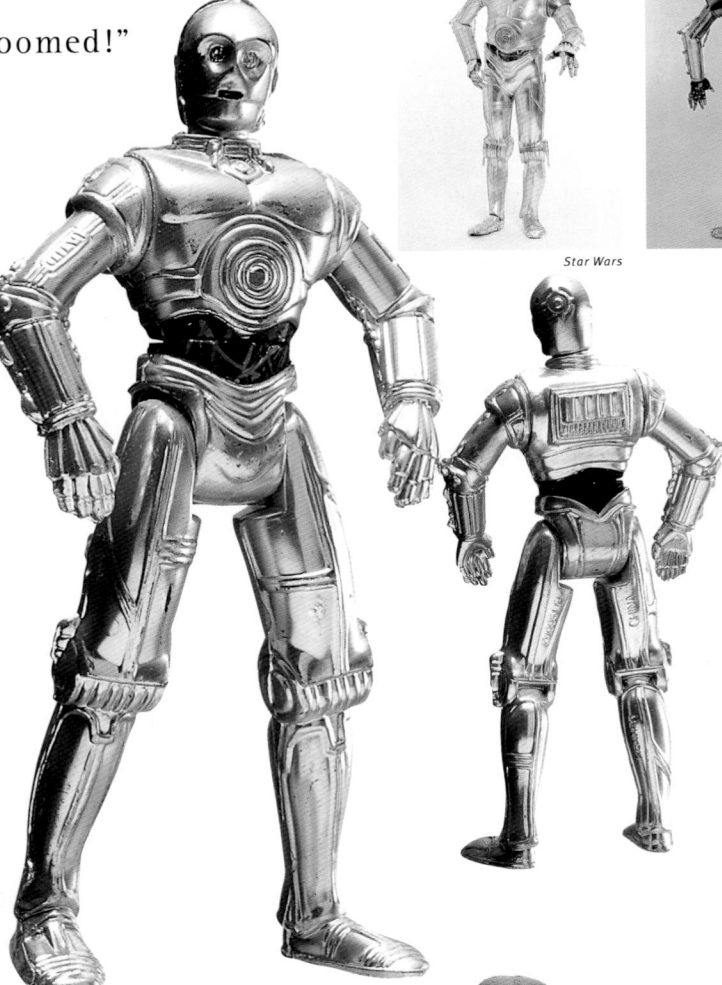

Star Wars

The U.S. version is vacuum-metalized in a "gold"-plated finish. In Japan, except for a small batch at the beginning of the run, C-3PO was first coated in a silver finish that was covered in a yellow glaze. This resulted in a greenish tint.

Star Wars

CARD VARIATIONS

1   ORANGE CARD (U.S.) .oo.
2   ORANGE CARD (JAPAN).
3   GREEN CARD WITHOUT FOIL STICKER .01.
4   GREEN CARD WITH FOIL STICKER .01.

PRINCESS LEIA ORGANA

The youngest ever elected to the Galactic Senate, Leia is also a leader of the Rebel Alliance. The young princess is captured while trying to deliver stolen Imperial plans to the Rebellion, but not before she sends an urgent plea for help to Obi-Wan Kenobi on the planet Tatooine.

WEAPONS   "Laser" Pistol

Assault Rifle

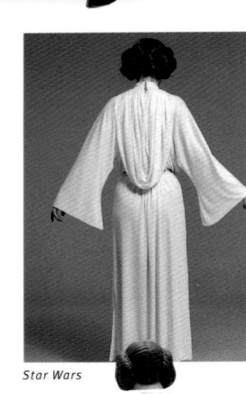

Star Wars

CARD VARIATIONS

ORANGE CARD .oo.

GREEN CARD WITH FOIL STICKER .01.

Star Wars

The first Leia was sculpted with a scowl on her face.

"Lando's not a system,
he's a man. Lando Calrissian."

LANDO CALRISSIAN

Friend or foe?

Han Solo's old buddy is the administrator of Cloud City on the gas giant Bespin. He's a gambler who lost the *Millennium Falcon* to Han in a game of sabacc. He is forced to betray his friend on Cloud City but later is instrumental in rescuing him from Jabba the Hutt. After becoming a general in the Rebellion, Lando helps to destroy the second Death Star at the helm of his old ship, the *Falcon*.

The Empire Strikes Back

LANDO CALRISSIAN
Heavy Rifle and Blaster Pistol!
AGES 4 & UP
WARNING

Lando's rifle is similar to a stormtrooper's but has a longer scope.

WEAPONS

Heavy Rifle

Blaster Pistol

A green-carded Lando Calrissian was available only in *Return of the Jedi* three-packs distributed at "warehouse" stores.

G Green Card .01

LUKE SKYWALKER

in X-wing Fighter Pilot Gear

"No, I'm not going to change my mind about this. We're going to the Dagobah system."

Hopping into his snowspeeder on the planet Hoth, Luke joins in the attack against the Imperial AT-AT walkers. He later flies to Dagobah to find the Jedi Master Yoda, mentor of Obi-Wan Kenobi. This version of Luke has the "bulked-up" look that characterized the launch of the new line. Hasbro quickly discovered, however, that fans wanted authenticity.

Luke Skywalker in X-wing Fighter Pilot Gear is dressed in the flight suit of the Rebel Rogue Squadron flight group. Luke wears this outfit during the battle of Hoth and while piloting his X-wing to Dagobah.

The Empire Strikes Back

WEAPONS

Lightsaber

Blaster Pistol

The Empire Strikes Back

CARD VARIATIONS

ON THE ORANGE CARD BOTH .00 AND .01 VERSIONS EXIST WITH THE LONG LIGHTSABER.

ORANGE CARD, SHORT LIGHTSABER WITH LONG LIGHTSABER TRAY.

ORANGE CARD, SHORT LIGHTSABER WITH SHORT LIGHTSABER TRAY.

GREEN CARD WITH FOIL STICKER .02.

As with Darth Vader, orange-carded versions can be found with short saber/short bubble, short saber/long bubble, or long saber/long bubble.

"Han, I can't make exceptions . . ."

BOBA FETT

The most fearsome bounty hunter in the galaxy hunts and finally captures the Corellian pirate Han Solo.

Jabba the Hutt threatens Han Solo, who owes Jabba a big debt. Han promises to "pay you back plus a little extra," but he doesn't deliver. So Jabba decides to hire a better bounty hunter than Greedo: the relentless Boba Fett, who rarely disappoints. There are many tales told of this Mandalorian armor-clad hunter, but no one knows where the truth ends and the legend begins.

The prototype.

Sawed-off Blaster Rifle

WEAPON

Return of the Jedi

The prototype.

CARD VARIATIONS

BOTH .00 AND .01 VARIATIONS ARE FOUND ON THE ORANGE CARD.

GREEN CARD WITH FOIL STICKER .02.

The first release had two half-circles on his hands. All later releases had full circles.

G | .02 | | S

Comparison of striped and full circle hand.

 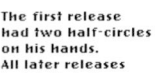

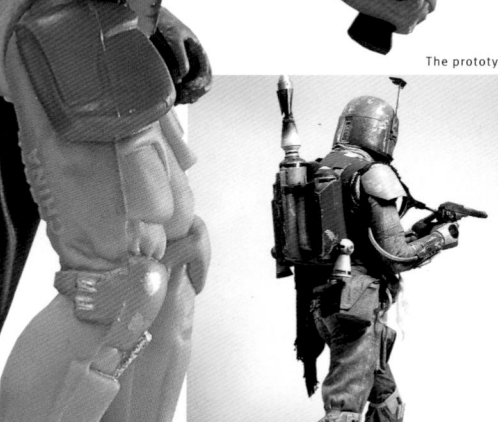

The prototype. The prototype.

Most photos of Boba Fett (such as those seen here) are of the prototype costume that was made around the time of the "Star Wars Holiday Special" (1978).

The prototype.

"Luminous beings are we, not this crude matter."

The Empire Strikes Back

The original Kenner Yoda is dressed in a cloth robe. The new Yoda has a more realistic look in plastic because of better sculpting and coloring.

The new Luke in Dagobah Fatigues is properly balanced and can stand only after Yoda is inserted into the backpack and hooked on. To fit the new Yoda, the backpack is slightly larger than the one in the film or with the original Kenner figure.

THIS VERSION WAS AVAILABLE ONLY FOR A SHORT TIME DURING THE INTRO-DUCTION OF THE GREEN CARDS—THE MORE COMMON ORANGE CARD DOES NOT HAVE A FOIL STICKER.

CARD VARIATIONS

ORANGE CARD WITH FOIL STICKER.

GREEN CARD WITHOUT FOIL STICKER.

WAVE 3 | **3.96**

YODA

ACCESSORY

Gimer Stick

Near the shore of the Dagobah swamp, Luke suddenly hears a voice from behind. The small green creature with pointed ears turns out to be Yoda, the Jedi Master whom the young Skywalker is searching for. For eight hundred years Yoda has trained Jedi. Now he reluctantly agrees to teach Luke—seemingly the last hope of the Rebel Alliance—the ways of the Force.

The Empire Strikes Back

WAVE 3 | **3.96**

LUKE SKYWALKER
in Dagobah Fatigues

While training in the ways of the Force, Luke feels the pain of his friends on Cloud City.

On the swamp planet Dagobah, Luke trains to become a Jedi Knight while carrying Yoda in his backpack. As Luke learns about the dark side of the Force, Yoda urges him not to take the path that Darth Vader followed.

The first release, long lightsaber/long bubble.

WEAPONS

Blaster Pistol

Luke's Lightsaber from *The Empire Strikes Back*

Lightsaber

This figure is the first in the new line that was not available in the original Kenner line.

CARD VARIATIONS

ORANGE CARD WITH SHORT SABER/LONG BUBBLE.

ORANGE CARD WITH SHORT SABER/SHORT BUBBLE.

Three different lightsaber packaging variations exist: short saber/short bubble, short saber/long bubble, and long saber/long bubble.

WAVE 3 · 3.96

"There isn't enough life on this ice cube to fill a space cruiser."

HAN SOLO
in Hoth Gear

Han Solo plans to leave the hidden Rebel base on the ice planet Hoth and make amends with Jabba the Hutt. Delayed by much-needed repairs to his *Millennium Falcon*, he learns that his comrade, Luke Skywalker, is lost and in terrible danger in the frigid night. Delaying his plans even further, Solo mounts a heroic search.

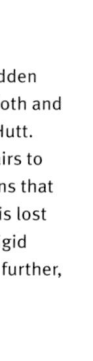

Blaster Pistol

Heavy Assault Rifle

WEAPONS

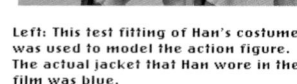

The Empire Strikes Back

CARD VARIATIONS

ORANGE CARD WITH OPEN HAND (1ST VERSION).

ORANGE CARD WITH CLOSED HAND (2ND VERSION). BOTH VERSIONS APPEAR ON THE .oo CARD.

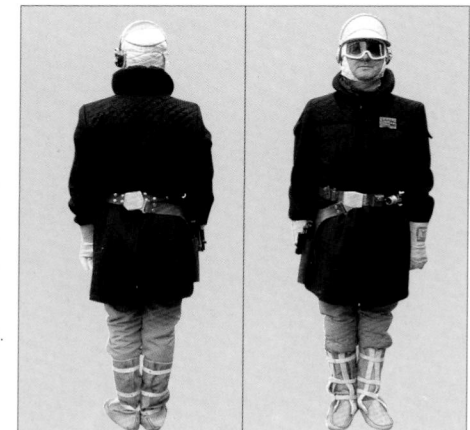
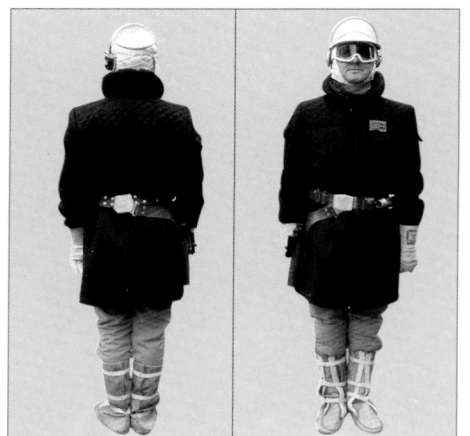

The Empire Strikes Back: Behind the Scenes

Left: This test fitting of Han's costume was used to model the action figure. The actual jacket that Han wore in the film was blue.

Above: Comparison of the closed and open hands. The first release had Han's right hand open, unable to hold a gun. Later releases had his hand closed.

WAVE 3 · 3.96

TIE FIGHTER PILOT

An elite corps that's eager to glorify the Empire, the TIE fighter pilots are fully trained and prepared for any combat, but their craft do not have life-support systems or hyper-drives, so just one mistake can mean death.

The chest apparatus is modeled after those seen in the second Death Star during the Emperor's arrival in *Return of the Jedi*, not the ones worn in *Star Wars*.

Return of the Jedi

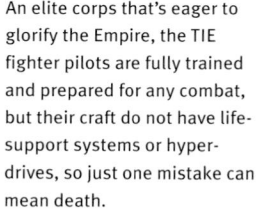

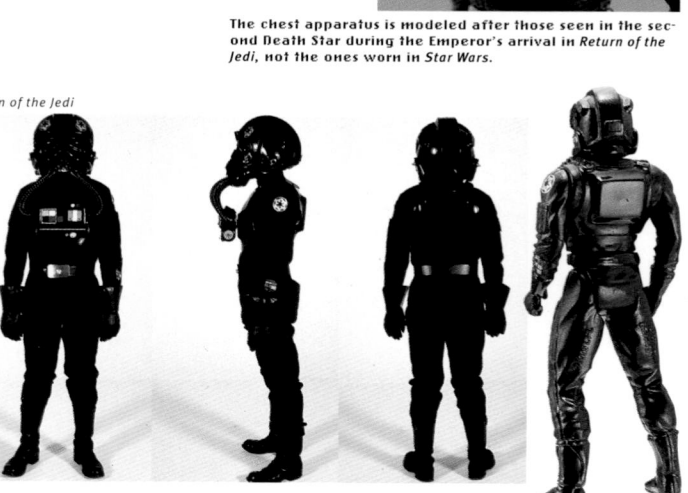

Imperial Blaster Pistol

Imperial Assault Rifle

WEAPONS

CARD VARIATIONS

1 ORANGE CARD WITH WARNING STICKER.
2 ORANGE CARD WITH WARNING.
3 GREEN CARD WITH FOIL STICKER .03.
4 GREEN CARD WITH FOIL STICKER .04.

The first release of the orange card included a warning sticker attached to the front. Later warnings were printed on the card.

"I do not want the Emperor's prize damaged. We will test this facility on Captain Solo."

HAN SOLO
in Carbonite Block

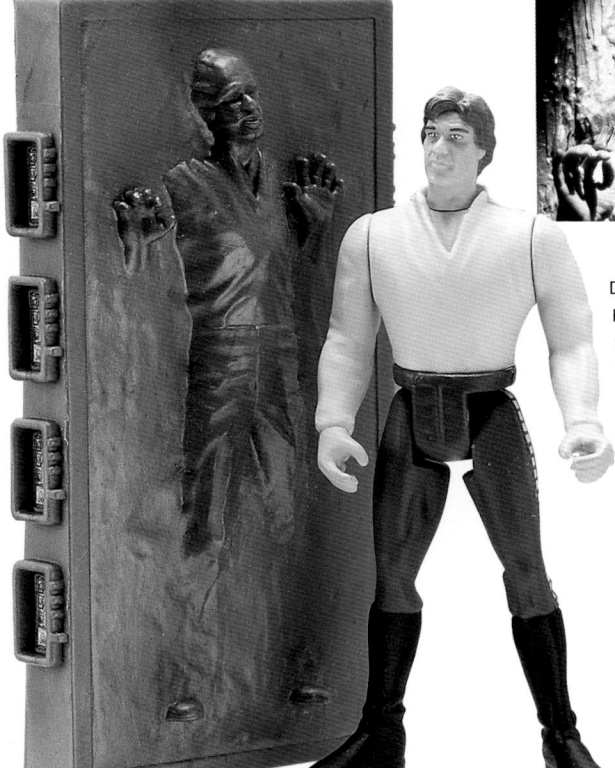

Comparisons of figure name variations.

Return of the Jedi

Darth Vader first freezes Han Solo as an experiment to ensure that the carbon-freezing process won't kill Luke Skywalker. Han spends nearly a year frozen in the block of carbonite.

The carbonite block from the original line was transparent, showing the figure within. The new block is opaque and has a clip on the back to secure the figure inside.

Right: Comparison of carbonite block with the block from the film.

ORANGE CARD WITH FIRST NAME (". . . WITH CARBONITE FREEZING CHAMBER") .oo.

ORANGE CARD WITH SECOND NAME ("IN CARBONITE BLOCK") .01.

Green carded version also available (not shown).

WEAPON

Heavy Assault Blaster

Han takes this gun from one of Jabba's skiff guards.

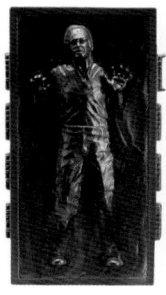
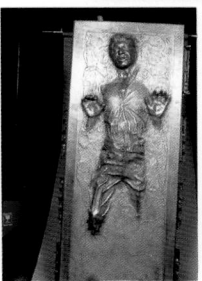

Return of the Jedi

Return of the Jedi

JEDI KNIGHT LUKE SKYWALKER

"I am Luke Skywalker, Jedi Knight and friend of Captain Solo."

Luke Skywalker tries to bluff his way with Jabba the Hutt, then he uses a Jedi mind trick to no avail. But Luke has another plan, and his allies are all in place to carry it out at precisely the right moment.

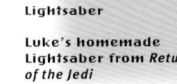

Lightsaber

Luke's homemade Lightsaber from *Return of the Jedi*

WEAPONS

Comparison of the variation in the vest colors. The tan vest (left) was released first and then quickly replaced with the version on the right.

ORANGE CARD WITH TAN VEST .oo.

ORANGE CARD WITH DARK VEST.

GREEN CARD WITHOUT FOIL STICKER.

For the release of *Return of the Jedi Special Edition*, U.S. theaters distributed a *Special Edition* Luke Jedi figure on opening night. The card has the *Special Edition* logo in place of the character photo.

Return of the Jedi

6.96 PRINCE XIZOR

Crime lord of the Black Sun organization and master of the ancient art of teräs käsi, Prince Xizor attempts to overthrow Darth Vader by planning the kidnapping and murder of Luke Skywalker. If he succeeds, he will be number two to the Emperor—and maybe even take his place.

WEAPON

Energy Blade Shields

6.96 LUKE SKYWALKER
in Imperial Guard Disguise

Disguised as an Imperial Guard, Luke sneaks into Xizor's palace on Coruscant in an attempt to free the captive Princess Leia and Chewbacca.

WEAPON

Tazer Staff

6.96 CHEWBACCA
in Bounty Hunter Disguise

Chewbacca disguises himself as the bounty hunter Snoova in order to gain entrance to Xizor's palace.

WEAPONS

Heavy Blaster Rifle

Vibro-Ax

6.96 DASH RENDAR

Once a Rebel snowspeeder pilot, Dash is personally hired by Leia to keep an eye on Luke.

Heavy Weapons Pack

WEAPONS

Blaster

series

6.96 LEIA
in Boushh Disguise

Return of the Jedi

Disguised as the Ubese
bounty hunter Boushh, Leia
enters Jabba's palace with the
"captured" Chewbacca. Leia
succeeds in thawing Han Solo
from the carbonite but Jabba is
not fooled and puts both Leia
and Han in chains.

The first Princess Leia action figure
from the new line seemed to be in
constant short supply and received
some criticism for its stern look. The
release of Leia as Boushh was meant
to satisfy any disappointed collectors.

Thermal Detonator

Return of the Jedi   *Return of the Jedi*

Jabba reaches out to sample a potential future meal.

Return of the Jedi

Return of the Jedi

WEAPON

Blaster Rifle

BOBA FETT VS. IG-88

Deluxe Two-Pack

With the release of the updated .01 card came the addition of "Vehicle of Choice" on the rear of the card. Another noticeable variation is the change in the size of the inner card nameplate found at the bottom of the bubble.

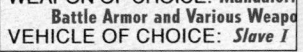

| AFFILIATION: Freelance WEAPON OF CHOICE: Mandalorian Battle Armor and Various Weapons _Slave 1_ | WEAPON OF CHOICE: Mandalori Battle Armor and Various Weapo VEHICLE OF CHOICE: _Slave 1_ |

The Empire Strikes Back

REGULAR FIGURE (LEFT) AND TWO-PACK VERSION (RIGHT)

The Empire Strikes Back

Boba Fett

Responding to Darth Vader's call, six bounty hunters assemble on the bridge of the Star Destroyer _Executor_. The most notorious is Boba Fett, wearing the armor of the old Mandalorian warriors who were defeated by the Jedi Knights. Fett tracks the _Millennium Falcon_ and collects two bounties on Han Solo.

The Empire Strikes Back

WEAPON

Sawed-off Blaster Rifle

The Empire Strikes Back

Too colorful? Or not flashy enough?

The paint job on the Boba Fett action figure in the Hasbro/Kenner two-figure set with IG-88 is based on the movie *The Empire Strikes Back*. The well-known color scheme of green, red, and blue was of the "prototype" Fett that was widely seen on television in the 1978 "Star Wars Holiday Special." In preproduction on *The Empire Strikes Back*, a more standardized Imperial soldier look was considered.

Artist Ralph McQuarrie and designer Joe Johnston initially depicted Fett as similar to a stormtrooper, in a white and black uniform. This photo shows an early Boba Fett mask beside the finished stormtrooper mask, suggesting that the Fett mask was also considered finished. This mask is white, while the actual Fett in *The Empire Strikes Back* was gray and green, with some reddish-brown accents. The less flashy *Empire* version wasn't as familiar to the public, since both large and small action figures were based on the color of the prototype and had been made before the actual movie. In *Return of the Jedi*, Boba Fett looked the same as he had in *Empire*. The new Hasbro line has a more authentic look for the figures, and the less flashy but more realistic paint job was chosen for both the large and the small action figure in the IG-88 two-pack.

The Empire Strikes Back

The prototype.

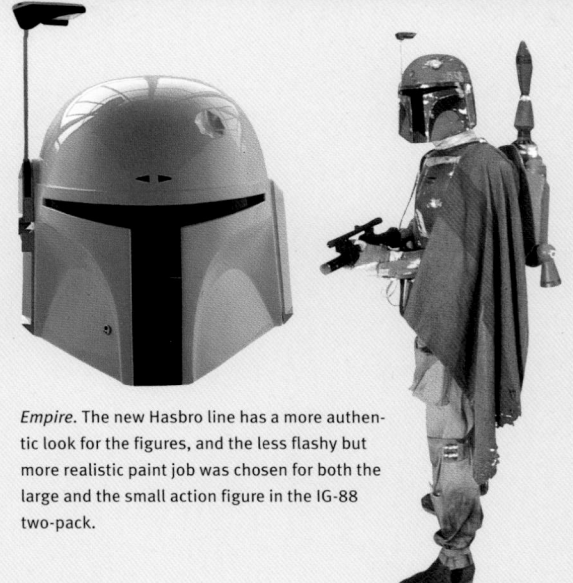

The Empire Strikes Back

IG-88

IG-88 is an experimental droid that escaped from a high-tech lab and became a bounty hunter. After being dismissed by Vader and leaving the *Executor*, IG-88 awaits the arrival of Boba Fett in deep space. He plans to steal the carbonite block containing Han Solo and collect Boba Fett's reward from Jabba the Hutt.

The Empire Strikes Back

The Empire Strikes Back

The Empire Strikes Back

The sculpting for the new IG-88 is similar to the original Kenner IG-88 first released in 1980. The new figure is more detailed and has a rotatable hip.

WEAPONS

Blaster Rifle

Blaster Rifle

PRINCE XIZOR VS. DARTH VADER
Deluxe Two-Pack

As can been seen above, the poses of the figures in this two-pack (second and last, above) are slightly different from the individually carded versions.

Force Pike

Lightsaber

As with the Boba Fett Vs. IG-88 two-pack, the Xizor Vs. Vader two-pack has two different sizes for the inner cardboard name tag.

WEAPON

Even though Prince Xizor and Darth Vader are packed together in a duel, they never confront each other directly in any other *Shadows of the Empire* media.

WEAPON

THE LIMITED ORANGE CARDS

These eight action figures were initially released for a short time on orange cards. Within weeks they were replaced by green cards with the new foil sticker design.

FOREIGN RELEASES

EUROPEAN MULTILINGUAL ORANGE CARDS

Figures released in Europe also have variations in the length of the lightsabers. Some figures could also be found with THX promotional brochures for the 1995/1996 *Star Wars Trilogy* video release.

CANADIAN BILINGUAL ORANGE CARDS

Some Canadian figures now come on three-language cards (English, French, and Spanish). Earlier Canadian releases were printed only in English and French and the top left of the card front wasn't die cut around the art of Vader's helmet.

Star Wars

SANDTROOPER

"All right, men,
load your weapons!
Stop that ship! Blast 'em!"

Even on desolate desert planets in the far corners of the galaxy, stormtroopers can be seen going about their duties, particularly in cities such as Mos Eisley.

Star Wars

Star Wars Special Edition

Star Wars Special Edition

Heavy Blaster Rifle

WEAPON

Equipped with rifle and backpack, each sandtrooper is uniquely weathered.

CARD VARIATIONS

1 ORANGE CARD .oo (NOTICE NAME: TATOOINE STORMTROOPER AND DIFFERENT WEAPON NAME).
2 GREEN CARD WITHOUT FOIL STICKER .01.
3 GREEN CARD WITH FOIL STICKER .01.
4 GREEN CARD WITH FOIL STICKER .02.

"Star Wars Holiday Special"

GREEDO

Greedo speaks Huttese to Han in the cantina:

"Chespoko toota kleesta ein honya ohska!"

("I've been looking forward to this for a long time!")

Poorly trained, a bad shot, and not very smart, Greedo pays for his deficiencies at the hands of Han Solo.

CARD VARIATIONS

ORANGE CARD .00. NOTICE THE NAME OF THE WEAPON HAS BEEN CHANGED.

GREEN CARD WITH FOIL STICKER .01.

GREEN CARD WITHOUT FOIL STICKER .01.

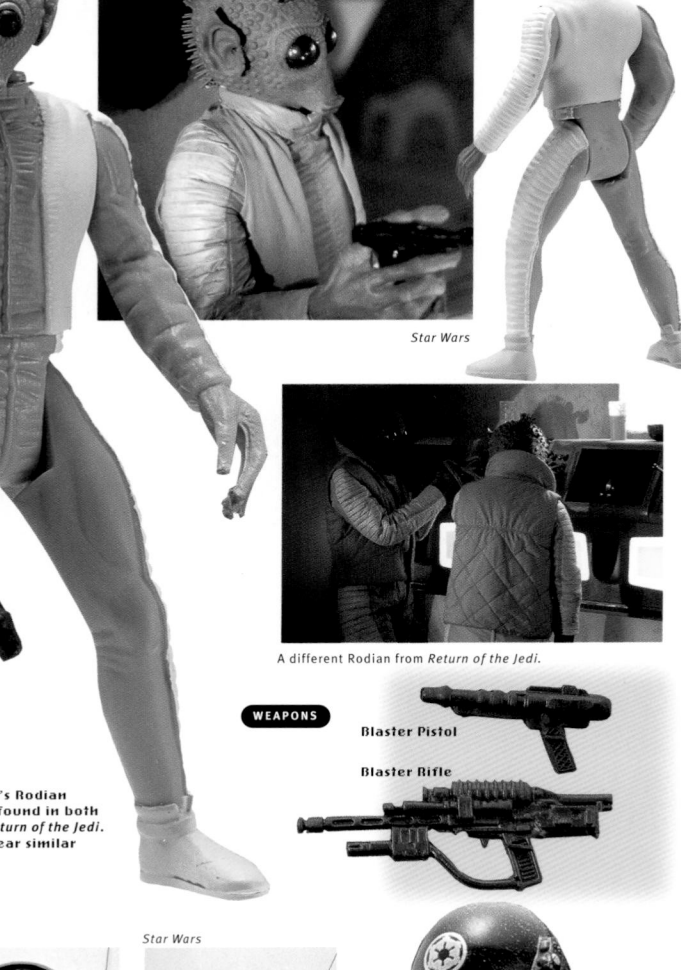

Star Wars

A different Rodian from Return of the Jedi.

Many of Greedo's Rodian species can be found in both *Star Wars* and *Return of the Jedi*. Most Rodians wear similar clothing.

WEAPONS

Blaster Pistol

Blaster Rifle

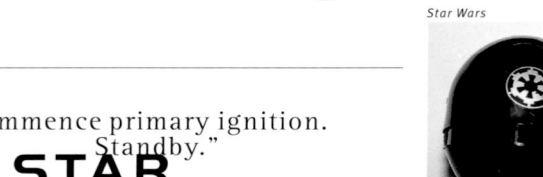

"Commence primary ignition. Standby."

DEATH STAR GUNNER

The Death Star gunners are in charge of antispacecraft turbolasers and the battle station's superlaser operation, as well as offensive and defensive maneuvers.

Star Wars

WEAPONS

Imperial Blaster

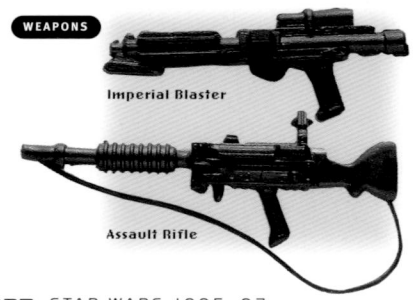

Assault Rifle

CARD VARIATIONS

1 FIRST RELEASED ON AN ORANGE CARD .00. NOTICE THE NAMES OF THE WEAPONS HAVE BEEN CHANGED.
2 GREEN CARD WITH FOIL STICKER .01.
3 GREEN CARD WITHOUT FOIL STICKER .01.
4 GREEN CARD WITH FOIL STICKER .02.

Star Wars   *Star Wars*

The original Gunner was modeled from the simple outfits used in *Return of the Jedi*. This new sculpt features the more complex armored outfit as seen in *Star Wars*.

"The droids belong to her.   She's the one in the message.   We've got to help her!"

LUKE SKYWALKER
in Stormtrooper Disguise

Star Wars

CARD VARIATIONS

ORANGE CARD .oo.

GREEN CARD WITH FOIL STICKER .01.

GREEN CARD WITHOUT FOIL STICKER .01.

.02

WEAPON

Luke knows that his destiny is to rescue the princess, but how can he and Han Solo have the freedom of movement to find her on a Death Star teeming with stormtroopers? Only by becoming stormtroopers themselves.

Imperial Issue Blaster

Though the name is different, the Luke stormtrooper blaster is the same as a regular stormtrooper's.

When compared with the regular stormtrooper (above left), Luke is not "a little short for a stormtrooper," as Leia remarked.

Star Wars

TUSKEN RAIDER

The Sand People howl and attack Luke.

Also known as Tusken Raiders, these fierce desert nomads usually keep to themselves. But they have been known to pick off roaming Jawas and go head-to-head in battle against the moisture farmers of Tatooine.

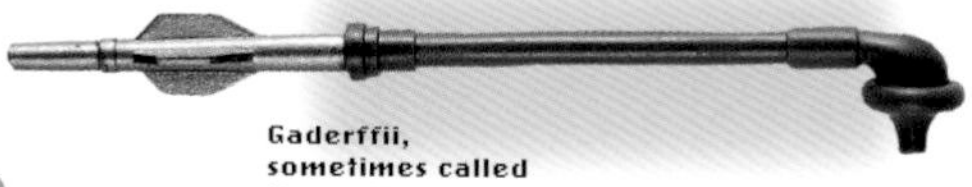

Gaderffii, sometimes called the gaffi stick.

WEAPON

Star Wars

Star Wars

The first release of the Tusken Raider had a left hand that was molded in a closed position (far left). The hand was later retooled in an open position to better grip the Gaderffii stick.

The legs and torso of the action figure are covered in mummy-like bandages.

CARD VARIATIONS

1   2

3   4

1 ORANGE CARD WITH CLOSED HAND ("GADERFFII STICK BATTLE CLUB") .oo.
2 ORANGE CARD WITH OPEN HAND .oo.
3 GREEN CARD WITH FOIL STICKER AND OPEN HAND .01.
4 GREEN CARD WITHOUT FOIL STICKER AND WITH CLOSED HAND (WEAPON NAME CHANGED TO "GADERFFII STICK") .01.

 .01

MOMAW NADON "HAMMERHEAD"

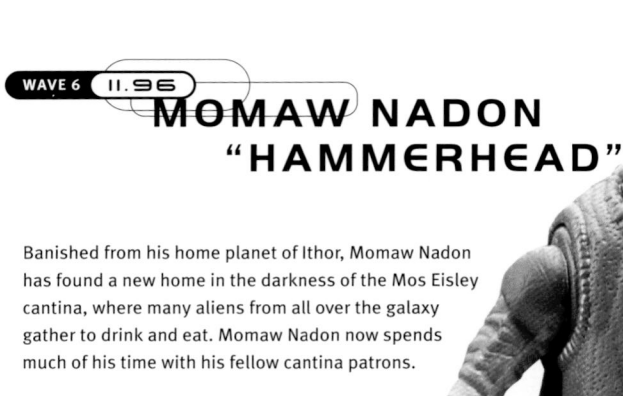

Banished from his home planet of Ithor, Momaw Nadon has found a new home in the darkness of the Mos Eisley cantina, where many aliens from all over the galaxy gather to drink and eat. Momaw Nadon now spends much of his time with his fellow cantina patrons.

Star Wars

Only the upper body and head of Hammerhead were made and appeared in the film. The action figure's body was sculpted based on Ron Cobb's original creature sketches for *Star Wars*.

WEAPON

Double-Barreled Blaster Rifle

CARD VARIATIONS

ORANGE CARD (NOTE "WITH DOUBLE-BARRELED LASER CANNON").

GREEN CARD WITH FOIL STICKER (NOTE "WITH DOUBLE-BARRELED BLASTER RIFLE").

GREEN CARD WITHOUT FOIL STICKER.

Hammerhead has a mouth on either side of his neck, resulting in "stereophonic" speech.

Star Wars

JAWAS

The Jawas are desert scavengers, and they never pass up a droid without an owner. After landing on the planet Tatooine, R2-D2 and C-3PO quarrel and decide to part ways. By chance, the same Jawas that find Artoo are the ones who find Threepio, reuniting them to be sold to Luke's Uncle Owen.

Star Wars

WEAPONS

Ionization Blaster

Jawa blasters from the film

Blaster Pistol

CARD VARIATIONS

ORANGE CARD (NOTE "WITH GLOWING EYES AND IONIZATION BLASTERS").

GREEN CARD WITH FOIL STICKER (NOTE "WITH GLOWING EYES AND BLASTER PISTOLS").

GREEN CARD WITHOUT FOIL STICKER.

Under the hood of the action figure there is a bandaged face that matches the costumes used for the Jawas in *Star Wars*.

"This R2 unit has a bad motivator. Look!"

R5-D4

Inside the Jawa sand-crawler is a veritable droid supermarket: EG power droids, C2-3 com-droids, but most noticeable to R2-D2 is an R5 unit with some basic similarities to himself. In fact, Luke mistakenly calls the R5-D4 an R2 unit.

R5-D4's body splits apart to reveal a firing missile. This function is similar to that of a cancelled "Attack R2-D2."

Star Wars

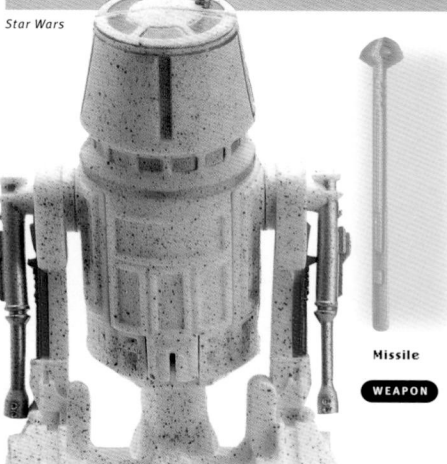

Missile

WEAPON

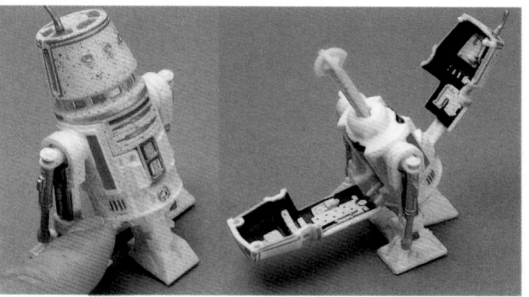

The internal missile is launched by pressing down on the yellow button on the lower body.

Star Wars

CARD VARIATIONS

 1
 2
 3
 4
 5

R5-D4 HAS HAD MANY CARD VARIATIONS IN A SHORT PERIOD OF TIME.

1 ORANGE CARD.
2 GREEN CARD WITHOUT FOIL STICKER AND NO WARNING.
3 GREEN CARD WITHOUT FOIL STICKER AND WITH WARNING STICKER.
4 GREEN CARD WITHOUT FOIL STICKER AND WITH PRINTED WARNING.
5 GREEN CARD WITH FOIL STICKER AND PRINTED WARNING.

The launching mechanism changed from the initial straight button to the current L-shaped button.

Both versions of the launching button can be found on both the orange and green cards.

Straight button

L-shaped button

Protocol Droids

R-3PO at Echo Base. *The Empire Strikes Back*

Many 3PO heads. *The Empire Strikes Back*

Silver U-3PO & C-3PO in the Blockade Runner. *Star Wars*

White K-3PO and C-3PO in the Echo Base command center.

E-3PO at Cloud City.

Close up of R-3PO.

Astromech Droids (R2 & R5 Units)

Red R2 unit. *Star Wars: Behind the Scenes*

Black R2 unit.

Biggs Darklighter's R2-Q2 unit, also seen in the Blockade Runner corridor. *Star Wars*

Transparent head is either an R1 or R3 droid.

R5 droid at a Rebel briefing. *Return of the Jedi*

Red leader's R5 unit.

Star Wars: Behind the Scenes

R5-M2 at Echo Base.

As is done by the filmmakers, some customizers repaint their droids to make as yet unproduced variations. Here, as seen in the films, are several droid variations created with different paint schemes.

Imperial R2 & R5 Units

Imperial R5 units.

Imperial R2 unit in the Death Star docking bay. *Return of the Jedi*

Rare photo of Darth Vader with two Imperial droids. *Return of the Jedi*

. . . And More

Blue & black R4 unit from the Rebel base on Yavin 4. *Star Wars*

R4-M9 was seen in the Blockade Runner and at Echo Base.

The Empire Strikes Back

Power droid from the streets of Mos Eisley.

EG-4 from Echo Base.

Another EG unit in Jabba's dungeon.

Various droids on the Death Star.

8D8 and a power droid.

BG-J38. The same body was used for 8D8.

EV-9D9 and R2-D2 in Jabba's dungeon.

The Empire Strikes Back

The Empire Strikes Back

BOSSK

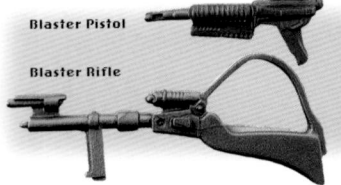

The Empire Strikes Back

Bossk the Trandoshan chases and hunts Chewbacca.

"Bounty Hunters? We don't need that scum!" As Admiral Piett shows his disdain, the reptilian bounty hunter Bossk expresses his own distaste for the Imperial officer: "Luxi bgwa auuff."

The detail of the Bossk figure is very precise, resulting in one of the most accurate figures in the line.

WEAPONS

Blaster Pistol

Blaster Rifle

CARD VARIATIONS

GREEN CARD WITH FOIL STICKER .00.

GREEN CARD WITHOUT FOIL STICKER .00.

GREEN CARD WITH FOIL STICKER .01.

Though the card printing hasn't changed, a new shape of the hook cutout can be seen.

"Luke, you must go to the Dagobah system."

LUKE SKYWALKER

in Hoth Gear

The Empire Strikes Back

Patrolling on his tauntaun, Luke is attacked by the wampa ice creature and later narrowly escapes from its cave. Unable to continue further, Luke collapses in the snow but is revived by the voice of Obi-Wan.

Lightsaber

Blaster Pistol

WEAPONS

CARD VARIATIONS

GREEN CARD WITHOUT FOIL STICKER .00.

GREEN CARD WITH FOIL STICKER .01.

The collection numbers on the card fronts refer to specific assortments. One for Rebels, two for droids and creatures, and three for Imperials, although that numbering scheme isn't always adhered to.

"Sir, it will take quite a while to evacuate the T-47s."

2-1B MEDIC DROID

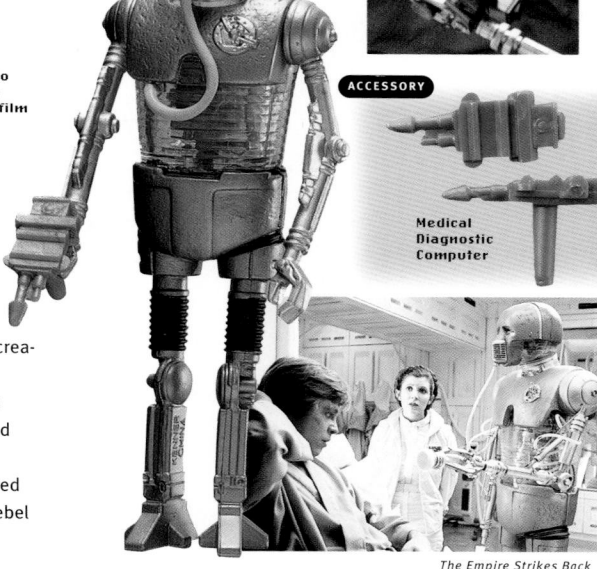

The Empire Strikes Back

The toy sculptors had to design the droid's legs themselves, since the film prop of 2-1B had only wooden rods from the knees down.

CARD VARIATIONS

GREEN CARD WITHOUT FOIL STICKER .00.

GREEN CARD WITH FOIL STICKER .01.

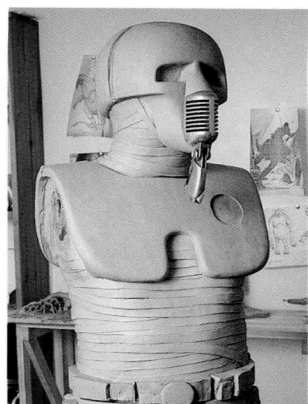

The Empire Strikes Back: Behind the Scenes

ACCESSORY

Medical Diagnostic Computer

After being attacked by the wampa snow creature, Luke is brought back to health by the droid medics 2-1B and FX-7. Later, 2-1B also tends to Luke's severed hand on board the Rebel medical frigate.

The Empire Strikes Back

AT-ST DRIVER

The AT-ST driver has the same gun as the stormtrooper, although the scope is a different length.

CARD VARIATIONS

GREEN CARD WITH FOIL STICKER .00.

GREEN CARD WITHOUT FOIL STICKER .01.

Return of the Jedi

In the forests of Endor, the Empire prefers the AT-ST over the AT-AT because of its greater maneuverability.

Return of the Jedi

WEAPONS

Blaster Pistol

Blaster Rifle

HOTH REBEL SOLDIER

"Echo station 3T8, we've spotted Imperial walkers!"

The Empire Strikes Back

The figure is bearded and thus is not representative of all other personnel.

CARD VARIATIONS

GREEN CARD WITH FOIL STICKER .00.

GREEN CARD WITHOUT FOIL STICKER .01.

The Rebels' modified snowspeeders are no match for the Imperial AT-AT walkers. Destruction of the shield generator is inevitable, but the enemy must be held off long enough to allow the evacuation of Echo Base.

WEAPON

Blaster Rifle

Han's coat is a separate piece from his body, although the sleeves are sculpted as part of the arms.

WAVE 8 4.97

HAN SOLO
in Endor Gear

"Take the squad ahead. We'll meet at the shield generator at 0300."

The Rebel strike team on Endor, led by Han Solo, must locate and storm the Imperial shield bunker. If they don't succeed in destroying the shield generator in time, the Rebel fleet approaching the second Death Star will be destroyed.

Han was originally released with the wrong colored pants (blue). Hasbro realized the error and later corrected the color to brown.

CARD VARIATIONS

GREEN CARD WITH FOIL STICKER .00.

GREEN CARD WITHOUT FOIL STICKER.

Return of the Jedi

The pants have the appropriate striping even though that detail isn't easily seen.

Return of the Jedi

WEAPON

Blaster Pistol

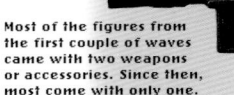

Most of the figures from the first couple of waves came with two weapons or accessories. Since then, most come with only one.

WAVE 8 4.97

LANDO CALRISSIAN
as Skiff Guard

Lando Calrissian is fully prepared to rescue Solo. The arrival of Luke Skywalker at Jabba's palace is key to the plan. Lando, disguised as one of Jabba's skiff guards, goes by the name Tamtel Screej. It is Lando who schemes to make Jabba angry with his last protocol droid and dispatches the bartender aboard Jabba's Sail Barge, thus making room for the arrival of R2-D2 and C-3PO, according to spin-off stories.

Return of the Jedi

Return of the Jedi

Return of the Jedi

Skiff Guard Force Pike

WEAPON

CARD VARIATIONS

GREEN CARD WITH FOIL STICKER .00.

GREEN CARD WITHOUT FOIL STICKER .00.

"Everything is proceeding
as I have foreseen.
Patience, Lord Vader."

EMPEROR PALPATINE

Return of the Jedi

The Galactic Emperor has declared his New Order throughout the galaxy and disbanded the Senate. Once his symbol of terror is completed, the second Death Star will force the Rebellion and the rest of the galaxy to their knees. Currently his concern is with the young Jedi Luke Skywalker, whom he hopes to turn to the dark side just as he turned Luke's father, Darth Vader.

CARD VARIATIONS

GREEN CARD WITH
FOIL STICKER .oo.

GREEN CARD WITHOUT
FOIL STICKER .oo.

GREEN CARD WITHOUT
FOIL STICKER .01.

Wave 8 figures are all from *Return of the Jedi*.

Return of the Jedi

The Emperor's name has been pronounced both as Palpa-"tine" and as Palpa-"teen."

The Emperor's legs are solid and sculpted in the shape of his cloak.

ACCESSORIES

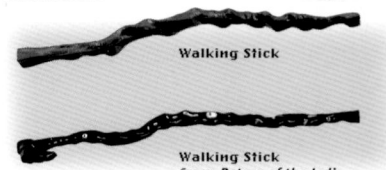

Walking Stick

Walking Stick
from *Return of the Jedi*

"Die wanna wanga!
Nee chadu so goodie?"

BIB FORTUNA

Jabba's majordomo, Bib Fortuna, attempts unsuccessfully to make two droids leave the entrance to Jabba's palace. Then a bounty hunter shows up with the Wookiee Chewbacca as prisoner. Next comes the black-cloaked Luke Skywalker, who claims to be a Jedi. What's going on here? Fortuna wonders.

Return of the Jedi

CARD VARIATIONS

GREEN CARD WITH
FOIL STICKER .oo.

GREEN CARD WITHOUT
FOIL STICKER .01.

The new Bib Fortuna has more precise color matching and sculpting than the original figure from the old line.

WEAPONS

Hold-out Blaster

Blaster from
Return of the Jedi

Return of the Jedi

Star Wars

GRAND MOFF TARKIN

CARD VARIATIONS

GREEN CARD COLLECTION 2 WITHOUT FOIL STICKER .00.

GREEN CARD COLLECTION 3 WITH FOIL STICKER .01.

GREEN CARD COLLECTION 3 WITHOUT FOIL STICKER .01.

WEAPONS

Blaster Rifle

Blaster Pistol

Grand Moff Tarkin is one of the most recognizable *Star Wars* characters, but an action figure in the likeness of actor Peter Cushing wasn't produced in the original line. Finally released in the current Hasbro/Kenner line, he is one of the most accurately sculpted figures.

The Empire's symbol of fear and the ultimate mobile fortress, the Death Star is now operational. Grand Moff Tarkin, who is assigned to operate the battle station, now has the ultimate power of the galaxy at his fingertips.

Star Wars

REBEL FLEET TROOPER

The Imperials have boarded! Princess Leia's captured consular ship fills with smoke and laser fire. The Rebel troops are unable to stop the invading stormtroopers. The captain of the ship, Antilles, is strangled by Darth Vader after refusing to reveal the location of the stolen Death Star technical readouts.

The figure's pants are brown; in the film they appear gray.

Star Wars

WEAPONS

Blaster Rifle

Blaster Pistol

An original Rebel blaster from the film

CARD VARIATIONS

GREEN CARD COLLECTION 2 WITH FOIL STICKER .00.

GREEN CARD COLLECTION 1 WITH FOIL STICKER .01.

GREEN CARD COLLECTION 1 WITHOUT FOIL STICKER .01.

WEEQUAY SKIFF GUARD

CARD VARIATIONS

GREEN CARD COLLECTION 2 WITH FOIL STICKER .00.

GREEN CARD COLLECTION 3 WITHOUT FOIL STICKER .01.

Return of the Jedi

Return of the Jedi

WEAPONS

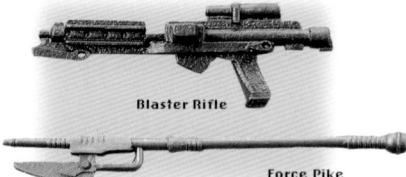

Blaster Rifle

Force Pike

"Move him into position. Put him in!"

On Jabba's orders, Weequay pushes Luke off the skiff's plank with his force pike. Luke catches the plank and launches himself upward to catch his lightsaber. Now it is Weequay's turn to worry.

There are several Weequay seen in the skiff/sail barge battle sequence. The figure was modeled after the individual who tried to push Luke into the mouth of the Sarlacc.

WAVE 9 · 7.97
ASP-7 DROID

A common labor droid with a short temper, the ASP droid can be seen in every corner of the Mos Eisley space-port. Marching, carrying, and loading, this multipurpose droid sometimes gets frustrated with his job, as can be seen when he smashes a taunting probe droid to the ground.

CARD VARIATIONS

GREEN CARD WITH FOIL STICKER .oo.

GREEN CARD WITHOUT FOIL STICKER .oo.

An ASP droid was first introduced in the multimedia adventure of *Shadows of the Empire* as Vader's training droid.

ACCESSORY

Spaceport Supply Rods

Star Wars Special Edition

WAVE 9 · 7.97
DENGAR

Dengar has a personal grievance to settle with Han Solo. Of the droids, aliens, and masked mercenaries assembled on the bridge of the Star Destroyer *Executor,* only Dengar reveals a human face. Wearing salvaged Imperial-issue armor, he later meets Bossk and Boba Fett at Jabba's palace.

The Empire Strikes Back

The Empire Strikes Back

CARD VARIATIONS

GREEN CARD WITH FOIL STICKER .oo.

GREEN CARD WITHOUT FOIL STICKER.

WEAPONS

Blaster Pistol

Blaster Rifle

Dengar's rifle from *The Empire Strikes Back*

Dengar was equipped with a backpack in *The Empire Strikes Back*. This backpack-less action figure may have been modeled from his appearance in *Return of the Jedi*.

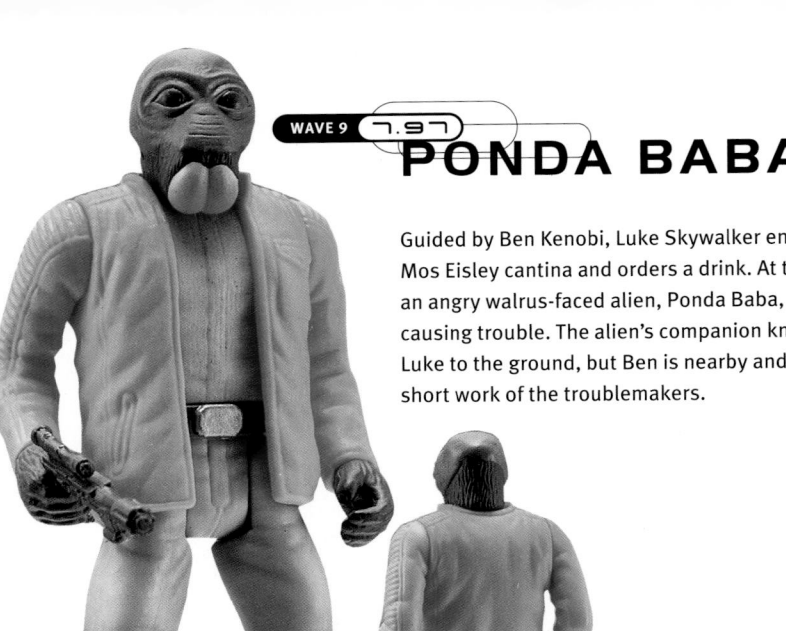

WAVE 9 7.97

PONDA BABA

Guided by Ben Kenobi, Luke Skywalker enters the Mos Eisley cantina and orders a drink. At the bar, an angry walrus-faced alien, Ponda Baba, starts causing trouble. The alien's companion knocks Luke to the ground, but Ben is nearby and makes short work of the troublemakers.

Holiday Special

WEAPONS

Blaster Pistol

Ponda Baba's pistol from *Star Wars*

Blaster Rifle

CARD VARIATIONS

GREEN CARD COLLECTION 2 WITHOUT FOIL STICKER .00.

GREEN CARD COLLECTION 3 WITH FOIL STICKER .01.

GREEN CARD COLLECTION 3 WITHOUT FOIL STICKER.

CARD VARIATIONS

GREEN CARD WITH FOIL STICKER .00.

GREEN CARD WITHOUT FOIL STICKER.

WAVE 9 7.97

4-LOM

Last of the mercenaries aboard the Star Destroyer *Executor* is the bounty hunter Zuckuss and his droid accomplice 4-LOM. Designed similarly to C-3PO, 4-LOM has an insectlike head and a slightly different torso. He has reprogrammed himself and plans crimes along with Zuckuss.

The Empire Strikes Back

In the older line the names 4-LOM and Zuckuss were reversed. The new line corrects the original mistake.

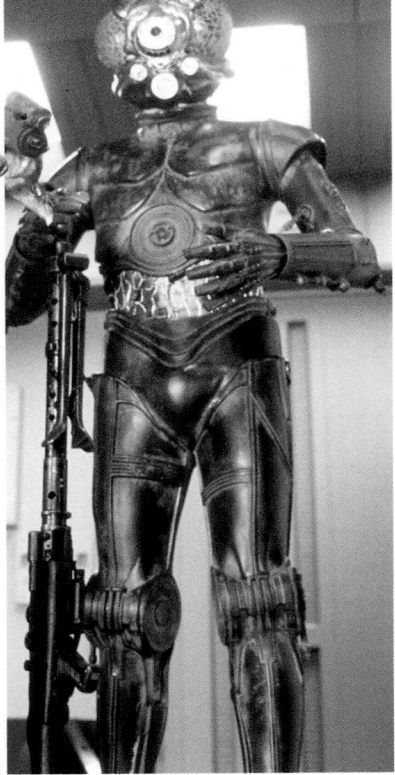

The Empire Strikes Back

WEAPONS

Blaster Pistol

Blaster Rifle

GARINDAN
(Long Snoot)

Around the time that Luke sells his landspeeder to the dealer Wioslea, Garindan spots two humans with a pair of droids. These must be the ones the Empire is searching for so thoroughly, he thinks. He smells a reward, and runs off to tell the stormtroopers before they escape.

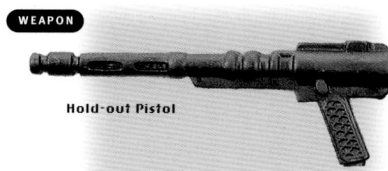

WEAPON

Hold-out Pistol

Garindan is a Kubaz from the planet Kubindi. He carries a comlink to aid in his snitching.

Star Wars

The release of the sandtrooper figure paved the way for the release of Garindan.

CARD VARIATIONS

GREEN CARD WITH FOIL STICKER .oo.

GREEN CARD WITHOUT FOIL STICKER.

Since he is labeled as collection 3 (Imperials), he can be considered an Imperial spy.

ADMIRAL ACKBAR
"We have no choice. Our cruisers can't repel firepower of that magnitude!"

Return of the Jedi

Alliance leader Mon Mothma introduces the Mon Calamari leader. Ackbar briefs the Rebels on the attack on the second Death Star and introduces the strategic leader, General Madine. During the battle, Ackbar is commander aboard the Rebel flagship *Home One*. He waits in vain for the planned deactivation of the Death Star's shield. He must now hold the Rebel fleet together as long as possible until the shield has been dropped.

Return of the Jedi

Other Mon Calamari officers wear darker-colored costumes.

WEAPON

Comlink/Wrist Blaster

Return of the Jedi

With each wave of figures, the detail and accuracy improves. Ackbar is one of the most accurate figures released.

CARD VARIATIONS

GREEN CARD WITH FOIL STICKER .oo.

GREEN CARD WITHOUT FOIL STICKER.

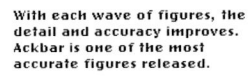

PRINCESS LEIA ORGANA

as Jabba's Prisoner

Disguised as the bounty hunter Boushh, Leia frees Han from his carbonite prison, but she is immediately captured and forced to remain by Jabba's side dressed in his favorite dancing girl costume. But Princess Leia will soon use her shackles to turn the tables on Jabba.

Return of the Jedi

In an action figure market that is dominated primarily by boys, female characters have always been sparse. But that is changing and more fantasy female characters are being produced. The Leia figure in her so-called "slave girl" outfit copies the revealing original costume very well.

Return of the Jedi

Return of the Jedi

ACCESSORY

Prisoner Chain

CARD VARIATIONS

GREEN CARD WITH FOIL STICKER.

BESPIN HAN SOLO

To remain with the Rebellion or pay off Jabba the Hutt? Han decides to postpone his visit to pay Jabba his debt in order to help the Rebellion destroy the first Death Star. He then aids them in their escape from Yavin and helps with the construction of the new Echo Base on the ice planet Hoth. Escaping the Imperial fleet, he and Leia end up on Cloud City on Bespin.

The Empire Strikes Back

The Empire Strikes Back

Surprisingly, while most of the later figures were slimmed down, Bespin Han Solo retains the beefed-up look seen in Wave 1.

WEAPONS

Han's pistol from *The Empire Strikes Back*

Blaster Pistol

Heavy Assault Rifle

CARD VARIATIONS

STAR WARS
THE POWER OF THE FORCE

BESPIN HAN SOLO
HEAVY ASSAULT RIFLE AND BLASTER

AGES 4 & UP
WARNING:
CHOKING HAZARD - Small parts.
Not for children under 3 years.

GREEN CARD WITH FOIL STICKER.

EMPEROR'S ROYAL GUARD

Wearing scarlet masks and robes, six Royal Guards descend from the Imperial shuttle to make way for Palpatine's arrival. The Emperor's bodyguards and gatekeepers are an elite corps selected from hundreds of thousands of stormtroopers. Standing side by side at the turbolift to the Emperor's chamber, they will punish even highly ranked officials who attempt to enter without permission.

A scene cut from Return of the Jedi

CARD VARIATIONS

GREEN CARD WITHOUT FOIL STICKER.

GREEN CARD WITH FOIL STICKER.

WEAPON

Return of the Jedi

Force Pike

The Royal Guards stand as tall as Darth Vader, about two meters high.

The red robes form a covering around a fully sculpted robed action figure.

Return of the Jedi

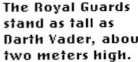
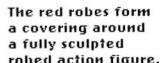

SNOWTROOPER

The snowtroopers are ready for any assault in frozen environments. Their mission on the frigid planet of Hoth is to prevent the escape of the Rebels and to take over their Echo Base.

Details such as the goggle lenses and the accurate chestplate and backpack show that the sculptor did in-depth research.

The Empire Strikes Back

The Empire Strikes Back

The Empire Strikes Back

The Empire Strikes Back

WEAPON

Blaster Rifle

NIEN NUNB

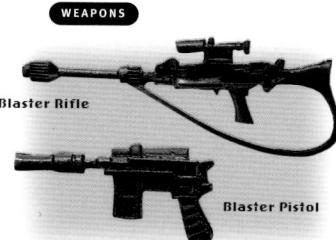

Return of the Jedi

Blaster Rifle

Blaster Pistol

Return of the Jedi

"Aterere yourere
mureare mou kay ahan."

The Rebel fleet assembles near the planet Sullust. Local pilots such as Nien Nunb are primed for the attack against the second Death Star. Living in an underground city, the Sullustan sense of orientation is also useful in deep space.

The mouse-like ears of the Sullustans are precisely copied. And Nien Nunb is not muscular at all.

MALAKILI

(Rancor Keeper)

Return of the Jedi

Return of the Jedi

Return of the Jedi

Malakili rarely has a hard time satisfying the rancor's hunger, as his boss Jabba the Hutt keeps dropping victims—or meals—into the rancor's pit. But when Jedi Knight Luke Skywalker drops in, he gives the rancor nothing but indigestion.

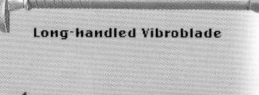

Long-handled Vibroblade

Malakili's weapon from *Return of the Jedi*

The vibroblade is a modified version of the Sand People's gaderffii stick.

HE'S NINE, NOT TEN

Early press material for *Return of the Jedi* in 1983 spoke of an alien B-wing pilot named Ten Numb, although no picture was shown. Soon after, a photo of Ten Numb in a prototype white flight suit was printed in a magazine. Some fans have noticed that what they thought was Nien Nunb at the Rebel briefing and at the Ewok celebration was actually Ten Numb. This can be confirmed by the B-wing pilot flight suit that he is wearing. The blue-vested Nien Nunb can be seen walking in the Rebel hangar during Han and Lando's good-byes. Because of the existence of Ten Numb, it seems that Nien is pronounced "nine."

Return of the Jedi

RANCOR KEEPERS

For the *Return of the Jedi* production, aliens and creatures are cataloged with archival numbers. The book *The Making of Return of the Jedi* lists number 55 as "Weeba Weeba's Appliances." The book *The Art of Return of the Jedi* classifies one of the rancor keepers as number 55. Thus, this second rancor keeper is apparently named Weeba Weeba.

A third keeper was the same species as Klaatu and is sometimes categorized as a green Nikto.

Return of the Jedi

Return of the Jedi

SAELT MARAE

(Yak Face)

Battle Staff

Tall enough to shoot hoops with the best!

Saelt Marae always drinks heavily and needs to lean against the nearest wall. Too drunk to give his name, he doesn't mind being called "Yak Face." Perhaps the best drink he has ever had was the one with Ree-Yees aboard Jabba's Sail Barge. It was also his last.

Return of the Jedi

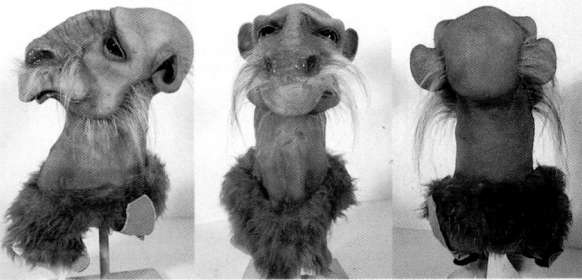

Return of the Jedi

One of the rarest figures in the original line, Yak Face comes to life again with a new name.

GAMORREAN GUARD

Return of the Jedi

One of the most massive figures in the new line.

The Gamorrean Guard is one of the bulkiest figures in the new line. C-3PO and R2-D2 have a hard time getting through to meet Jabba the Hutt since their path is blocked by the pig-like Guards.

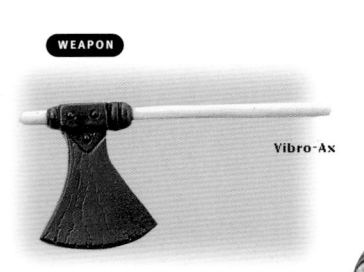

Vibro-Ax

Hasbro/Kenner's efforts at precision and accuracy are very successful with the release of this figure. He's almost identical to his appearance in the film.

Return of the Jedi

EV-9D9

"You're a feisty little one but you'll soon learn some respect. I have need for you on the master's sail barge."

G .00

R2-D2 and C-3PO are taken to the droid control room to meet the supervisor droid EV-9D9. The two droids are given tasks as part of Jabba the Hutt's staff. Threepio is assigned to be Jabba's new translator droid, while Artoo becomes a bartender on the sail barge.

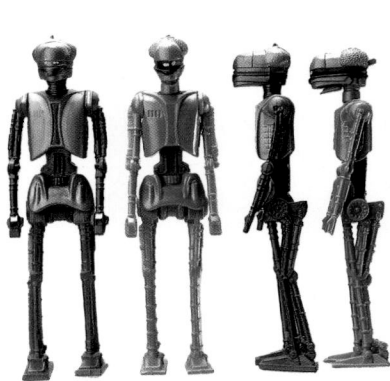

Hasbro left (1 and 3).
Kenner right (2 and 4).
The new action figure has a more realistic paint job.

Return of the Jedi

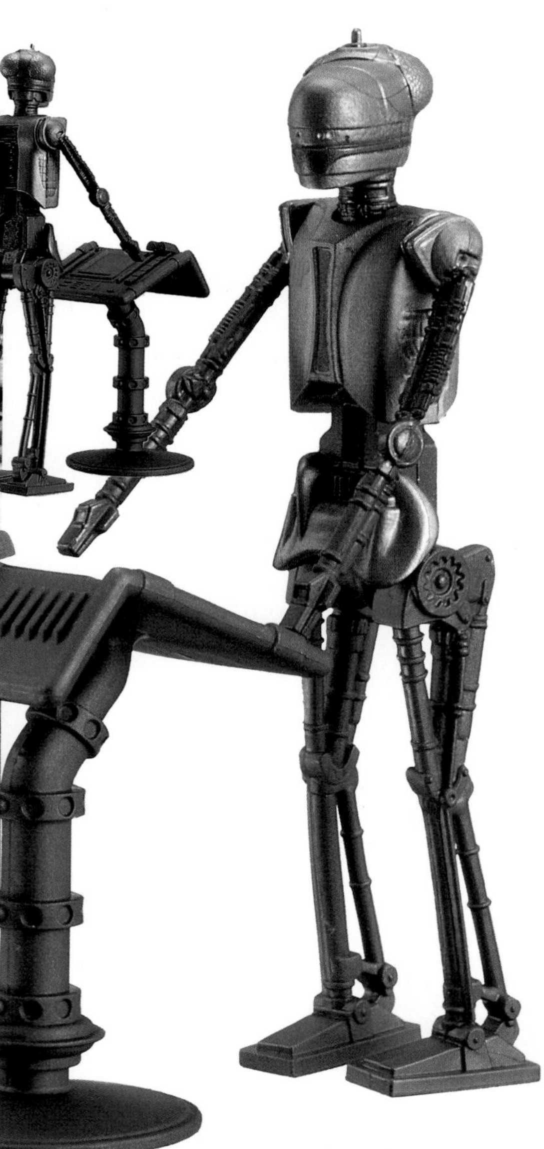

Return of the Jedi

The action figure for EV-9D9 has three eyes, just like the film prop.

LUKE IN CEREMONIAL OUTFIT

The end of an adventure, or just the beginning?

After Luke succeeds in destroying the Death Star, he joins Han Solo and Chewbacca in an awards ceremony. Walking through a stone corridor, they approach the ceremony stage where a luminous Princess Leia presents medals to Luke and Han. Even R2-D2 is there, completely repaired and cleaned up.

Luke's face was resculpted before production began.

CARD VARIATIONS

GREEN CARD COLLECTION 2 WITH FOIL STICKER .00.

GREEN CARD COLLECTION 1 WITH FOIL STICKER .01.

G .01

The earlier face sculpting for ceremonial Luke was used in catalog photos only.

Star Wars

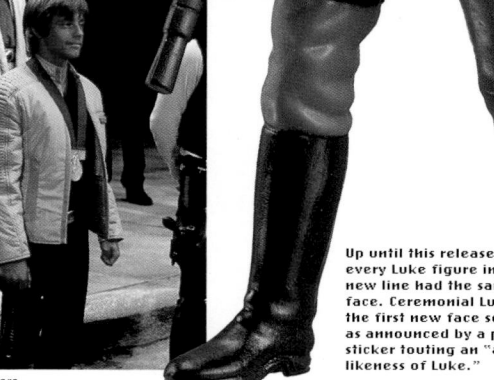

Up until this release, every Luke figure in the new line had the same face. Ceremonial Luke has the first new face sculpt, as announced by a package sticker touting an "all new likeness of Luke."

WEAPON

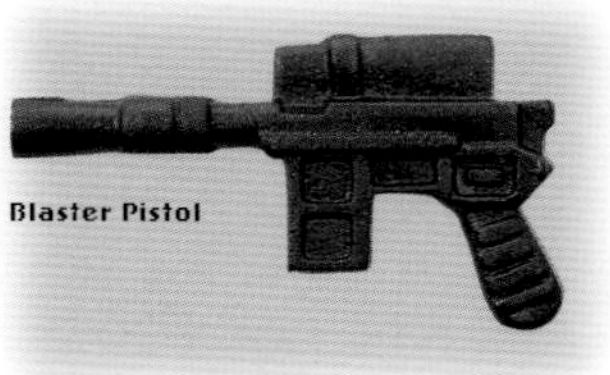

Blaster Pistol

promotional figures

11.95 HAN SOLO
in Stormtrooper Disguise

Star Wars

The body of the Stormtrooper Han Solo figure is sculpted differently than that of the standard stormtrooper. This figure hasn't been released on a card, but a slightly different sculpting is available in the Death Star Escape three-pack.

Han as a stormtrooper was a mail-away offer with the purchase of Kellogg's Froot Loops. No weapons were included. The figure squats a bit, but it is nearly the same size as the Luke stormtrooper.

1.97 SPIRIT OF OBI-WAN KENOBI

Return of the Jedi

To promote the release of the *Star Wars Special Edition* to theaters, Frito-Lay offered the Spirit of Obi-Wan as a mail-away offer with the purchase of specially marked bags of chips. Kenner included one of five different coupons with the Spirit of Obi-Wan figure: Two different *Star Wars* toy in-store rebate coupons, a mail-in coupon for a special five-dollar *Star Wars* rebate, an offer for a special pop-up cantina display, and a redemption slip for a B'omarr Monk action figure.

The head and arms of this figure are not poseable.

5.97 CANTINA BAND MEMBER
(Figrin D'an)

The Jawa Trader section in the *Star Wars Insider* titled this figure Figrin D'an, but with the five different instruments included, the figure can play 6 different characters (two band members play the Fanfar).

Star Wars

Star Wars

Bandfill

ACCESSORIES

Kloo Horn   Fanfar   Fizzz   Ommni Box

Nalan Cheel with Bandfill

9.97 B'OMARR MONK

Hasbro's *Star Wars* website provided information on how to receive a B'omarr Monk figure by mail. A small number of coupons included with the Spirit of Obi-Wan offer also provided the offer. The character can be seen in *Return of the Jedi* walking near the gate to Jabba's palace just as C-3PO and R2-D2 enter.

In fiction, these spiderlike droids are said to be the next life stage of the monks and others, keeping their brains alive in nutrients while they contemplate the spiritual aspects of life. Other sources refer to the B'omarr Monks as perimeter droids.

Return of the Jedi

Return of the Jedi

Return of the Jedi

3.97 LUKE SKYWALKER

Jedi Knight Theater Edition

With the U.S. release of *Return of the Jedi Special Edition* on March 14, 1997, movie theaters distributed a total of nearly 150,000 of these specially carded figures to the first people who attended the opening night's screenings. The Mann Chinese theater in Hollywood distributed 2,500 of these at a special screening a day early. The figure is the same as the one sold in stores; only the packaging is different.

NOT FOR RETAIL SALE

Jedi Knight Luke Skywalker™

Star Wars

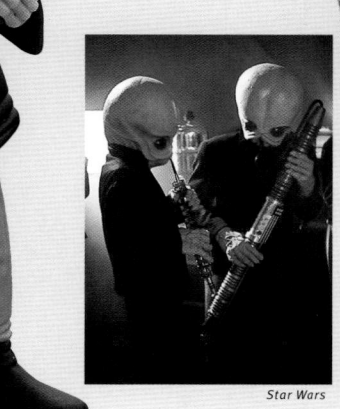

Star Wars

Tech M'or with Ommni Box

Figrin D'an with Kloo Horn

Doikk Na'ts with Fizzz

Ickabel G'ont or Tedn Dahai with Fanfar

deluxe figures

1.97
PROBE DROID

"We've picked up something outside the base of zone twelve, moving east. An Imperial probe droid."

Launched from the underbellies of Star Destroyers, probe droids are scattered into space. One reaches Hoth and emerges from its pod to search for any indication of the Rebels' secret base.

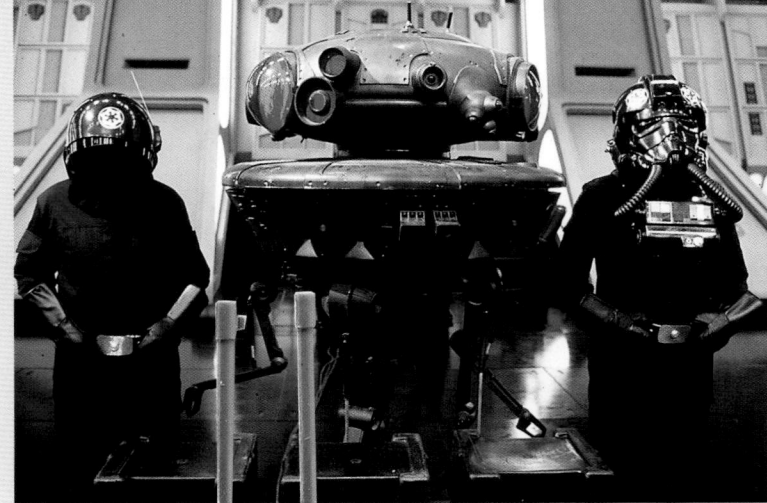

Return of the Jedi

Probot inside the second Death Star.

FIRST RELEASE OF THE DELUXE PROBE DROID HAD A WARNING STICKER PLACED ON THE CARD FRONT (.oo CARD). LATER RELEASE HAD THE WARNING PRINTED DIRECTLY ON THE CARD (.o1).

The Empire Strikes Back

Full-size prop.

The Empire Strikes Back

New Hasbro version (left)
Older Kenner version (right)

CARD VARIATIONS

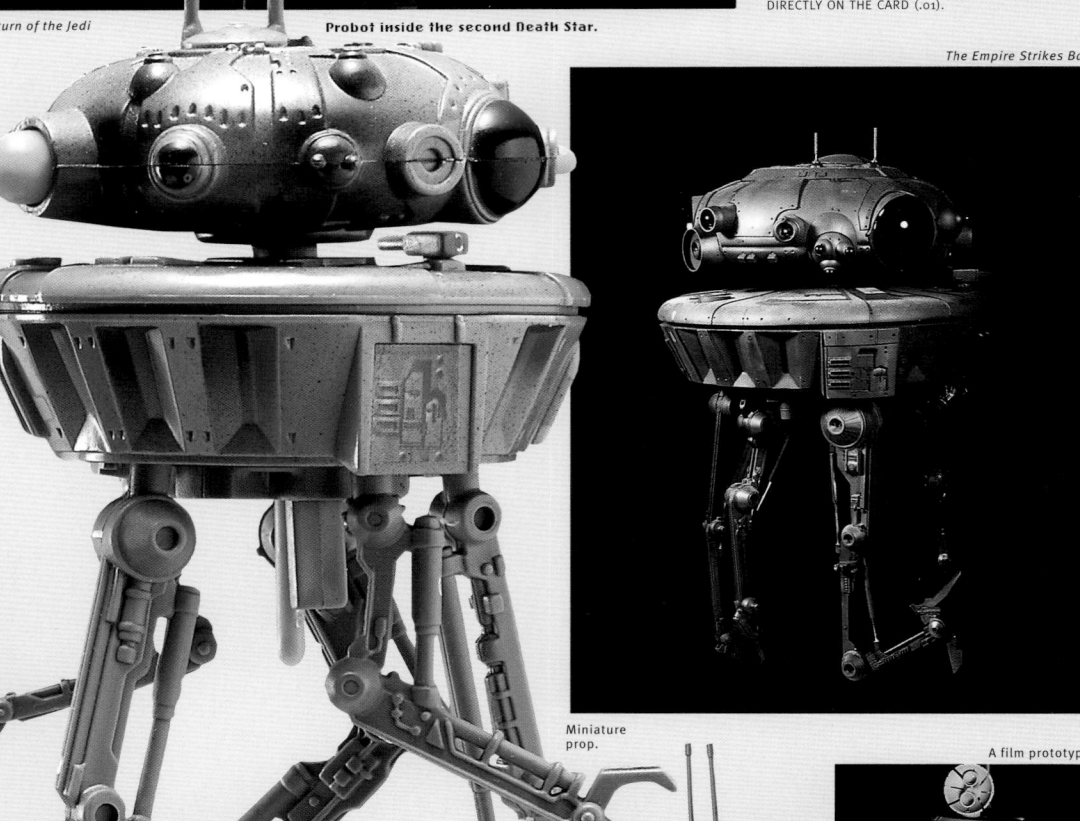

Miniature prop.

A film prototype.

The figure can stand on its own with its three longest legs. Even the legs are accurately sculpted.

CARD BACKS OF BOTH THE .oo AND .o1 CARD VARIATIONS.

CARD BACK OF THE .o2 CARD.

The Empire Strikes Back

To add larger toys to the collection and increase playability, Kenner/Hasbro introduced the deluxe figure line. Earlier releases were more toy oriented and weren't a part of the film universe. Later releases included accessories that were actually found in the films.

7.96
LUKE SKYWALKER
with Desert Sport Skiff

This Luke can be distinguished from the carded version by the hole found in his back.

Wings spring open into flight position and the front missile fires.

7.96
HAN SOLO
with Smuggler Flight Pack

The flight pack harness straps are molded directly onto Han's torso.

7.96
CROWD CONTROL STORMTROOPER

A weathered body and a hole in his back are the main differences from the standard carded stormtrooper.

EAPONS PACK SPEED: :
YEAPONRY: Photon Torpedo,

As a result of Luke Skywal

EAPONS PACK SPEED: :
YEAPONRY: Proton Torpedo,

As a result of Luke Skywa

THE .oo CARD SAYS "PHOTON" WHILE THE .01 CARD SAYS "PROTON."

1.97
BOBA FETT
with Wing Blast Rocketpack

Deluxe Boba Fett is taller than the standard Boba Fett and is more precise in proportion.

The Empire Strikes Back

7.97

"Stop the *Falcon*! Hurry up and assemble the blaster cannon!"

SNOWTROOPER

with E-Web Heavy Repeating Cannon

The deluxe line was made more exciting to collectors with more accurate film-related figures.

The Echo Base shield is down. In addition to the Imperial walker troops, a direct landing party led by Darth Vader makes its way into the Rebel base. Most of the personnel have evacuated, but the snowtroopers find the *Millennium Falcon* attempting to leave the hangar bay.

Tripod cannon, generator container, and power conduit are all portable and can be assembled where necessary.

The Empire Strikes Back

Deluxe Snowtrooper differs slightly in pose and details from the standard carded version.

7.97

HOTH REBEL SOLDIER

with Anti-Vehicle Laser Cannon

"Aim for the walkers' legs!"

The Rebels are assembled for the Imperial attack. In the battle trench, soldiers await, aiming their weapons at the distant targets. They thought that the remote-controlled dish-shaped lasers would work fine, until they saw the size of the metal beasts.

The Rebel soldiers have different molds even though they look similar.

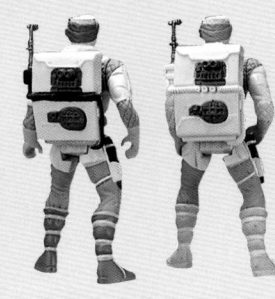

The Empire Strikes Back

The standard figure, with a sculpted beard, was more personalized. The deluxe figure can be any one of the many other soldiers.

In comparison to the film prop, the toy cannon was reduced in size.

electronic power F/X figures

2.97 DARTH VADER

The figure can be moved around on its base, and the lightsaber illuminates.

 .00

The proportions are close to the standard Vader carded release.

2.97 BEN (OBI-WAN) KENOBI

 .00

Although the batteries increase the size of his upper back, the figure is not changed much from the original release.

The two bases interlock to form one large action diorama.

Star Wars

The climactic lightsaber battle between Vader and Kenobi can be recreated with the special background included.

2.97 R2-D2

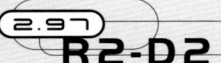 .02

Buyers can recreate R2-D2's encounter with the Jawas in the canyon, or his first meeting with Obi-Wan in the Jundland Wastes.

Pressing a button on the front of R2 causes his red sensor to light up and starts his beeping and chirping sounds.

7.97 EMPEROR PALPATINE

 .01

Pressing a button on his back simulates his flashing Force lightning.

Return of the Jedi

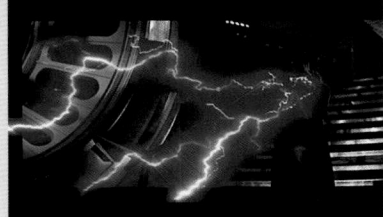

The Emperor tries to destroy Luke Skywalker after failing to turn him to the dark side.

7.97 JEDI KNIGHT LUKE SKYWALKER

 .00

Luke's base can be connected with Darth Vader's base. The duel from *Return of the Jedi* can be recreated with the special extended background included with Luke.

action figure multipacks

Originally only five thousand sets were going to be produced, but demand for all the sets resulted in production being increased.

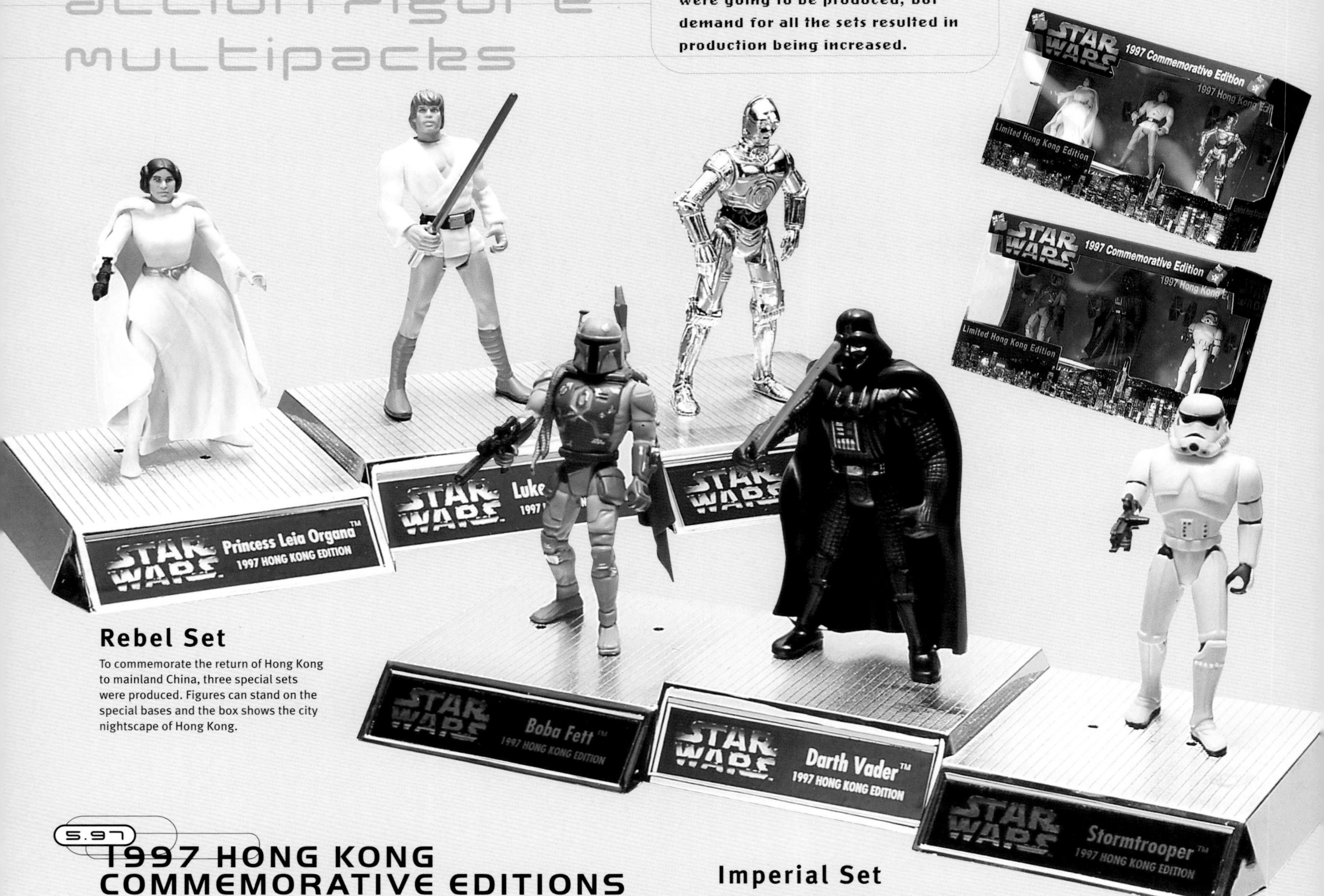

Rebel Set

To commemorate the return of Hong Kong to mainland China, three special sets were produced. Figures can stand on the special bases and the box shows the city nightscape of Hong Kong.

5.97

1997 HONG KONG COMMEMORATIVE EDITIONS

A celebration of twenty years of *Star Wars* and the return of Hong Kong to China.

Imperial Set

China is now where the majority of the world's toys are produced. These sets are a salute to the history of China and Hong Kong and a hope for the future. The packaging is similar in shape and style to the Cinema Scene three-packs or the 12-inch Collector Series dolls.

5.97

12-INCH COMMEMORATIVE SET

Back of box shows the Hong Kong nightscape with the *Star Wars* logo. The three figures are identical to the figures released in single packs, but the bonus three trading cards are unique to this set.

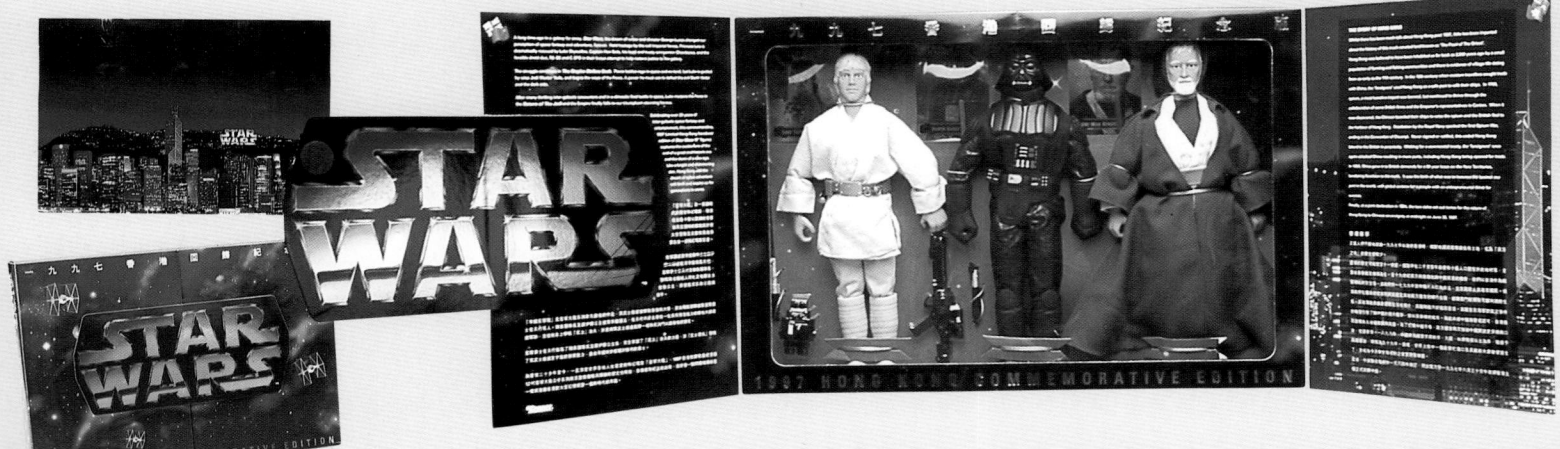

Star Wars

With the success of the standard carded figures and the unexpected popularity of the 12-inch Collector Series, the next step was a new series of multipacks that have unique or differently sculpted figures. They are much more appealing in their Cinema Scene packaging than the multipacks from the original Kenner line.

6.97 DEATH STAR ESCAPE

WEAPON

This three-pack recreates the trio en route to rescuing Leia from the Detention Block. Each figure is different from its original release.

Blaster Rifle

Initially released as a Toys "Я" Us exclusive, the set was later sold everywhere.

The helmet detail is sharper than the previous release.

Han now comes with a gun and his stance has been altered. Han on the left is the Kellogg's mail-away version.

Chewbacca's arms are shackled, but overall he is very similar to the first release.

Luke has also been reposed for the set with wider arms.

9.97 CANTINA SHOWDOWN

The figures in this set are much more dynamically sculpted than the original carded versions.

Initially released as a Wal-Mart exclusive, the set was later sold everywhere.

Blaster Pistol

Dr. Evazan's blaster from *Star Wars*

WEAPONS

Blaster Pistol

Lightsaber

Star Wars

Dr. Evazan is available only in this set.

Proportionally, Ponda Baba is slightly larger than his carded version.

While other figures have been slimmed down for subsequent releases, Obi-Wan is slightly bulkier in this set.

Star Wars

creature assortments

8.97

JABBA THE HUTT WITH HAN SOLO

The original scene with Jabba and Han in the docking bay was deleted from the initial release of *Star Wars*. With that scene restored in the *Star Wars Special Edition*, Hasbro introduced a new Jabba the Hutt. The sculpting was based on the somewhat slimmer look in the *Special Edition* rather than the fatter version that appears in *Return of the Jedi*.

Jabba's eyes are transparent.

Star Wars Special Edition

Jabba's tail swings left and right as his head is turned back and forth.

The new sculpted Han is more accurate and slimmer than the carded release.

Blaster Pistol

WEAPON

8.97

RONTO WITH JAWA

Star Wars Special Edition

The Jawa included with the ronto is midsized between the two previously released carded Jawas.

This Jawa has only one foot hole rather than the normal two that the others have.

When the hind leg is turned, the ronto swings its head, causing the Jawa to fall off and swing.

Star Wars Special Edition: Behind the Scenes

Blaster Pistol

WEAPON

At the start, the *Star Wars* characters were all newly sculpted while most of the vehicles were created using the old molds from the 1970s and 1980s. But what about creatures? With the release of the *Special Edition* came the chance to introduce some new creatures to the toy line. Both Jabba and the dewback have changed much since their previous appearances, and the ronto is a totally new creature. Rather than use the old molds, Hasbro set out to sculpt totally new, up-to-date versions.

8.97
DEWBACK WITH SANDTROOPER

G .01

In the original *Star Wars*, the dewbacks were very simplistic. In the *Special Edition*, the dewbacks are much more animated and detailed, and the toy has also been given a totally new look.

The sandtrooper included in this set has a gray shoulder pouldron rather than the previously released orange one. Minor changes in the sculpting of the backpack also distinguish him from the carded release.

Star Wars Special Edition: Behind the Scenes

The new dewback has been changed dramatically from its original look. It is more muscular, with large, sand-anchoring feet.

Battle Lance

WEAPONS

Blaster Rifle

Star Wars Special Edition

The tail is a little shorter than the film dewback, but otherwise it's precise in every way.

By swinging the tail from side to side, the dewback lifts its head and closes its mouth. The dewback must be a vegetarian, as evident from the shape of its teeth.

"What can we do next?"

a look ahead

In a period of less than three years, from the summer of 1995 to Christmas 1997, the toy makers at Hasbro/Kenner released more action figures and variations than in the eight years of the original *Star Wars* trilogy line. There were 101 new ones in all, if you count that each instrument included with the cantina band member figure provides for five separate characters. So, did Kenner designers despair of finding other characters to shrink to four inches or less?

Of course not! The *Star Wars* films are so dense and meaty, that even without sculpting or painting variations, Kenner could more than double the number of figures. They made a running start toward doing just that, as can be seen in the 1998 Update section starting on page 155.

Some of the choices were obvious. A sentimental fan favorite was Biggs Darklighter, whose most important scene in *Star Wars* ended up on the cutting room floor. Princess Leia Organa in her ceremonial dress and necklace became a cornerstone of the four-piece Princess Leia assortment of two-packs, which used soft goods for the first time in the new figure line. Kenner also chose Captain Piett, one of the few Imperial officers to survive Darth Vader's rage. The line included the aliens Ishi Tibb and Lak Sivrak, an alien who was in the cantina during *Star Wars*, but was replaced with a newer alien in the *Star Wars Special Edition*.

But perhaps the most eagerly anticipated figure was Darth Vader with a removable mask and helmet. Kenner had tried for years to produce such a figure, but it took modern manufacturing technology to get it just right.

All those figures still didn't deplete the possibilities. For one thing, Kenner has again gone into the expanded *Star Wars* universe, like it did earlier with *Shadows of the Empire*. This time it has tested fans' interest in buying figures of characters that exist only in novels, comic books, or video games— and it hasn't even scratched the surface with the handful released in 1998.

The release of Mace Windu, a preview figure from *Star Wars: Episode I*, is just the start of an entire new group of humans, aliens, creatures and droids who live in George Lucas' "used" galaxy. But there will always be room for more classic characters from the first trilogy. So if you haven't yet seen your particular favorite, perhaps a character whose screen time was so short it was nearly subliminal, don't give up hope. His/her/its name is more than likely on some Kenner designer's list, waiting to work its way to the top.

Biggs Darklighter

Princess Leia

Captain Piett

Anakin Skywalker, with his mask and helmet removed

Ishi Tibb

Logray the Ewok

Dice Ibegon and Lak Sivrak

Dice Ibegon and Ketwol

1991

vehicles and playsets

Hasbro/Kenner Toys

One of the main reasons that the 3³/₄-inch standard was originally developed for *Star Wars* action figures back in 1977 was that the film had so many interesting environments and vehicles. Kenner officials knew that producing an extensive line of playsets and spacecraft to fit the then-prevailing 12-inch standard would have sent the prices far too high for the average buyer. So a new standard was introduced and the company had the chance to duplicate in toys some of the most fanciful and exciting settings and vehicles ever produced for motion pictures.

7.95 ELECTRONIC X-WING FIGHTER

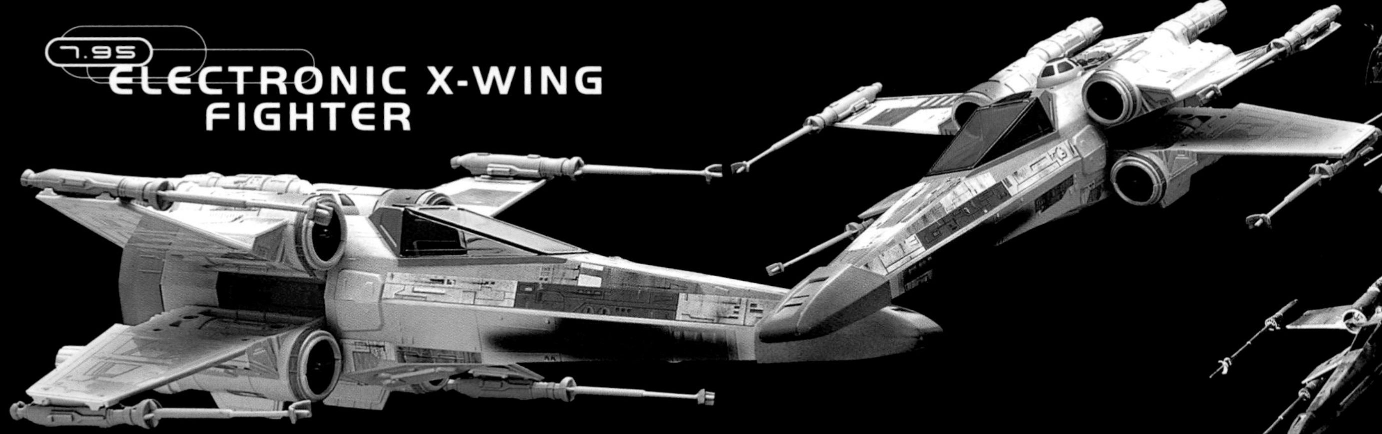

Star Wars

"This is Red Five. I'm going in!"

The X-wing fighter was launched as the first vehicle in the new line just as it was the first some 20 years ago. The same molds were used, but new sounds directly from the film were added, while the light from the fuselage has been removed. The main difference is a dramatic new paint job instead of the previous paper stickers.

Star Wars

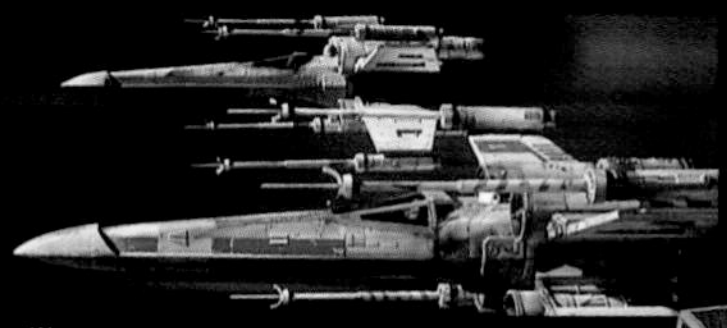

Star Wars

Star Wars

Star Wars

7.95 TIE FIGHTER

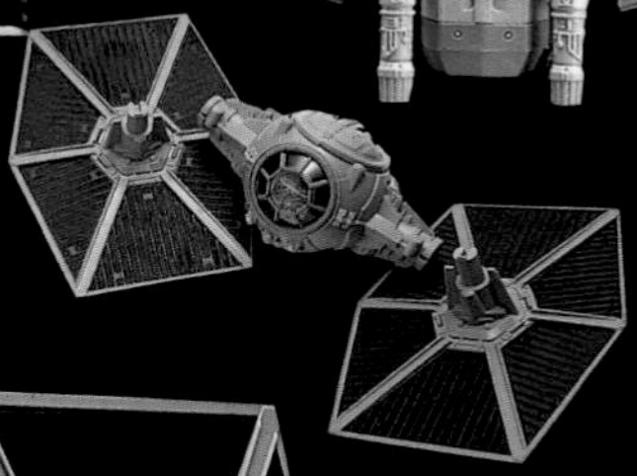

"Here they come! Three marks at two ten!"

The TIE fighter's wings are smaller in proportion to the body to make the toy more compact. The electronics have been removed for the new release. Again, most of the same molds were used, but the solar panel detail is now sculpted instead of a sticker.

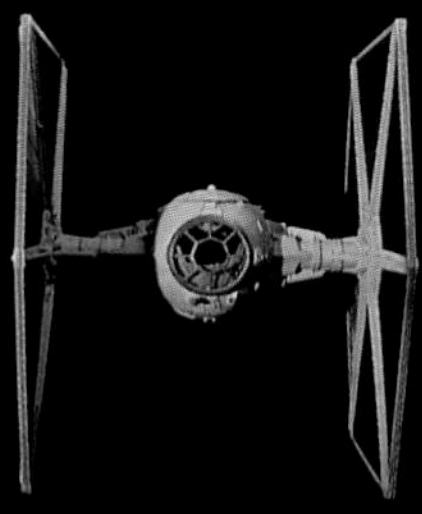

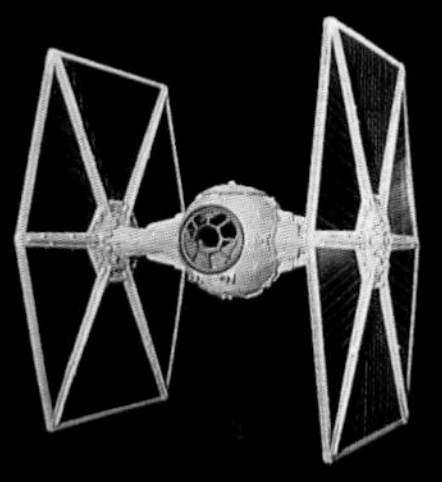

Star Wars

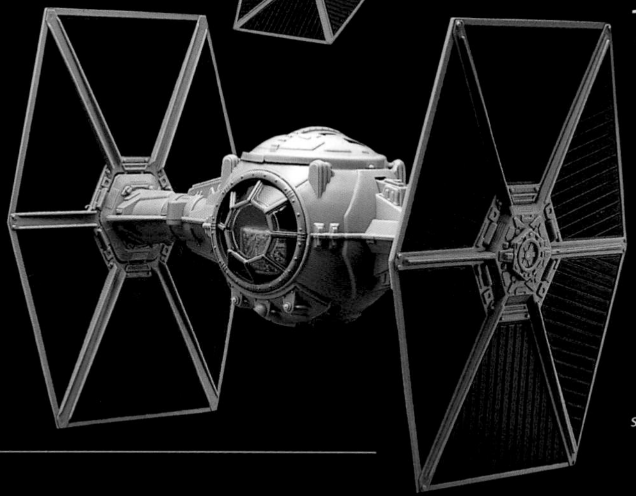

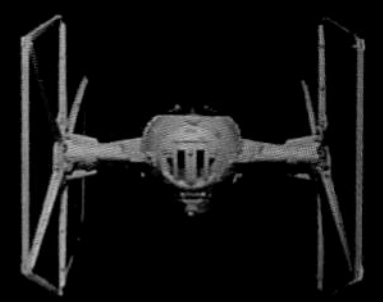

Star Wars

7.95 "You'll have to sell your speeder." LANDSPEEDER

"That's OK. I'm never coming back to this planet again."

The landspeeder's color and painted detail has improved markedly from the original release, although the sculpting is basically the same. A damaged engine has been added at the rear.

Star Wars Special Edition

Star Wars Special Edition

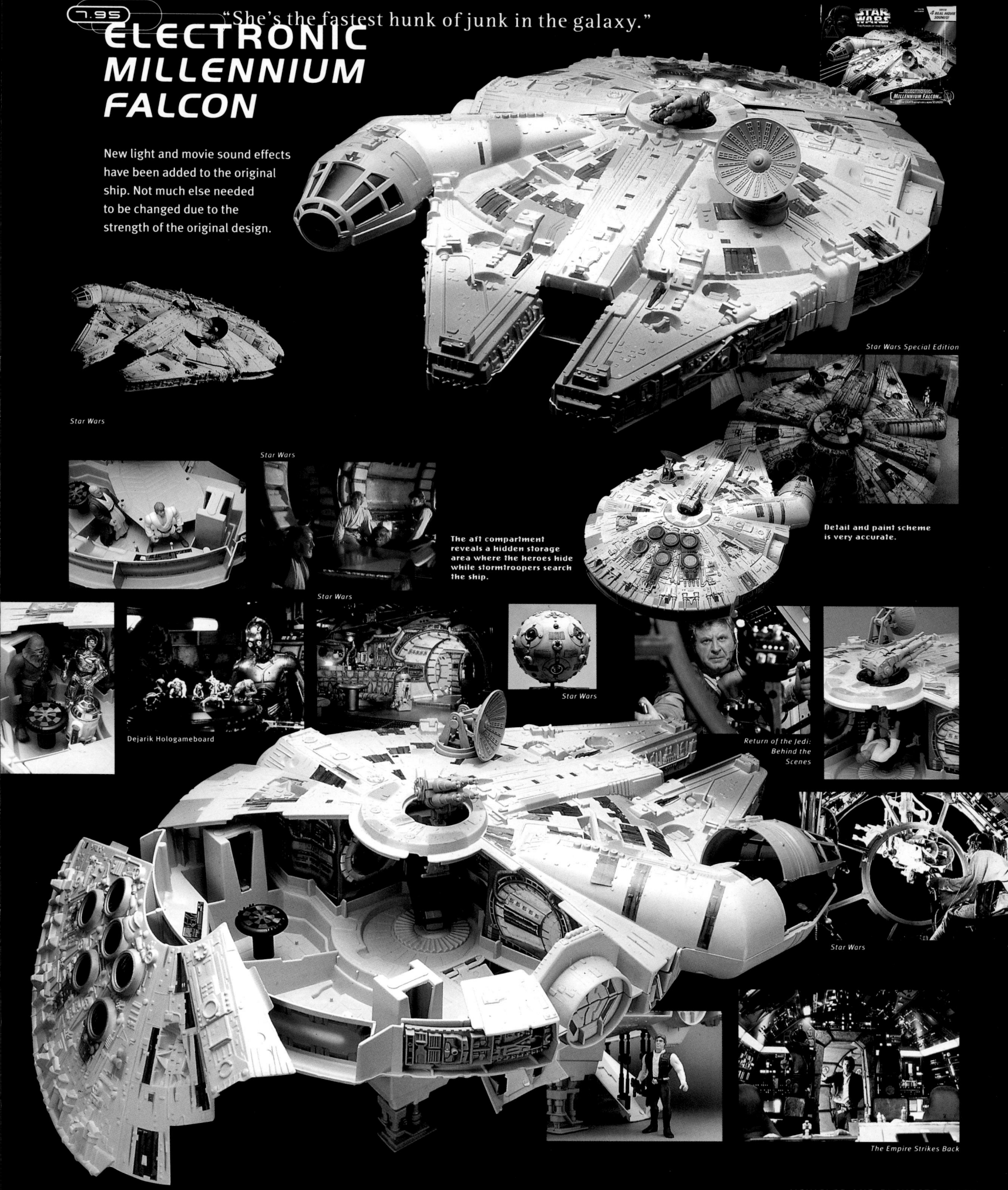

7.95

"She's the fastest hunk of junk in the galaxy."

ELECTRONIC
MILLENNIUM
FALCON

New light and movie sound effects
have been added to the original
ship. Not much else needed
to be changed due to the
strength of the original design.

Star Wars Special Edition

Star Wars

Star Wars

The aft compartment
reveals a hidden storage
area where the heroes hide
while stormtroopers search
the ship.

Detail and paint scheme
is very accurate.

Star Wars

Dejarik Hologameboard

Star Wars

*Return of the Jedi:
Behind the
Scenes*

Star Wars

The Empire Strikes Back

IMPERIAL SPEEDER BIKE

"Go for help! Go!"

The basic proportion of the speeder bike is the same. The paint scheme is different and the handle bars have been resculpted. The T-bar (used to hold the original action figures on the seat) seems unnecessary.

Lowering the landing struts causes the rear thruster flaps to open.

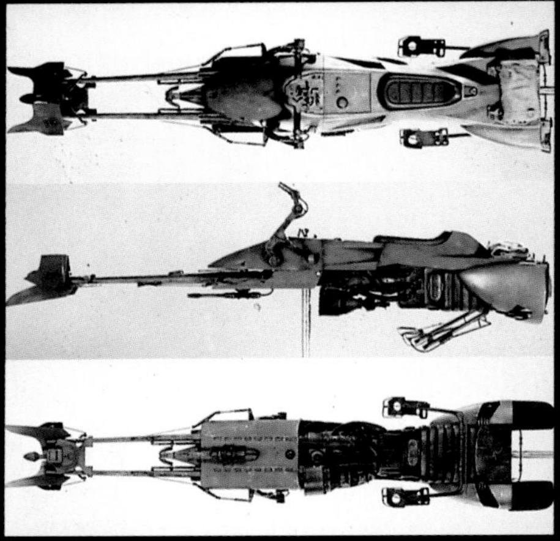

Return of the Jedi

Return of the Jedi

The scout trooper does not have holes in his feet.

Return of the Jedi

Return of the Jedi

SWOOP BIKE

Luke is attacked by a swoop gang in *Shadows of the Empire.*

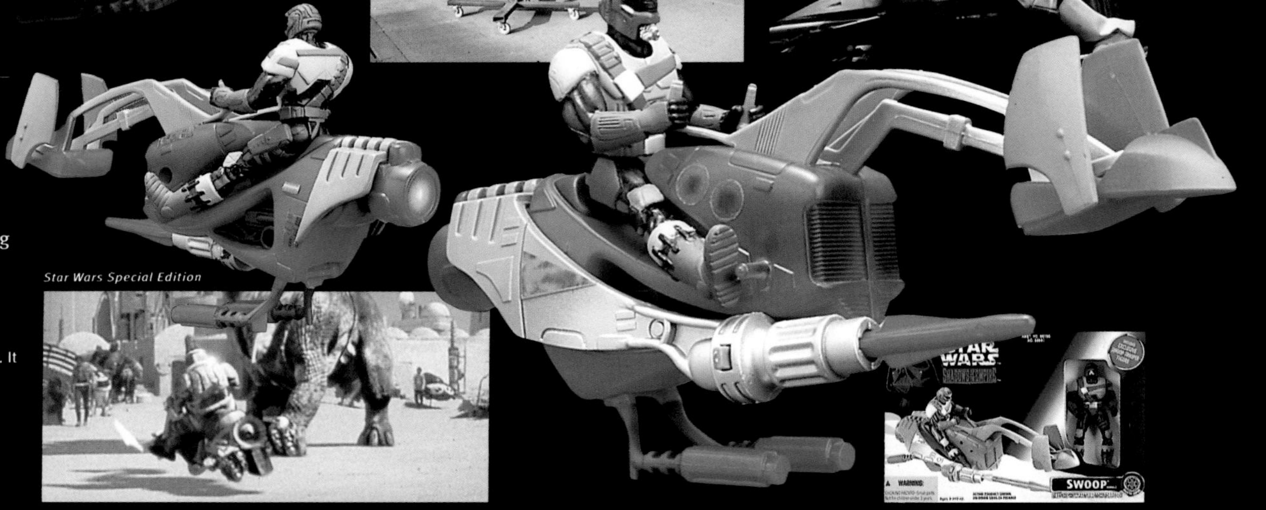

The swoop was used in *Shadows of the Empire* and then later appeared in the *Star Wars Special Edition.* It leads to a startled ronto and some unlucky Jawas.

Star Wars Special Edition

DASH RENDAR'S *OUTRIDER*

"It's OK, Lebo. I'm a dead man to them."

Totally new molds for vehicles were first introduced with the swoop and the *Outrider* from the multimedia project, *Shadows of the Empire.* The cockpit and center section rotate.

The *Outrider*, a spin-off of the *Millennium Falcon*'s freighter design, pleased George Lucas so much that it makes a brief appearance at Mos Eisley in the *Star Wars Special Edition.* The *Outrider* should be close to the same size as the *Falcon*, but the toy is much smaller.

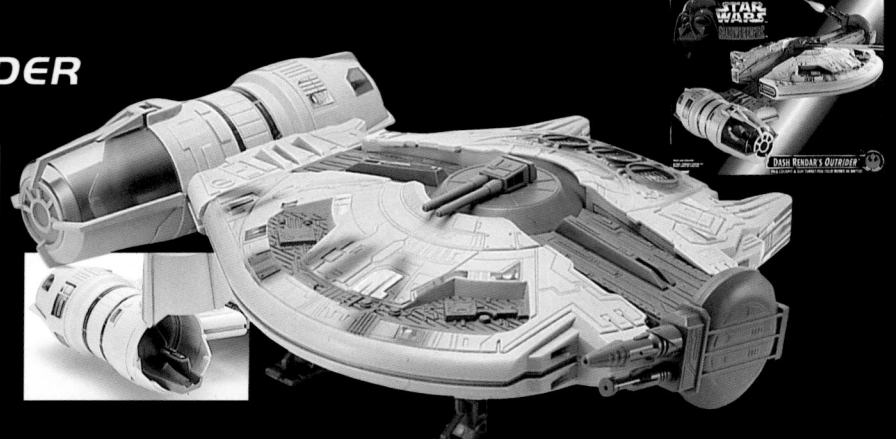

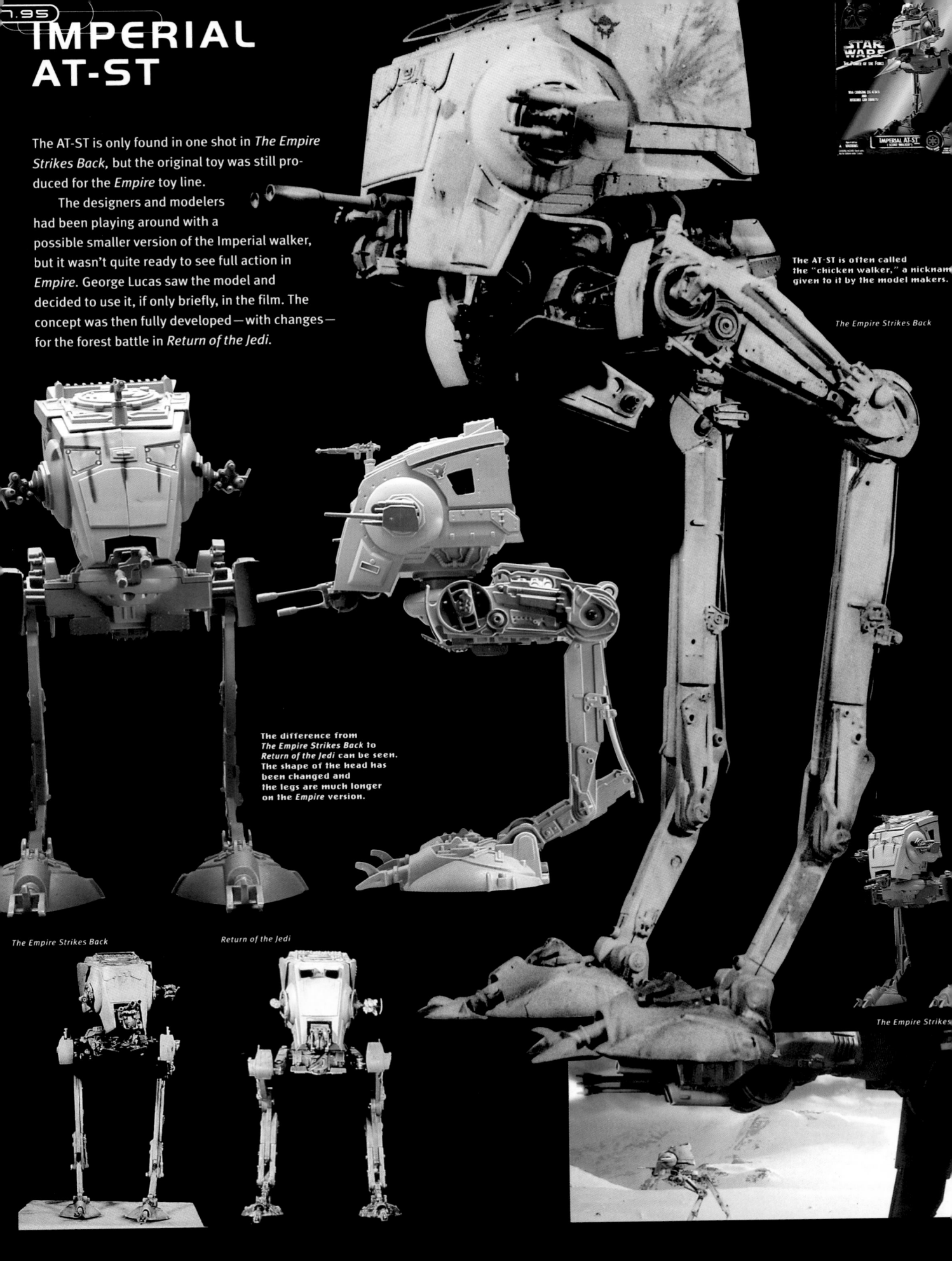

IMPERIAL AT-ST

The AT-ST is only found in one shot in *The Empire Strikes Back,* but the original toy was still pro-duced for the *Empire* toy line.

The designers and modelers had been playing around with a possible smaller version of the Imperial walker, but it wasn't quite ready to see full action in *Empire.* George Lucas saw the model and decided to use it, if only briefly, in the film. The concept was then fully developed—with changes—for the forest battle in *Return of the Jedi.*

The AT-ST is often called the "chicken walker," a nickname given to it by the model makers.

The Empire Strikes Back

The difference from *The Empire Strikes Back* to *Return of the Jedi* can be seen. The shape of the head has been changed and the legs are much longer on the *Empire* version.

The Empire Strikes Back

Return of the Jedi

The Empire Strikes

The Empire Strikes

use your harpoons and tow cables!

ELECTRONIC REBEL SNOWSPEEDER

The Empire Strikes Back

turn a prop vehicle into a toy, most the modeling has to be altered in der to accommodate the action figures. Because this, the ships tend to be slightly smaller in scale than e figures. However, proportionally, the snowspeeder is more to ale with the action figures than any of the other larger ships.

BOBA FETT'S SLAVE I

STAR WARS
THE POWER OF THE FORCE

STAR WARS
SHADOWS OF THE EMPIRE

BOBA FETT'S SLAVE I

BOBA FETT'S SLAVE I

Originally released in a purple-accented *Shadows of the Empire* box, *Slave I* later shipped in the standard green Power of the Force box.

Empire Strikes Back

"Put Captain Solo in the cargo hold."

With its new weathered paint job and improved decals, *Slave I* is a major step up from its original release. In order to properly seat the Boba Fett action figure in the cockpit, the backpack must be removed first.

The Empire Strikes Back

The Empire Strikes Back

The Empire Strikes Back

The Empire Strikes Back

The Empire Strikes Back

The Empire Strikes Back

The Empire Strikes Back

The Empire Strikes Back

ACCESSORY

STAR WARS
THE POWER OF THE FORCE

WITH
REAL MOVIE
SOUNDS!
• LASER CANNON FIRE
• ENGINE FLY-BY
SOUNDS

ELECTRONIC
REBEL SNOWSPEEDER

CRUISEMISSILE TROOPER

A cousin of the original line's minirigs, this vehicle was never in any of the *Star Wars* films. These "off camera" vehicles were designed to be sold at a lower price point. Only the trooper's head is included with the toy.

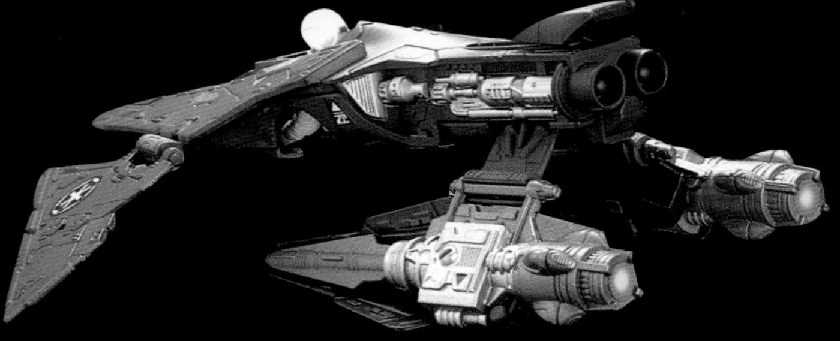

LUKE'S T-16 SKYHOPPER

"I used to bull's-eye womp rats in my T-16 back home."

Luke's model of a T-16 was seen in *Star Wars*, but this is the first time a T-16 toy has been produced. The model design was later modified and turned into an Imperial shuttle in *Return of the Jedi*.

Star Wars

The model seen in the film was built by Colin Cantwell as a proposal for an actual prop ship that was never used.

Star Wars

Star Wars

Star Wars

SPEEDER BIKE

with Luke Skywalker in Endor Gear

"Keep on that one. I'll take these two!"

Speeder Bike Luke comes equipped with poncho, lightsaber, and a blaster.

The figure of Luke in Endor gear does not have holes in his feet.

Return of the Jedi

Return of the Jedi

DARTH VADER'S TIE FIGHTER

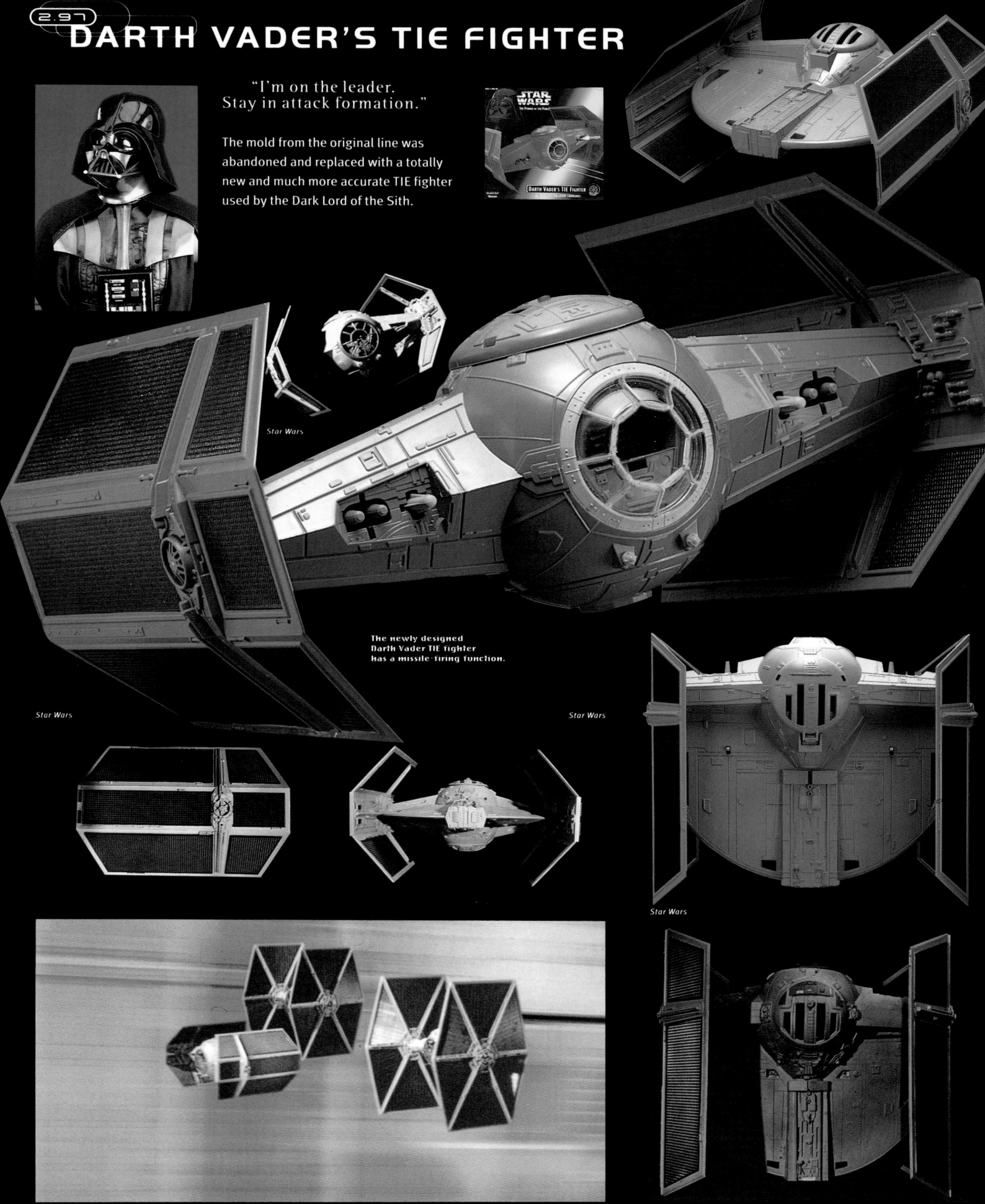

"I'm on the leader.
Stay in attack formation."

The mold from the original line was
abandoned and replaced with a totally
new and much more accurate TIE fighter
used by the Dark Lord of the Sith.

Star Wars

The newly designed
Darth Vader TIE fighter
has a missile-firing function.

Star Wars

Star Wars

Star Wars

Star Wars

Star Wars

(10.96) DETENTION BLOCK RESCUE

Rescue the Princess!

This was the first *Star Wars* playset —
or playset section — from Hasbro/Kenner.

Star Wars

(10.96) DEATH STAR ESCAPE

Swing over the core shaft!

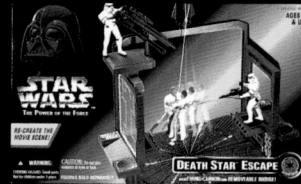

A small but nicely designed
replica of the chasm that Luke
and Leia had to swing across to
escape oncoming stormtroopers.

Star Wars

(8.97) HOTH BATTLE

Prepare for
the attack!

The Empire Strikes Back

The generator
and laser cannons
are reminiscent of the
Micro Collection playset
in 1982.

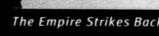

The Empire Strikes Back

(8.97) ENDOR ATTACK

Battle at the shield bunker!

Without the help of the
Ewoks and their primitive
weapons, a Rebel victory
would have been doubtful.

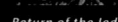
Return of the Jedi

7.97 SPEEDER BIKE

with Leia in Endor Gear

Return of the Jedi

Return of the Jedi

This is the third version of the speeder bike toy—each has slightly different markings and decoration, and each has a different action figure. Again, the figure doesn't have holes in the feet to fit pegs in a stand.

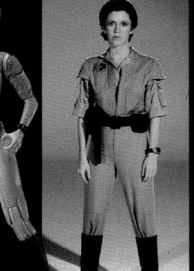

Return of the Jedi

6.97 A-WING FIGHTER

First shown in *Return of the Jedi*, the A-wing fighter came late in the original line and is now a very difficult toy for collectors to find mint and in the original box. Thus there was great excitement—and some fear—when it was announced that the A-wing was making a comeback.

Prior to the release of the A-wing, only the smaller-sized vehicles included exclusive figures. But the only way to get the A-wing pilot figure was by purchasing the vehicle.

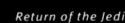

Return of the Jedi

Return of the Jedi

Return of the Jedi

Return of the Jedi

Return of the Jedi

ELECTRONIC IMPERIAL AT-AT WALKER

With thundering footsteps,
the metal monster approaches!

The largest of the new *Star Wars* toys uses basically the same tooling from the first Kenner release, but Hasbro/Kenner has updated the AT-AT with all new lights, sound effects, and dialog from *The Empire Strikes Back*.

The Empire Strikes Back

The Empire Strikes Back

General Veers in the AT-AT's cockpit. The commander himself leads the ground assault to assure Darth Vader that there won't be any more fatal mistakes.

The Empire Strikes Back

The Empire Strikes Back

The Empire Strikes Back

The Empire Strikes Back

The Empire Strikes Back

The AT-AT driver, also included with the toy, is a perfect replica of the costumed actor from the film.

The "chin" guns, a new feature, light up and make authentic movie sounds when they are pulled back and forth.

The Empire Strikes Back

The Imperial walker is the perfect size for recreating Luke's heroism in planting the explosive charge. In the interior of the main compartment, a view screen lights up to show targets.

The Empire Strikes Back

To enable the AT-AT to hold two action figures (included with the toy in the new version), the head was made to a larger scale than the rest of the body.

12-inch figures

ASSORTMENT 1 8.96
LUKE SKYWALKER

First release:
Dark blue background, macrobinoculars on belt, lightsaber handle unpainted.
Second release:
Macrobinoculars packaged in bubble on background.
Further releases:
Light blue background, lightsaber handle painted.

The European trilingual editions came packaged without the front flap on the box. Hasbro/Kenner went to a similar design worldwide in 1998.

ASSORTMENT 1 8.96
HAN SOLO

Earliest releases have a dark blue background, which was later changed to light blue.

ASSORTMENT 1 8.96
OBI-WAN KENOBI

Ben was first released with a dark blue background, an unpainted lightsaber handle and a silver belt buckle. Later releases had a light blue background, a painted saber handle, and a gold belt buckle.

ASSORTMENT 1 8.96
DARTH VADER

Originally released with a dark blue background and an unpainted lightsaber handle, the most recent releases have light blue backgrounds and painted detailing on the lightsaber. Since Hasbro used the same body for all of its early 12-inch dolls, Darth Vader is no taller than the other characters.

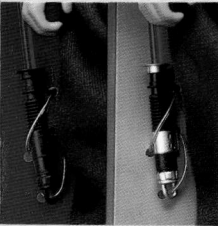

The demand for larger action figures was initially met by using existing G.I. Joe bodies. New heads, accessories, and costumes were created, and the results are the first *Star Wars* dolls or "collector figures" since their cancellation in 1980. They have been successful beyond all expectations.

LUKE SKYWALKER

in Bespin Fatigues

The back of the box shows that Chewbacca was to be released in this assortment. Production problems would later delay him to Assortment 4.

LANDO CALRISSIAN

Kenner had plans to release a Lando doll in 1980, but the 12-inch line was discontinued before it could be produced and only a couple of prototypes still exist.

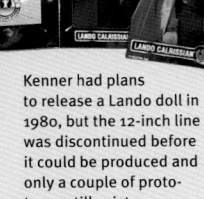

TUSKEN RAIDER

Two different Tusken Raiders were released, one with a gaderffii stick and the other with macrobinoculars and a blaster.

PRINCESS LEIA

The figure's hair is rooted but cannot be styled as the original doll's could. Twenty years ago Kenner called the style "star puffs."

LUKE SKYWALKER

in X-wing Gear

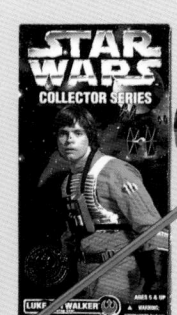

Luke's flightsuit and helmet have very accurate details and accessories.

STORMTROOPER

The figure seems a bit too chunky, and thus the armor doesn't fit as well as it could have.

BOBA FETT

The Empire Strikes Back

The armor is modeled after the style used in *The Empire Strikes Back*. The gun is from *Return of the Jedi*.

ASSORTMENT 4 · 9.97
CHEWBACCA

After several delays, the large Chewbacca finally arrived. The standard G.I. Joe body was abandoned, and Chewbacca was built around a taller, bendable doll. Unlike the original doll, this Chewbacca has "real" fur.

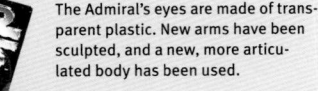

ASSORTMENT 4 · 9.97
ADMIRAL ACKBAR

The Admiral's eyes are made of transparent plastic. New arms have been sculpted, and a new, more articulated body has been used.

ASSORTMENT 4 · 9.97
C-3PO

The droid is beautifully finished with gold plating. Threepio is articulated at the head, shoulders, hip, legs, knees, and ankles.

ASSORTMENT 4 · 9.97
TIE FIGHTER PILOT

This pilot is modeled after the *Return of the Jedi* costume, since there is no side tube on the life-support pack.

SPECIALS · 7.97
HAN SOLO & LUKE SKYWALKER
in Stormtrooper Gear

Star Wars

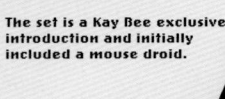

The set is a Kay Bee exclusive introduction and initially included a mouse droid.

Star Wars

Star Wars

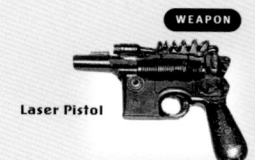

WEAPON

Laser Pistol

SANDTROOPER

Initially an exclusive introduction to comics stores and a few warehouse chains, the trooper has an orange shoulder pouldron indicating rank.

GREEDO

A J.C. Penney exclusive introduction, the poor-aiming bounty hunter comes with a gun molded into his hand.

GRAND MOFF TARKIN & IMPERIAL GUNNER

An F.A.O. Schwarz exclusive introduction, the set is enhanced with an interrogator droid and a special printed background of the Death Star corridor.

Star Wars

This is the first time an interrogator droid has been produced. Its scale is a little smaller than that of the dolls.

The gold seal on the boxes was made easier to read with the addition of black lettering and detailing. Most of the initial 12-inch figure boxes are the same dimension, but hefty dolls such as the stormtrooper required a deeper box.

SPECIALS 9.97

CANTINA BAND

Sounds of the band filled the Mos Eisley cantina.

The cantina band members were released to Wal-Mart as an exclusive introduction. All six figures are identical, but each comes with a unique instrument, and the box carries a sticker with the band member's name. These initially were the most limited of the large figures, with only about 6,500 of each variety released.

Ickabel G'ont with Fanfar   Doikk Na'ts with Fizzz   Figrin D'an with Kloo Horn   Tech M'or with Ommni Box   Tedn Dahai with Fanfar   Nalan Cheel with Bandfill

SPECIALS 9.97

ELECTRONIC POWER F/X OBI-WAN KENOBI VS. DARTH VADER

The Death Star duel can be recreated with lights and original movie sounds.

The set was a J.C. Penney exclusive introduction, and it was initially available only through the Penney Christmas catalog. Priced at around $100, the set was a slow seller and was discounted by the retailer shortly after Christmas.

Each of the figures speaks its own lines from *Star Wars* and comes with an illuminated lightsaber activated by a touch of a button.

LUKE SKYWALKER VS. WAMPA

A massive snow-covered claw nearly does Luke in.

The Empire Strikes Back

This special two-pack was released to Target stores as an exclusive introduction and immediately sold out. When supplies were replenished in early 1998, the yellow stains on the wampa's fur were less pronounced, leading some collectors to proclaim the second wampa a "variation."

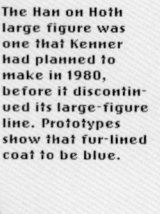

HAN SOLO & TAUNTAUN

Paying little heed to a Rebel officer's warning of extreme cold, Han mounts his tauntaun to search for Luke.

One of the most sought-after specials, the set was introduced only at Toys "Я" Us. In many cases, the toys never made the shelves as eager buyers bought them from cartons in the aisles. Considered the high point of the new Hasbro line so far, the sculpting of the tauntaun is nearly as precise as an actual Lucasfilm model.

The Han on Hoth large figure was one that Kenner had planned to make in 1980, before it discontinued its large-figure line. Prototypes show that fur-lined coat to be blue.

The Han and Tauntaun set comes with accurately detailed macrobinoculars and a scanner.

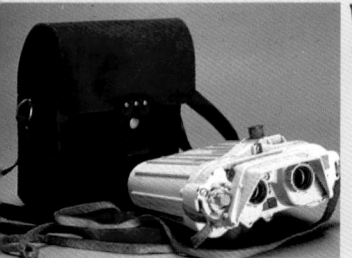

The Empire Strikes Back   *The Empire Strikes Back*

action figure storage cases

1995
OFFICIAL COLLECTOR CASE

The case, basically a black plastic box with flimsy inserts and a piece of printed cardboard riveted on, is identical to collector cases that Hasbro/Kenner produced for other action figure lines such as Superman.

The updated electronic C-3PO case uses the same basic mold as a carry case from the 1980 line. Blinking lights and Threepio's original film voice are activated by a button at the droid's mouth.

10.96
C-3PO ELECTRONIC CARRY CASE

The Luke Skywalker figure and the Wedge Antilles figure that came with the *Falcon* case both wear the flight suits of the snowspeeder pilots.

Blaster Pistol

WEAPON

The Empire Strikes Back

9.97
MILLENNIUM FALCON CARRY CASE

WEDGE ANTILLES with **BLASTER PISTOL**

The first release of the case included Wedge Antilles painted as he appears on the package front, with white stripes down his sleeves and a flight helmet identical to Luke's. Later versions corrected the error. The stripes on the sleeves were removed and the helmet was painted with Wedge's unique decorations.

1977-81

Star Wars was a surprise hit when it was released in May 1977. It had everything: creatures, droids, aliens, spaceships, good guys versus bad guys, a beautiful and feisty princess... but, anxious kids wanted to know, where were the cool toys? As surprised by the phenomenon as anyone, Kenner Products worked overtime to produce them. But it was still nine long months before the first action figures started shipping. No matter, because *Star Wars* was still in full force. By the time the phenomenon cooled, more than 250 million action figures had been sold.

EARLY BIRD CERTIFICATE PACKAGE

In 1977, movies weren't considered candidates for a successful toy license, and most companies weren't interested in taking on *Star Wars* in advance. Kenner Products took a gamble, but except for some puzzles and board games it was able to rush into production, there weren't any toys ready for Christmas 1977. Instead, against the advice of most marketers, Kenner sold an "empty box," an Early Bird Certificate Package that contained, among other things, a certificate to send away for the first four action figures that would ship in the first few months of 1978.

EARLY BIRD MAIL-IN OFFER

The first four figures released (Luke Skywalker, Princess Leia Organa, Chewbacca, and R2-D2) came packed with plastic foot pegs to be used with a cardboard stage and backdrop in the Early Bird package. The items came in a plastic tray shipped in a plain white mailer box. The earliest sets included Luke with a double-telescoping lightsaber and/or Chewbacca with a greenish-colored bowcaster.

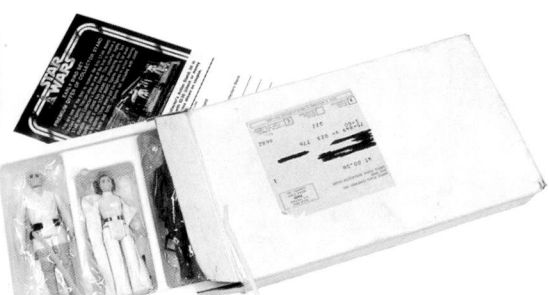

LUKE, BEN, AND VADER
with Telescoping Lightsabers

The earliest versions of the lightsabers had an extremely thin extending tip that would almost double the size of the standard saber. Many Luke Skywalker figures with these double-telescoping sabers were included with the Early Bird kit. Some can also be found on cards. Darth Vader and Obi-Wan Kenobi with double-telescoping lightsabers are much rarer, and they are extremely difficult to find on cards, though some exist at least as sales samples.

Carded telescoping Luke Skywalker. Notice that the tip of the saber is pushed in.

Below: Telescoping lightsaber fully extended on left and fully retracted on right.

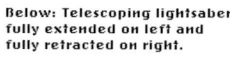

LUKE SKYWALKER

Luke was sometimes painted with yellow hair and sometimes with brown. Both versions are available on several of the card styles below. Note the change of photo on the *Return of the Jedi* card.

STAR WARS CARD

Star Wars

Kenner decided to make Luke Skywalker's action figure lightsaber yellow even though it appears more bluish-white in the films.

The original Luke Skywalker figure is representative of Kenner's older line, having a gentle face, slim body, and not much color.

CARD VARIATIONS

STAR WARS CARD

EMPIRE CARD

JEDI CARD

JEDI CARD

ARTOO-DETOO (R2-D2)

STAR WARS CARD

Star Wars

EMPIRE CARD

R2-D2 has a paper decal for body detail.

Artoo's head is chrome plated and makes a clicking sound when rotated.

The original R2-D2 action figure packaged on an *Empire Strikes Back* card is fairly rare since the sensorscope version was released soon after the card change.

PRINCESS LEIA ORGANA

With no makeup, the Princess still appears elegant.

STAR WARS CARD

The only major female character in the *Star Wars* trilogy, Princess Leia Organa was the only human female character in the 93-character toy line as well.

CARD VARIATIONS

EMPIRE CARD

JEDI CARD

WEAPON

Laser Pistol

Many of the main character figures had their photos changed on the card during the *Return of the Jedi* toy release. But Leia retained the original picture from her *Star Wars* card.

CHEWBACCA

STAR WARS CARD

Not a dog, not a wolf . . . it's a Wookiee.

The sculpting of the fur on Chewbacca shows some of the simplicity of the original line and the difficulty of capturing some of the strange creatures that came from the imagination of George Lucas.

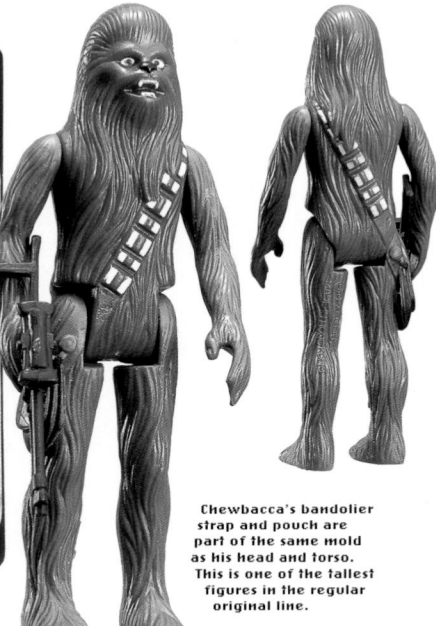

Chewbacca's bandolier strap and pouch are part of the same mold as his head and torso. This is one of the tallest figures in the regular original line.

WEAPON

Bowcaster

CARD VARIATIONS

EMPIRE CARD

JEDI CARD

JEDI CARD

POWER OF THE FORCE CARD

SEE-THREEPIO (C-3PO)

C-3PO has a subtle gold metallic tone.

Assembled differently than the other figures, C-3PO has a metal fastener visible on his back. Such a mechanical look, impermissible with the others, seems perfectly proper here.

Star Wars

A new C-3PO, with removable limbs, was released for *The Empire Strikes Back*, although the original version was available on *Empire* packaging as well. But some of the newer versions were accidentally packaged on the older version's cards, so watch for the telltale small bag packed behind the figure.

CARD VARIATIONS

STAR WARS CARD

EMPIRE CARD

DARTH VADER

As with other action figures of main characters, Vader's packaging photo was changed for the release of *Return of the Jedi* to freshen the line.

The Darth Vader figure is accurate in relative height, but appears too slim compared to the muscular actor.

Throughout the trilogy, Vader's figure was one of the few without variations or changes.

STAR WARS CARD

CARD VARIATIONS

STAR WARS CARD (JAPAN)

EMPIRE CARD

JEDI CARD

JEDI CARD

POWER OF THE FORCE CARD

Star Wars

STORMTROOPER

STAR WARS CARD

The stormtrooper is the loyal foot soldier of the Empire.

The stormtrooper's helmet is sculpted as part of its body, thus preventing natural head movement. This is another figure that stayed the same throughout the entire run.

Laser Rifle

WEAPON

Star Wars

CARD VARIATIONS

EMPIRE CARD

JEDI CARD

POWER OF THE FORCE CARD

HAN SOLO

This smuggler has a swelled head!

STAR WARS CARD

One of the few major Kenner mold changes occurred with Han. First released with a small head, he was later resculpted with a larger head. This second version was used until the end of the toy line.

A small number of the earlier, small-head Han Solos have appeared on *The Empire Strikes Back* cards. This is because with the change from *Star Wars* to *Empire* packaging, stores sent many of the older figures back to the manufacturer to be repackaged.

Star Wars

CARD VARIATIONS

STAR WARS CARD (JAPAN)

EMPIRE CARD

WEAPON

Blaster Pistol

STAR WARS CARD

EMPIRE CARD

JEDI CARD

BEN (OBI-WAN) KENOBI

"Your powers are weak, old man."

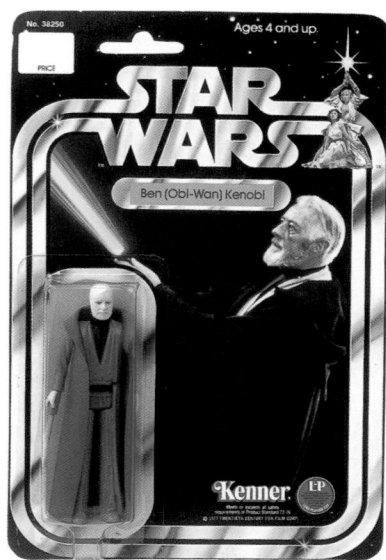

STAR WARS CARD

Among the variations found with Obi-Wan Kenobi are lightsaber changes, paint changes, and card variations.

Ben can be found with both white and gray hair.

CARD VARIATIONS

EMPIRE CARD

EMPIRE CARD

JEDI CARD

JEDI CARD

POWER OF THE FORCE CARD

SAND PEOPLE
(Tusken Raider)

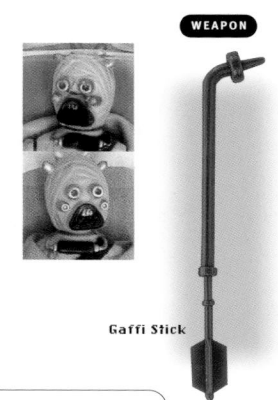

A little-known variation is in the cheek tubes on the Tusken Raider's face. Both solid and hollow tubes exist. The character's name as printed on the card also changed.

WEAPON

Gaffi Stick

CARD VARIATIONS

STAR WARS CARD   *STAR WARS* CARD (JAPAN)   *EMPIRE* CARD   *JEDI* CARD

JAWA

The earliest release of the Jawa included a vinyl cape rather than a "richer looking" cloth cape. The vinyl-caped Jawa is so rare and expensive today that many bootlegs have been made—even some appearing to be mint on original cards.

STAR WARS CARD

 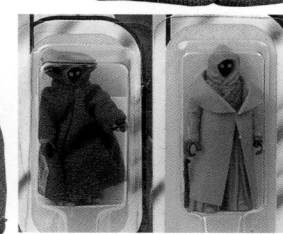

WEAPON

Blaster Pistol

CARD VARIATIONS

STAR WARS CARD   *EMPIRE* CARD   *JEDI* CARD   POWER OF THE FORCE CARD

DEATH SQUAD COMMANDER
(Star Destroyer Commander)

The officer in the packaging photo wears a gray uniform like the figure, but most of the officers with this style helmet wore black uniforms in the film.

Star Wars

STAR WARS CARD

WEAPON

Blaster Pistol

Originally called the Death Squad Commander, this figure's name was changed to Star Destroyer Commander.

Very early releases on *The Empire Strikes Back* cards still have the Death Squad Commander name. The name change came soon after.

CARD VARIATIONS

EMPIRE CARD   *JEDI* CARD

The Empire Strikes Back

GREEDO

In the *Special Edition,* Greedo shoots first.

Greedo's head is modeled, as shown by this close-up of the alien, who was brought back from the dead for the 1978 "Star Wars Holiday Special."

If the body parts were right, the costume wasn't. Instead of the green jacket with yellow arm stripes and an orange vest from the film, the Greedo action figure vestments appear to be those used by a background cantina creature with four arms.

"Star Wars Holiday Special"

STAR WARS CARD

EMPIRE CARD

WEAPON

Blaster Pistol

JEDI CARD

WALRUS MAN

CARD VARIATIONS

STAR WARS CARD

EMPIRE CARD

JEDI CARD

The figure of Walrus Man, another background cantina creature, is quite different in its shape, color, and details from the alien in the film.

WEAPON

Blaster Pistol

HAMMERHEAD

CARD VARIATIONS

STAR WARS CARD

EMPIRE CARD

JEDI CARD

Hammerhead was an awkward figure to package. It could fit in the blister-card bubble only when its head was turned to one side.

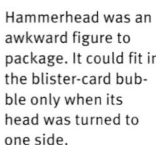

WEAPON

Blaster Pistol

SNAGGLETOOTH

"Star Wars Holiday Special"

Snaggletooth fooled the Kenner designers.

Using a fairly vague photo as reference, Kenner first produced a tall blue Snaggletooth, included in the Sears Cantina Playset. It quickly corrected the figure, making him shorter and dressed in a red outfit for his carded release. Snaggletooth's species is known as Snivvian. The name of the Snivvian who appears in the cantina is Zutton.

CARD VARIATIONS

STAR WARS CARD

EMPIRE CARD

JEDI CARD

Once a cantina patron, then a Cloud City citizen, and later a sail barge passenger, the Snivvian characters got around a lot in George Lucas' galaxy.

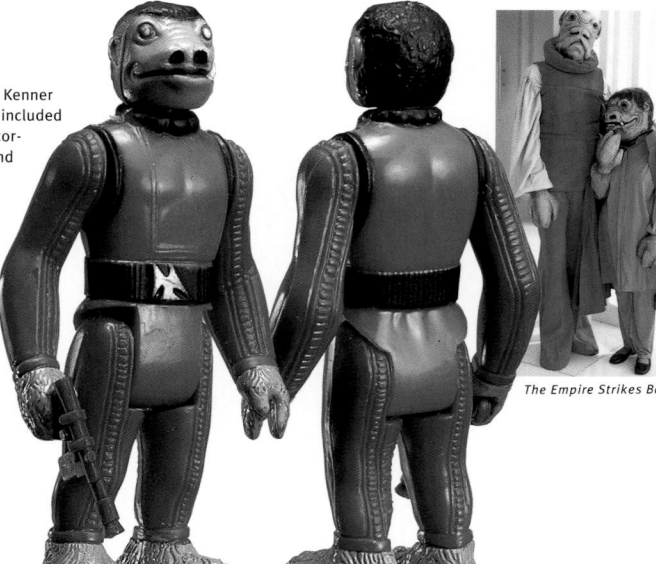

The Empire Strikes Back

Return of the Jedi

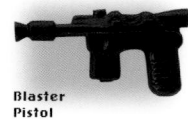

Blaster Pistol

WEAPON

LUKE SKYWALKER

X-wing Pilot

The figure has undergone frequent name variations.

While the figure is supposed to represent Luke as an X-wing pilot, it could as easily be another of his squadron compatriots.

WEAPON

Blaster Pistol

CARD VARIATIONS

Luke Skywalker: X-Wing Pilot

STAR WARS CARD

Luke Skywalker (X-Wing Pilot)

EMPIRE CARD

Luke Skywalker (X-Wing Fighter Pilot)

JEDI CARD

Luke Skywalker (X-Wing Fighter Pilot)

POWER OF THE FORCE CARD

R5-D4

"This R2 unit has a bad motivator. Look!" **I'm afraid that's an R5 unit, Luke!**

Although the action figure has only red markings, the actual R5-D4 in the film has some blue detailing as well.

There's a dramatic change from this original figure to the new Hasbro/Kenner version. In the film, since Luke calls it an "R2 unit," some call this droid R2-AG4.

CARD VARIATIONS

R5-D4

STAR WARS CARD

R5-D4

EMPIRE CARD

Arfive-Defour (R5-D4)

JEDI CARD

DEATH STAR DROID

This Insectoid droid appears throughout the trilogy.

A golden insect droid in the Jawa sandcrawler is RA-7, and a black one near the Death Star turbo lift is 5DK-RA-7.

Star Wars

The design and detailing of the Death Star Droid is similar to that of C-3PO.

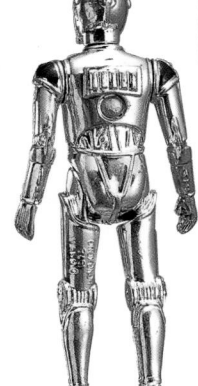

CARD VARIATIONS

STAR WARS CARD

EMPIRE CARD

JEDI CARD

POWER DROID

"Gonk . . . gonk . . . gonk."

The power droids are of the EG production series. Each is slightly different. Perhaps the action figure was modeled after EG-6 as seen in the Jawa sandcrawler.

Star Wars

Return of the Jedi

Not many detailed photos of power droids exist. The photo on the left is the power droid at the Lars homestead. The other is a power droid being tortured in Jabba's dungeon.

CARD VARIATIONS

PowerDroid

STAR WARS CARD

Power Droid

EMPIRE CARD

Power Droid

JEDI CARD

A threat of danger,
even in a piece of molded plastic.

BOBA FETT

STAR WARS CARD

EMPIRE CARD

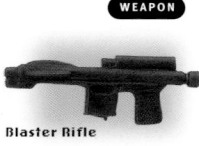

WEAPON

Blaster Rifle

JEDI CARD

JEDI CARD

The twenty-first action figure in the Kenner line had only appeared in an animated segment of the "Star Wars Holiday Special" at the time of its release. It was nearly two years before the theatrical release of *The Empire Strikes Back.*

FREE BOBA FETT WITH PURCHASE OF ANY FOUR STAR WARS ACTION FIGURES (See details on back)

What happened to the rocket-firing Boba Fett?

The packaging for the second wave of *Star Wars* action figures features a burst announcing a mail offer for Boba Fett.

The card was printed showing the rocket-firing feature but was later covered with a plain black sticker or information on Boba Fett's appearance in *The Empire Strikes Back.* In the mail-away version, Kenner included a note explaining the design change.

The Boba Fett offer was printed showing the initial rocket-firing feature. But the art was covered after the decision was made to permanently glue the rocket into the backpack when toys from another line were recalled after reports of children being injured by firing projectiles. The rocket-firing Boba Fett went through several safety changes. When the L-shaped firing mechanism slot was found to be unsafe, Kenner tried a J shape before the firing function was scrapped. No "firing" Fetts were ever sent out to consumers. However, an unknown number of prototypes are in collectors' hands.

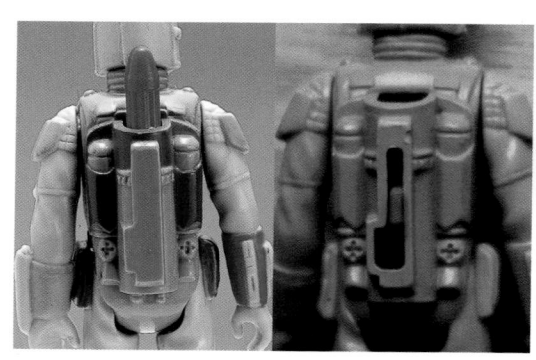

promotions and foreign packaging

DISPLAY STAND OFFER

All the galaxy's a stage— for action figures.

The Action Display Stand came with a backdrop showing a stylized Death Star and a space battle. There was a thin printed strip for the front of the stand, instructing kids where to place their first twelve figures. As for the promised action, each of the three levers in front turned the bases of four figures, giving them at least limited movement.

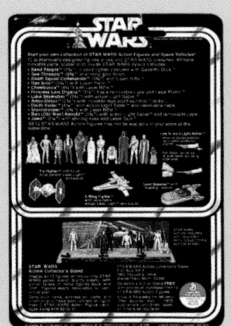

The display stand was offered through a coupon redemption included with the set of four Early Bird kit figures. It was sent in a plain mailing box.

The display stand was also offered on action figure cardbacks and later was sold in a display box in toy departments and stores.

| STORMTROOPER | DEATH SQUAD COMMANDER | DARTH VADER | SAND PEOPLE | | CHEWBACCA | PRINCESS LEIA |
| JAWA | SEE THREEPIO | BEN KENOBI | LUKE SKYWALKER | HAN SOLO | | ARTOO DETOO |

CARD BACK VARIATIONS

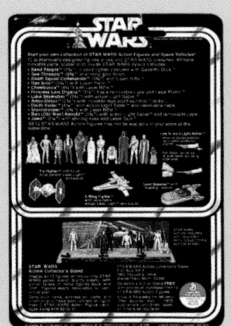
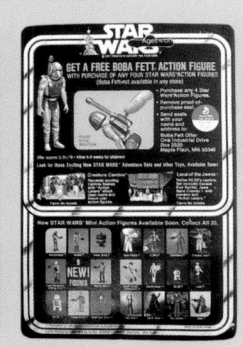
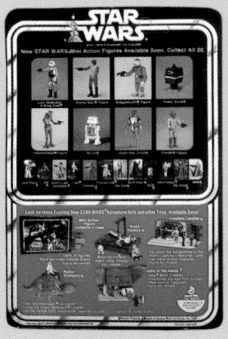
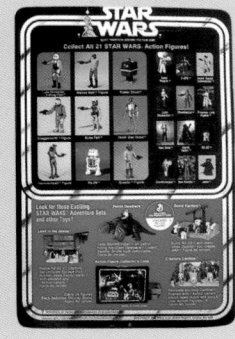

Card backs underwent many changes.

There were four main variations for *Star Wars* cards. The original twelve-back is the most widely sought. The Boba Fett offer back promoted twenty action figures, as did another, which promoted vehicles and playsets. The last card included a photo of Fett and urged "Collect All 21 *Star Wars* Action Figures."

FOREIGN CARDS

The figures became a worldwide phenomenon.

CANADIAN

The front of the Canadian packaging looks similar to the U.S. version, while the back repeats the *Star Wars* logo in French and uses two languages to describe the offerings.

BRITISH

The first Palitoy releases in England used a large logo on the front, which was later reduced in size. One cardback promoted the British chipboard Death Star playset.

ITALIAN

European countries issued different cards as well. An Italian version is pictured here. Clipper from Belgium (not pictured) also had different cards.

FRENCH

This Meccano card from France shows a Snaggletooth, although its existence on a French card has never been verified.

JAPANESE

Takara of Japan released the original twelve figures on U.S. cards with a Japanese Takara sticker. Nine of the figures were identical, but there are slight differences in sculpting in the Japanese versions of Darth Vader, C-3PO, and the stormtrooper.

Not available in all regions of the United States, these were department store exclusives. Note the "Android" set, not "Droid."

HERO SET

VILLAIN SET

ANDROID SET

SPECIAL ACTION FIGURE SETS

Rare action figure collectibles: action figure three-packs.

An "Exclusive" joins the "Special."

The same set names—except for "Android"—were used for the second series although the figures were changed.

The second series of three-packs included an exclusive fold-out photo back-drop of scenes from the film to increase play value—and sales.

FIRST SERIES

SECOND SERIES

HERO SET

DROID SET

VILLAIN SET

CREATURE SET

the empire strikes back

Kenner Toys

1981–82

The year 1980 brought the much-anticipated sequel to *Star Wars*. Three years was a long time to wait, but the release of new toys helped make the time pass more quickly. With *The Empire Strikes Back* came a new set of action figures, twenty-seven in all to add to the existing twenty-one, which were now sold with new *Empire* packaging.

LUKE SKYWALKER
(Bespin Fatigues)

Having gone to Bespin despite Yoda's warnings, Luke searches for his endangered friends, Leia and Han. He is drawn to the carbon-freezing chamber, where he confronts the ultimate enemy, Darth Vader. The action figure's face is basically the same as the original Luke, although the figure is slightly taller. Early figures have light yellow hair, while later ones have more of a dirty blond look.

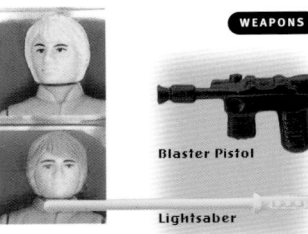

WEAPONS

Blaster Pistol

Lightsaber

CARD VARIATIONS

EMPIRE CARD   *EMPIRE* CARD   *JEDI* CARD

HAN SOLO
(Hoth Outfit)

WEAPON

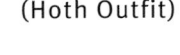

Blaster Pistol

Captain Han Solo departs from Echo Base alone to search for Commander Skywalker in a blizzard. He finds Luke, but his tauntaun collapses and dies. To keep his friend warm, he uses Luke's saber to cut the beast's belly. The original figure wears a dark-blue snowproof jacket, though the latest Hasbro version is dark brown.

CARD VARIATIONS

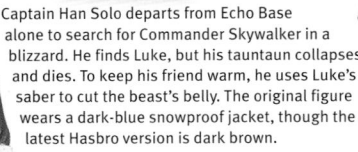

EMPIRE CARD   *JEDI* CARD

LEIA ORGANA
(Bespin Gown)

On Bespin, Leia's elegant gown is a step up from the military jumpsuit she had been wearing, but the discovery of a disassembled C-3PO is a clear indication that the Princess might have to put her battle gear back on.

The Empire Strikes Back

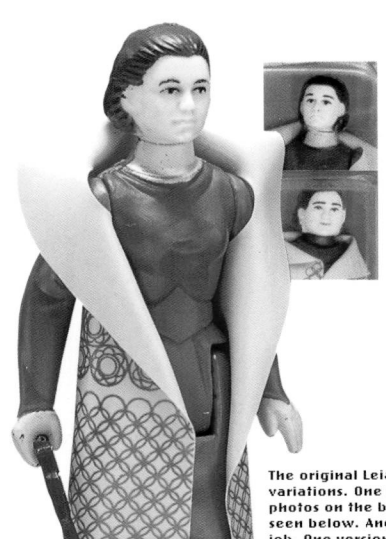

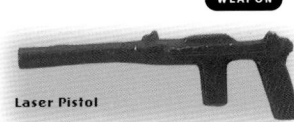

WEAPON

Laser Pistol

The original Leia Bespin has many variations. One is the difference in photos on the backing card as seen below. Another is the paint job. One version comes with a flesh-painted neck and collar and is called "flesh collar" Leia. Another comes with an unpainted red-brown plastic neck and is called "turtle-neck" Leia.

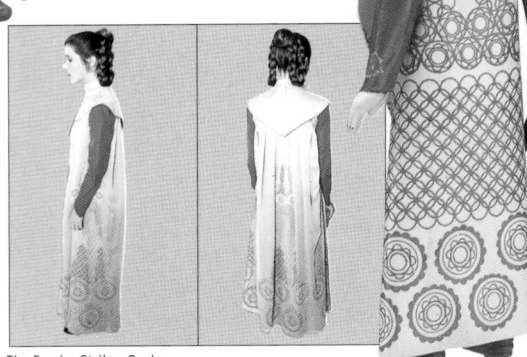

The Empire Strikes Back   *The Empire Strikes Back*

CARD VARIATIONS

EMPIRE CARD   *EMPIRE* CARD   *JEDI* CARD

BOSSK

Bossk is summoned
by Lord Vader to hunt for Han Solo.

One of the cantina creatures was nicknamed "Croc"
by the film crew. The mask got cataloged as "Saurin"
and was repainted for use as the bounty hunter
Bossk, complete with new arms, legs, and costume.

Compared with the new
Hasbro/Kenner version, the
older version is much less
detailed and not nearly as
accurate, especially the
facial detail.

CARD VARIATIONS

EMPIRE CARD

JEDI CARD

WEAPON

Blaster Rifle

IG-88

It's called Phlutdroid,
Assassin Droid, or just IG-88.

Photos of the back of IG-88 haven't been published,
so the accuracy of the back sculpting—which is very
similar to the front—remains unclear.

The Empire Strikes Back

The Empire Strikes Back

Blaster Pistol

WEAPONS

Blaster Rifle

CARD VARIATIONS

EMPIRE CARD

JEDI CARD

Earlier releases of IG-88 are
molded in plain gray plastic.
Later releases included a fine
glittery coating that made the
figure look more metallic.

REBEL SOLDIER

From handling tauntauns to defending Echo Base,
the work of Hoth's Rebel soldiers is essential
to the survival of the Rebellion.

The particular outfit worn by
the Rebel soldier in the original line
has not yet made its way to the
new Hasbro/Kenner line.
Note the brown vestlike jacket.

The Empire Strikes Back

WEAPON

Blaster Rifle

CARD VARIATIONS

EMPIRE CARD

JEDI CARD (UNRELEASED "REVENGE"
VERSION)

The Empire Strikes Back

**Rebel soldiers fighting
against intruding wampas
in a deleted scene from
The Empire Strikes Back.**

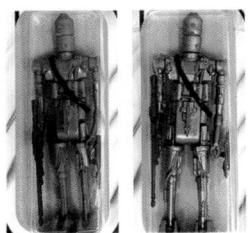

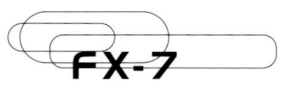

FX-7

FX-7 is pretty spiffy for a mere assistant.

An aide to the chief medical droid 2-1B, this FX-7 droid made only a brief appearance in *The Empire Strikes Back*, yet the prop is very detailed.

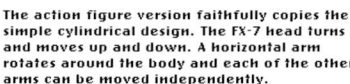

The action figure version faithfully copies the simple cylindrical design. The FX-7 head turns and moves up and down. A horizontal arm rotates around the body and each of the other arms can be moved independently.

CARD VARIATIONS

EMPIRE CARD

JEDI CARD

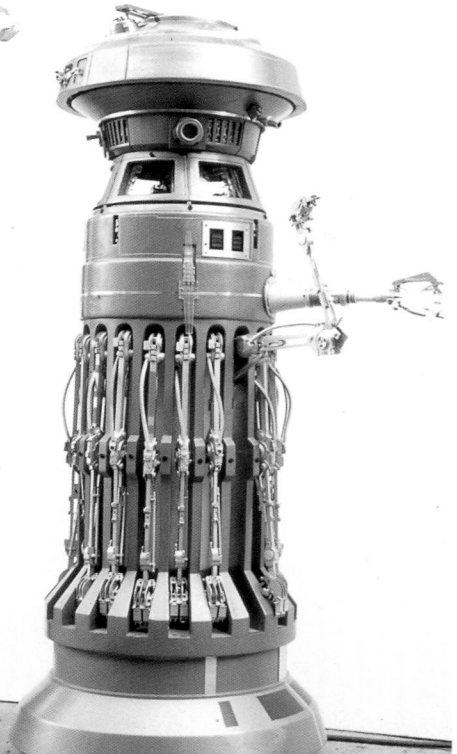

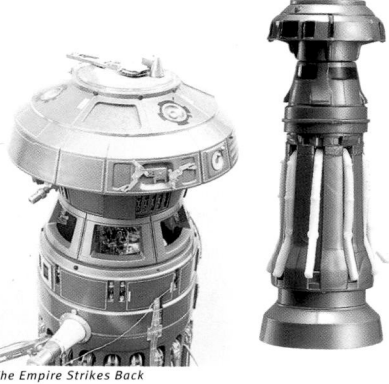

The Empire Strikes Back

The Empire Strikes Back

The Empire Strikes Back

The Empire Strikes Back   *The Empire Strikes Back*

IMPERIAL STORMTROOPER

(Hoth Battle Gear)

Stormtroopers + Snow = Snowtroopers on Hoth

Using mighty AT-ATs, the Imperial forces led by Darth Vader succeed in invading and occupying the Rebels' Echo Base. The stormtroopers in special cold-weather gear are now most often referred to as snowtroopers.

CARD VARIATIONS

EMPIRE CARD

JEDI CARD

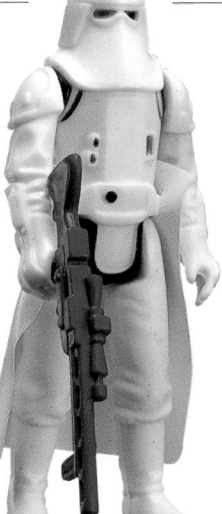

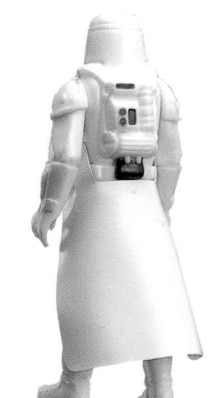

Detailing in the older Kenner line is much less true to the films than the new *Star Wars* toys, as seen here. But for the time, the sculpting was superior to other toy lines and made for great playability.

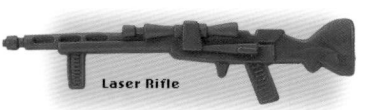

Laser Rifle

WEAPON

LANDO CALRISSIAN

Friend or foe? Imperial or Rebel? Lando must make a choice.

Lando Calrissian misses by only moments the lift-off of Boba Fett in his ship *Slave I*, carrying away his precious cargo, Han Solo frozen in carbonite. Knowing that the Empire will take over control of Cloud City, Lando orders all inhabitants to evacuate.

Laser Pistol   **WEAPON**

In early releases Lando doesn't have white paint on his eyes or teeth. Later releases add the white highlights to the facial detail.

CARD VARIATIONS

EMPIRE CARD   *EMPIRE* CARD   *JEDI* CARD

BESPIN SECURITY GUARD

"Palace" guards stand duty in the city in the clouds.

Not yet under the dominion of the Empire or the Rebellion, the citizens of Cloud City have their own paramilitary organization for protection, the Bespin security guards.

The Empire Strikes Back

CARD VARIATIONS

Laser Pistol

WEAPON

EMPIRE CARD   *JEDI* CARD

Figure Factoids
THE DISAPPEARING ALIEN SECURITY GUARD

The citizens of Bespin's Cloud City consist of many different species and races. This exotic-looking alien security guard was considered for use in *The Empire Strikes Back* but apparently was never filmed. The gold piping on his uniform and a different neck treatment presumably indicate officer rank.

The Empire Strikes Back: Behind the Scenes

YODA

The ever-wise Jedi Master.

Released later in *The Empire Strikes Back* line to preserve the surprise for filmgoers, the look and detail of the Yoda action figure—especially for its size—made it one of the standouts of the original action figure line. In many countries, the character was considered "cute."

ACCESSORY

Gimer Stick

The Empire Strikes Back

CARD VARIATIONS

EMPIRE CARD   *EMPIRE* CARD   *JEDI* CARD

Yoda's major variations are the color of his skin, the snake, and the cane. In the earliest releases, Yoda had very light green skin, which got much darker with later releases. Yoda's snake, originally orange, eventually became brown. His cane also went from a lighter to a darker brown. As seen in the photos below, the snake's sculpting was also slightly altered, changing the way it wrapped around Yoda's body.

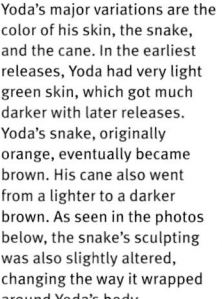

JEDI CARD   POWER OF THE FORCE CARD

LEIA
(Hoth Outfit)

Stormy times for a princess.

In *The Empire Strikes Back*, Leia has one worry after another. Her Hoth escape is a success, but just barely. The chase through the asteroid belt leads to another narrow escape. She and her party arrive safely at Cloud City, but concern for their safety only increases—for good reason.

The Empire Strikes Back

The Empire Strikes Back

EMPIRE CARD

JEDI CARD

From *Empire* to *Jedi*, Leia's name changed on the card packaging, with her title and last name being added.

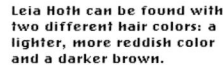

Leia Hoth can be found with two different hair colors: a lighter, more reddish color and a darker brown.

WEAPON

Blaster Pistol

REBEL COMMANDER

The Rebels make a valiant stand against Imperial AT-ATs.

The Rebel commander scans the horizon for enemies with his macrobinoculars. Then, to his shock, he sees immense Imperial walkers heading straight for the shield generators.

The Empire Strikes Back

CARD VARIATIONS

Blaster Rifle

WEAPON

The action figure is based on the Rebel officer who shouts "Come on!" after a "lassoed" walker trips and collapses.

EMPIRE CARD   *JEDI* CARD

AT-AT DRIVER

The AT-ATs lead the attack against Echo Base.

These well-armored Imperials are the pilots of the Empire's most feared land vehicle, the All Terrain Armored Transport, or walker. From their high control cabin, they can spot Rebels at a distance and blow them out of existence. But they must exert some caution because the AT-ATs have weaknesses.

WEAPON

Blaster Rifle

Imperial insignia on the driver's helmet came in two slightly different colors, scarlet and a truer red.

The Empire Strikes Back

CARD VARIATIONS

EMPIRE CARD   *JEDI* CARD

Like the stormtrooper action figure, the AT-AT driver's helmet is fixed and nonmovable.

2-1B
(Too-Onebee)

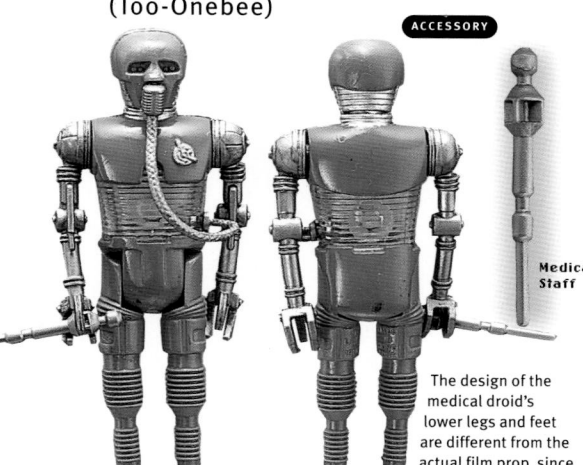

ACCESSORY

Medical Staff

The design of the medical droid's lower legs and feet are different from the actual film prop, since it wasn't detailed below the knee.

CARD VARIATIONS

2-1B

EMPIRE CARD

Two-Onebee (2-1B)

EMPIRE CARD

Too-Onebee (2-1B)

JEDI CARD

IMPERIAL COMMANDER

Commanders cannot fail Lord Vader.

The rank of Commander is simply a generic title for all uniformed Imperial Officers. From the detachment Commander Praji to Moff Jerjerodd, who supervises the construction of the second Death Star, all serve Lord Vader to his liking—or die.

Sculpting, rank, and package photo show that General Veers was the model for this figure. However, the black color of the uniform suggests a lower ranked officer, and Veers was made into a separate figure.

Star Wars

The Empire Strikes Back

CARD VARIATIONS

EMPIRE CARD

JEDI CARD

Blaster Rifle

WEAPON

Return of the Jedi

UGNAUGHT

Small in stature, Ugnaughts run Cloud City.

The species of small beings known as Ugnaughts have been hired to perform the simple yet dangerous labor tasks on Cloud City. The Ugnaughts are inhabitants of Gentes in the Anoat system. Three species of Ugnaughts can be seen working together in Cloud City. The chief Ugnaught is known by the name Ugloste.

A fanged Ugnaught was chosen as the action figure model. The figure's apron can be found in lavender, green, or blue.

The Empire Strikes Back

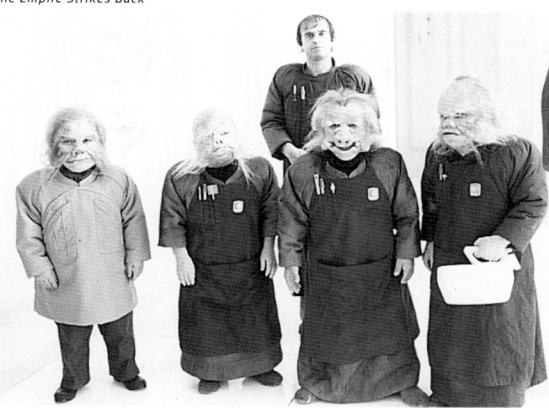

ACCESSORY

Ugnaught's Bag

CARD VARIATIONS

EMPIRE CARD

JEDI CARD

The Empire Strikes Back

The Empire Strikes Back

An Ugnaught also makes a brief appearance in *Return of the Jedi*.

The Empire Strikes Back

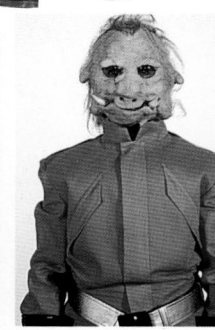

Return of the Jedi

LOBOT

Lando's obedient, expressionless aide.

Lobot, the cyborg aide of Lando Calrissian, betrays no emotion. The permanently attached interface on his head allows him to work closely with the computers that run Cloud City.

The Empire Strikes Back

The Empire Strikes Back

The Empire Strikes Back

CARD VARIATIONS

Lobot is not very tall, and his height has been translated well to the action figure.

EMPIRE CARD

JEDI CARD

WEAPON

Laser Pistol

DENGAR

This bounty hunter is a damaged human with scavenged armor.

Wearing battered Imperial armor (a snowtrooper's chest plate and sandtrooper's knee pads), Dengar is one of six bounty hunters who respond to Lord Vader's call.

The Empire Strikes Back

The original action figure replicates Dengar's backpack from the film, but the new Hasbro/Kenner figure comes without any back equipment.

The Empire Strikes Back

CARD VARIATIONS

EMPIRE CARD

JEDI CARD

WEAPON

Laser Rifle

HAN SOLO
(Bespin Outfit)

Han escapes the Imperial fleet
only to confront another crisis.

Not fully repaired, the *Millennium Falcon*
makes an emergency evacuation from
the Hoth Echo Base. After being chased into
an asteroid field by the Empire's TIE squadrons,
Han and the *Falcon*'s passengers barely
escape being lunch for a space slug.

The Empire Strikes Back

The Empire Strikes Back

This is Han's apparel on
Bespin as well as Hoth.

WEAPON

Laser Pistol

CARD VARIATIONS

EMPIRE CARD

JEDI CARD

SEE-THREEPIO (C-3PO)
with Removable Limbs

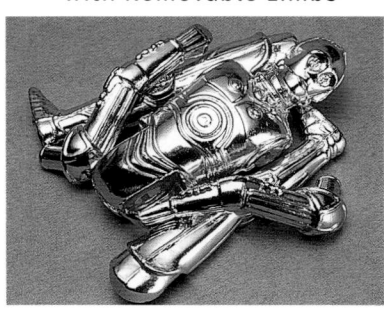

The Empire Strikes Back

"At least you're still in one piece!
Look what happened to me!"

While following a voice that he thought was R2-D2, C-3PO is shot to pieces by
stormtroopers. Chewbacca later discovers and barely rescues the dismem-
bered droid. Putting him partially together, Chewie carries Threepio on his
back during their escape from Cloud City; all the droid does is complain.

CARD VARIATIONS

EMPIRE CARD

JEDI CARD

POWER OF THE
FORCE CARD

C-3PO was reissued
with a new remov-
able-limbs feature
and a plastic carry
net.

ARTOO-DETOO (R2-D2)
with Sensorscope

R2-D2 has countless gadgets and tools.

Artoo scans the frigid Hoth tundra for
his missing master Luke. His sensorscope lets
the small droid scan in all directions and for
many kilometers.

The Empire Strikes Back

The action figure's sen-
sorscope more closely
resembles the periscope
that Artoo used in the
Dagobah swamp after
Luke's X-wing crashed.

CARD VARIATIONS

EMPIRE CARD

JEDI CARD

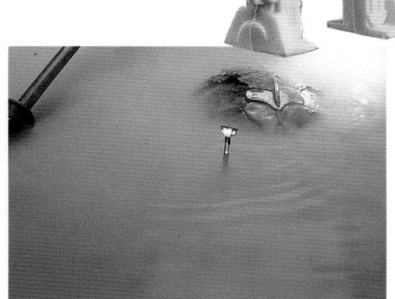

The Empire Strikes Back

LUKE SKYWALKER

in Hoth Gear

About to head back to base, Luke is knocked out from behind.

Patrolling the ice plains of Hoth,
Luke is preparing to return to Echo Base.
He ignores the unease of his tauntaun
and is attacked by a wampa snow beast
and hauled to its ice cavern.

AT-AT COMMANDER

General Veers takes command of the Imperial attack force.

Wearing an armored chest plate
and assault helmet, General Veers
takes charge of the lead Imperial walker
and eventually succeeds in destroying
the Rebels' power generator.

The Empire Strikes Back

WEAPON

Blaster Pistol

CARD VARIATIONS

EMPIRE CARD   *JEDI* CARD

WEAPON

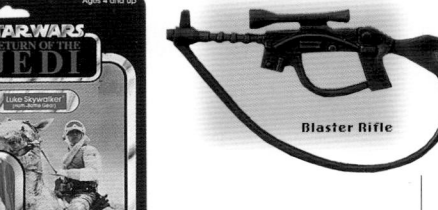

Blaster Rifle

While Han Solo wears
his own unique cold-
weather jacket, Luke
wears the standard-issue
Rebel soldier jacket.

CARD VARIATIONS

EMPIRE CARD   *JEDI* CARD

The "AT-AT Commander" figure
was originally going to be
named "General Veers." That
version exists on some
Canadian department store in-
pack promotions.

CLOUD CAR PILOT

Cloud cars patrol and defend Cloud City.

The patrolling cloud cars fire a warning shot at the
Millennium Falcon upon its arrival at Cloud City. There
is a brief appearance of what is possibly a cloud car
pilot within the halls of Cloud City. But his helmet and
uniform are different from that of the action figure.

The Empire Strikes Back

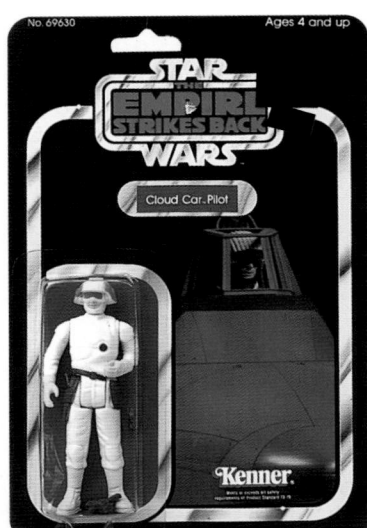

EMPIRE CARD

CARD VARIATIONS

JEDI CARD

The style and color of the action figure are
modeled after the prop vehicle's figure
used in the film.

ACCESSORIES

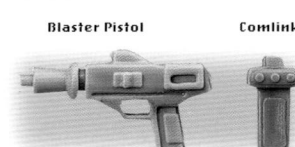

Blaster Pistol   **Comlink**

BESPIN SECURITY GUARD

Bespin guards push Han Solo in carbonite.

The Empire Strikes Back

CARD VARIATIONS

EMPIRE CARD

JEDI CARD

WEAPON

Blaster Pistol

In *The Empire Strikes Back*, Cloud City is a cosmopolitan setting where many races and species mingle. So it is only natural that there are black human security guards as well as white ones.

This second security guard is more realistic in shape and color than the first one produced.

ZUCKUSS

(now 4-LOM)

A droid bounty hunter joins the assembly aboard the *Executor*.

This droid was called Zuckuss in the original Kenner line, although it was rechristened to fit the naming conventions of the *Star Wars* galaxy. His head is somewhat similar to the head of 4-LOM (now Zuckuss).

WEAPON

Blaster Rifle

CARD VARIATIONS

EMPIRE CARD

JEDI CARD

Still mysterious is the droid's body color. In the film it looks metallic brown. The original Kenner figure is metallic gray, while the newer Hasbro/Kenner figure has rusty orange weathering. Photos from the Lucasfilm archives indicate a metallic dark blue.

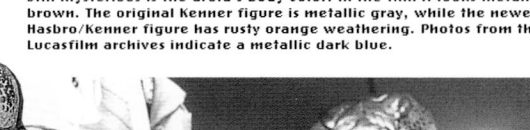

The Empire Strikes Back

4-LOM
(now Zuckuss)

Alien bounty hunter from the planet Gand.

The shortest of the bounty hunters, the alien once known as 4-LOM has now had his name corrected to Zuckuss. There are very few reference photos available for this character. His head is similar in shape to the droid that is now called 4-LOM.

The Empire Strikes Back

The Empire Strikes Back

The new Hasbro action figure line has corrected the character's name to Zuckuss, a change brought about originally by West End Games.

WEAPON

Blaster Rifle

The Empire Strikes Back

IMPERIAL TIE FIGHTER PILOT

Only the elite were good enough to be TIE pilots.

While there were no screen appearances in *Empire*, the TIE pilot figure was released first on an *Empire* card. The difference between the pilots from *Star Wars* and *Return of the Jedi* is the presence in the first film of a tube coming out of the left side of the life-support system.

The actual color of the prop helmet is metallic dark gray rather than the flat black of the figure.

WEAPON

Blaster Pistol

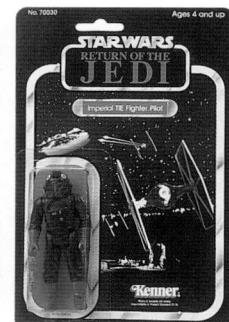

Star Wars

SPECIAL ACTION FIGURE SETS

Three-packs

Three-packs are scarce and highly collectible.

Similar to the special department store sets for *Star Wars, The Empire Strikes Back* sets were issued in 1980, 1981, and 1982. It is now very difficult to acquire a complete set. The second and third assortments share the same set names: Bespin, Rebel, and Imperial.

HOTH REBELS

BESPIN ALLIANCE

REBEL SET

BESPIN SET

IMPERIAL SET

BESPIN SET

Six-packs

With *Empire,* larger-sized figure packs appeared.

The first *Empire* six-pack (above right) was available just after the release of the first three-pack assortment. The six-pack containing Yoda (below right) was released later.

CARD BACK VARIATIONS and Mail-Away Offers

Mail-in offers expanded the *Star Wars* universe.

Four-piece L-shaped plastic stands could be arranged in many different layouts and included interchangeable backgrounds of film scenes.

Before any figures were released of characters that first appear in *The Empire Strikes Back*, a secret action figure offer was printed on the earliest *Empire* cards. The figure was Bossk.

Accessories from the Survival Kit were later separated and packed along with several vehicles as department store specials.

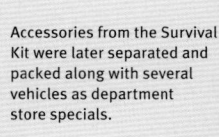

The last offer of a figure from *The Empire Strikes Back* was for 4-LOM. The offer was either in the form of a sticker or printed on the action figure cards.

The last offer appearing on an *Empire* card was for Admiral Ackbar from *Revenge of the Jedi*.

BRITISH

In England, Kenner *Star Wars* action figures were released through Palitoy. For *The Empire Strikes Back*, the first carded figures had a midsize Palitoy logo printed on the front. The second series had a large logo, and the third series a small logo. The final series had no logo but just a black bar under the film title.

JAPANESE

In Japan, Kenner figures were sold in plastic bags enclosed in small and colorful boxes by the toy company Popy. Only fifteen of the *Empire* figures were in this line.

Kenner Toys

return of the jedi

1983

The final chapter in the original *Star Wars* trilogy arrived in 1983. *Return of the Jedi* was to be the most complex of the films, tying up many loose ends. Early production photos whetted the appetites of a legion of fans. Kenner's action figures, also eagerly anticipated, proved to be closer than ever to the look of the film, with greater detailing and the use of new materials.

ADMIRAL ACKBAR

A Mon Calamari commands the Rebel fleet.

Many alien species have joined the Rebellion by *Return of the Jedi*, including the Mon Calamari led by Admiral Ackbar.

Return of the Jedi

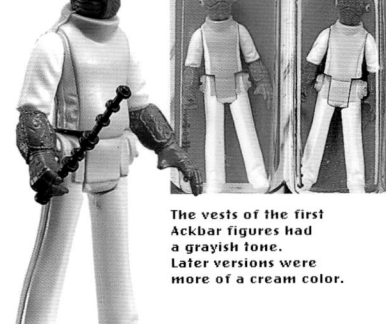

The vests of the first Ackbar figures had a grayish tone. Later versions were more of a cream color.

ACCESSORY

Ackbar's Command Stick

CARD VARIATIONS

JEDI CARD	*JEDI* CARD

GAMORREAN GUARD

The "pig guards" protect Jabba's palace.

Powerful-looking but stupid Gamorrean guards greet C-3PO and R2-D2 near the gate of Jabba's palace. The guards know the droids will quickly become captives in thrall to their master.

WEAPON

Vibro-Ax

Although it appears primitive, a Gamorrean guard's vibro-ax can be deadly in fights. With only the slightest touch, an ultrasonic generator located in the vibro-ax handle produces vibrations that give the blade great cutting power.

CARD VARIATIONS

SPECIAL COLLECTORS COIN

JEDI CARD	POWER OF THE FORCE CARD

LUKE SKYWALKER
(Jedi Knight Outfit)

Once again, Skywalker to the rescue.

Luke Skywalker, now a Jedi Knight, enters Jabba's palace. The figure is accurate including the color of the cloth robe. The gun was the one he grabbed from one of Jabba's guards before he fell into the rancor pit.

Return of the Jedi

WEAPONS

Blaster Pistol

Lightsaber

There are many packaging variations. The first lightsaber was blue, the second green. Several variations in the robe include its color, a snap or sewn collar, and how it was packaged in the plastic blister.

CARD VARIATIONS

JEDI CARD	*JEDI* CARD

SPECIAL COLLECTORS COIN

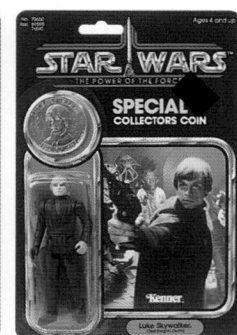

JEDI CARD	POWER OF THE FORCE CARD

PRINCESS LEIA ORGANA

(Boushh Disguise)

A thermal detonator gets everyone's attention.

The disguised princess' rescue plan works fine until Jabba, monitoring her every step, springs his trap and shackles her as his slave.

WEAPON

Blaster Rifle

Inside the mask of the bounty hunter Boushh is the face of Princess Leia, well sculpted and in proportion despite the helmet.

JEDI CARD

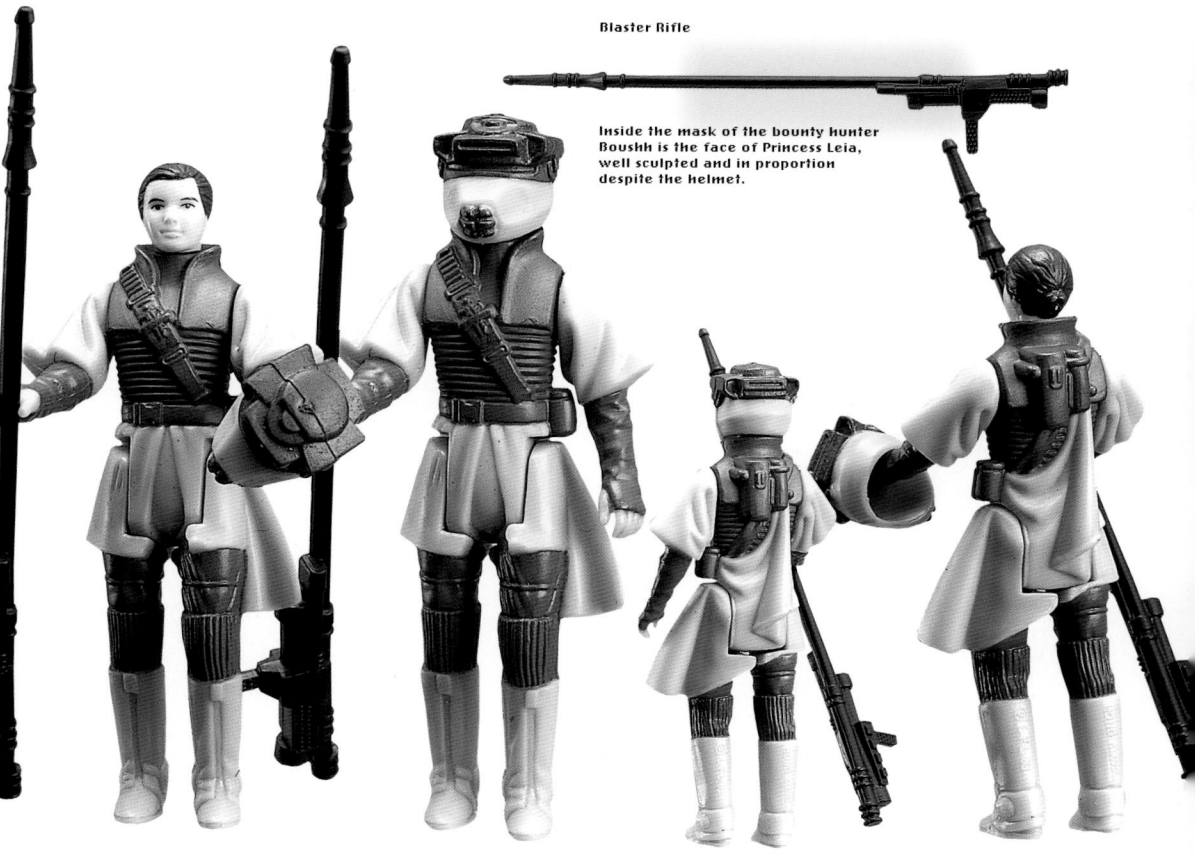

EMPEROR'S ROYAL GUARD

The Royal Guard protects the Emperor.

Before the Emperor descends down the ramp of the Imperial shuttle, six Royal Guards clear his way onto the Death Star.

Some cards hide misprinted serial numbers with a sticker.

JEDI CARD

ACCESSORY

The cloth robe may tone down the brightness of the "Crimson Guard," but the mask and other parts are well sculpted.

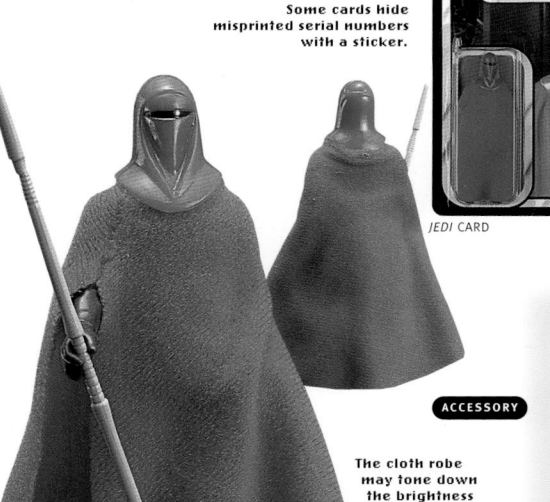

Force Pike

CHIEF CHIRPA

Return of the Jedi

Return of the Jedi

Battle Staff

Head of his tribe's Council of Elders, the strong-willed Chirpa befriends the Rebel strike force sent to the moon of Endor. His warriors are courageous and skillful despite being vastly outnumbered. Chief Chirpa has gray fur and carries a reptilian staff denoting his rank. He wears the teeth, horns, and bones of animals he has hunted.

The sculpting of the fur on the Ewoks is much improved from the original Chewbacca action figure detailing.

JEDI CARD

ACCESSORY

LOGRAY

A floating C-3PO amazes the Ewok medicine man.

Logray, an Ewok shaman who stands alongside Chief Chirpa, provides predictions and advice, but he has no way of predicting the "magical powers" of the golden "god" C-3PO.

One of the most accurately sculpted action figures, the Logray figure looks very much like Lucasfilm's costume reference photos.

Return of the Jedi

JEDI CARD

ACCESSORY

Shaman Staff

KLAATU

Klaatu enjoys the party at Jabba's palace.

The name Klaatu pays homage to the 1950's film *The Day the Earth Stood Still*, which supplied two other alien names to the *Star Wars* galaxy. Klaatu also appears on Jabba's sail barge.

Return of the Jedi

Some Klaatu figures are dressed in a thicker fur while others have a much thinner loin cloth. Some also have tan arms (not shown).

WEAPON

Force Pike

CARD VARIATIONS

JEDI CARD   *JEDI CARD*

WEEQUAY

His chief enjoyment is feeding victims to the Sarlacc.

There are at least three different Weequays in *Return of the Jedi*. The character is sometimes called Queequeg after the character in the novel *Moby Dick*.

JEDI CARD

Force Pike

While at first glance the old version seems similar to the Hasbro/Kenner Weequay Skiff Guard, a closer look shows how the current line's sculpting is superior.

WEAPON

REBEL COMMANDO

The Rebels must take over the bunker before their fleet arrives!

When you're outnumbered, hand-to-hand combat isn't always the best strategy. Han Solo lures a scout behind the Imperial bunker into the hands of waiting Rebel troops. But it's a trap in more ways than one.

The Endor troops wear camouflaged jump suits, but the ability to paint action figures at that time was quite limited. Therefore, the original figures are dressed in plain green.

JEDI CARD

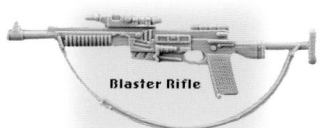

Blaster Rifle

JEDI CARD

GENERAL MADINE

Return of the Jedi   *Return of the Jedi*

Once an Imperial officer, he becomes a major Rebel leader.

General Crix Madine introduces many innovative tactics to the Rebel forces, working on ground strategy while Admiral Ackbar develops space combat techniques.

When the Alliance learns that the Empire is building a second Death Star above the forest moon of Endor, General Madine helps devise an ultimately successful plan to have a small strike team led by Han Solo deactivate the uncompleted Death Star's energy shield—located on Endor's moon—so that the battle station can be attacked.

Return of the Jedi

The scenes of Madine piloting a Rebel cruiser never made it into *Jedi*.

Return of the Jedi

LANDO CALRISSIAN
(Skiff Guard Disguise)

Through his mask, Lando's eyes show his determination.

Lando disguises himself as a skiff guard and infiltrates the palace of Jabba the Hutt, waiting for his chance to aid in the rescue of Han Solo. Han returns the favor, saving Lando's life by snatching him from the maw of the Sarlacc in the Tatooine desert.

JEDI CARD

The skiff guard helmet is removable and comes in a separate blister section so buyers can see Lando's face.

WEAPON

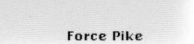

Force Pike

NIEN NUNB

Lando's new partner: the pilot Nien Nunb.

Nien Nunb, of the Sullustan species, is the copilot of Gold Leader (Lando Calrissian) aboard the *Millennium Falcon* during its assault on the second Death Star. He should not be confused with the B-wing pilot Ten Numb.

Return of the Jedi

JEDI CARD

Nien Nunb's outfit is similar to a B-wing pilot's flight suit. The breathing apparatus has been replaced with a blue vest.

WEAPON

Blaster Pistol

BIKER SCOUT

Biker scouts patrol the forest moon of Endor.

Return of the Jedi

The trees and brush of the forest moon make it difficult for most vehicles to maneuver. So the Empire uses speeder bikes and highly trained pilots as its scouts.

WEAPON

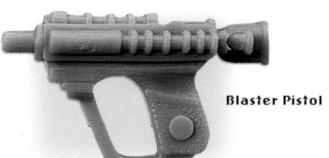

Blaster Pistol

Several molding variations can be found in the face and body sculpting. Figures were manufactured in Hong Kong, Macao, Taiwan, and Mexico.

CARD VARIATIONS

JEDI CARD

JEDI CARD

POWER OF THE FORCE CARD

SQUID HEAD

Tessek skulks about Jabba's palace.

A Quarren or "Squid Head," Tessek flees his homeworld of Mon Calamari after an Imperial invasion and ends up as an accountant for crime lord Jabba the Hutt. But he plots against his boss. Jabba insists that he accompany his party out to the Pit of Carkoon to execute a number of Rebels. Tessek escapes just as Jabba's sail barge is blown up.

Return of the Jedi

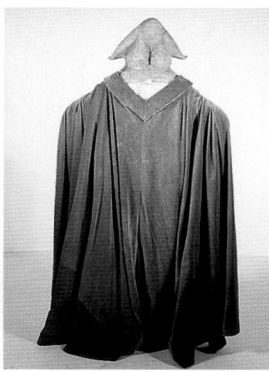

In the film, Squid Head was a minor background character. However, he was one of the first figures to be released for *Return of the Jedi*.

JEDI CARD

WEAPON

Blaster Pistol

REE-YEES

This alien can't hold his Sullustan gin very well.

Ree-Yees' name is a partial anagram of "Three Eyes." In *Return of the Jedi*, the Gran from the planet Kinyen holds C-3PO's mouth to shut him up.

Return of the Jedi

WEAPON

Blaster Rifle

Ree-Yees' weapon could be a Kenner original, since no prop reference photo can be found.

JEDI CARD

BIB FORTUNA

Jabba the Hutt's majordomo.

A member of the Twi'lek species, Bib Fortuna has the pronounced head-tails of all natives of Ryloth. He is obsequious to Jabba even as he plots to kill him and take over his illegal businesses.

JEDI CARD

WEAPON

Battle Staff

As with Ree-Yees, Fortuna's battle staff can't be found in any prop reference photo.

NIKTO

Aboard a skiff, he protects Jabba's sail barge.

The Nikto are a humanoid species with flat faces, multiple nostrils, and four small horns protruding from their foreheads. Several Niktos are hired by Jabba the Hutt as skiff guards. One of them gets thrown to the Sarlacc.

Other Niktos in *Return of the Jedi* include the pilot of the skiff on which Luke Skywalker is a captive and a deck gunner of the sail barge.

Return of the Jedi

Battle Staff

WEAPON

JEDI CARD

POWER OF THE FORCE CARD

Return of the Jedi

Return of the Jedi

8D8

Even droids can be punished!

The droid 8D8 is in the middle of torturing a power droid when R2-D2 and C-3PO arrive. A thin-faced, white-colored droid with an almost humanoid face, pincers for hands, and pistons operating its legs, 8D8 works under EV-9D9 in Jabba the Hutt's droid operations center.

The figure's sculpting is a little bulkier than the film droid, but otherwise the proportions hold true to the original.

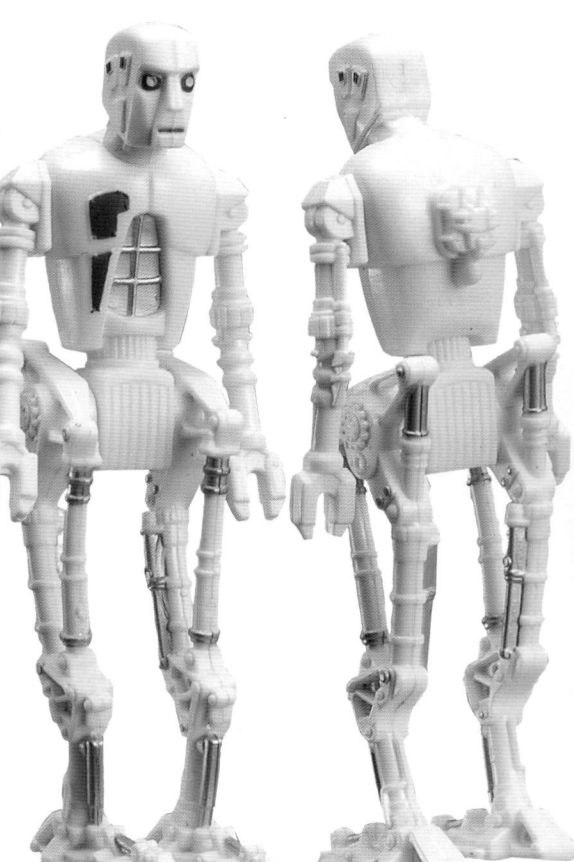

JEDI CARD

Return of the Jedi

PRINCESS LEIA ORGANA
(Combat Poncho)

Leia is dressed for forest combat.

Princess Leia's helmet and poncho serve her well while literally flying over the terrain on one of the Empire's swift speeder bikes. The action figure's helmet and poncho are removable.

JEDI CARD

POWER OF THE FORCE CARD

The figure's legs are pliable enough to be bent in order to seat Leia on a speeder bike toy.

WEAPON

Blaster Pistol

WICKET W. WARRICK

As nosy as an . . . Ewok.

Full of curiosity, the young Ewok Wicket W. Warrick draws close to inspect an unconscious Princess Leia. Each is spooked by the other at first, but a friendship grows that leads to the Ewoks helping the Rebels fight the Imperial forces.

Return of the Jedi

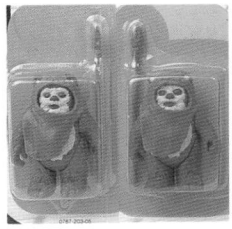

Even for its small size, the sculpting of Wicket is fairly accurate to the film counterpart. Two variations can be found, one with the spear packed on the left, the other with it packed on the right.

Spear

WEAPON

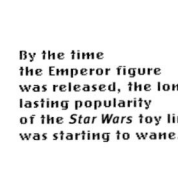

CARD VARIATIONS

JEDI CARD

JEDI CARD

POWER OF THE FORCE CARD

THE EMPEROR

The corrupter of the Force.

To develop an interesting toy assortment, a mixture of major and minor characters was used. The Emperor, who had a major role in the film, was not released until the second wave of *Jedi* figures.

By the time the Emperor figure was released, the long-lasting popularity of the *Star Wars* toy line was starting to wane.

ACCESSORY

Walking Stick

CARD VARIATIONS

JEDI CARD

POWER OF THE FORCE CARD

Return of the Jedi

KLAATU

(Skiff Guard Outfit)

Death to betrayers of the mighty Jabba!

There are at least four different Klaatus in *Return of the Jedi*. The first was introduced as a figure in the first *Jedi* wave. The second is represented by this figure and can be seen on the deck of the sail barge. The third was one of the rancor keepers, and the fourth was possibly on the second skiff.

JEDI CARD

Return of the Jedi

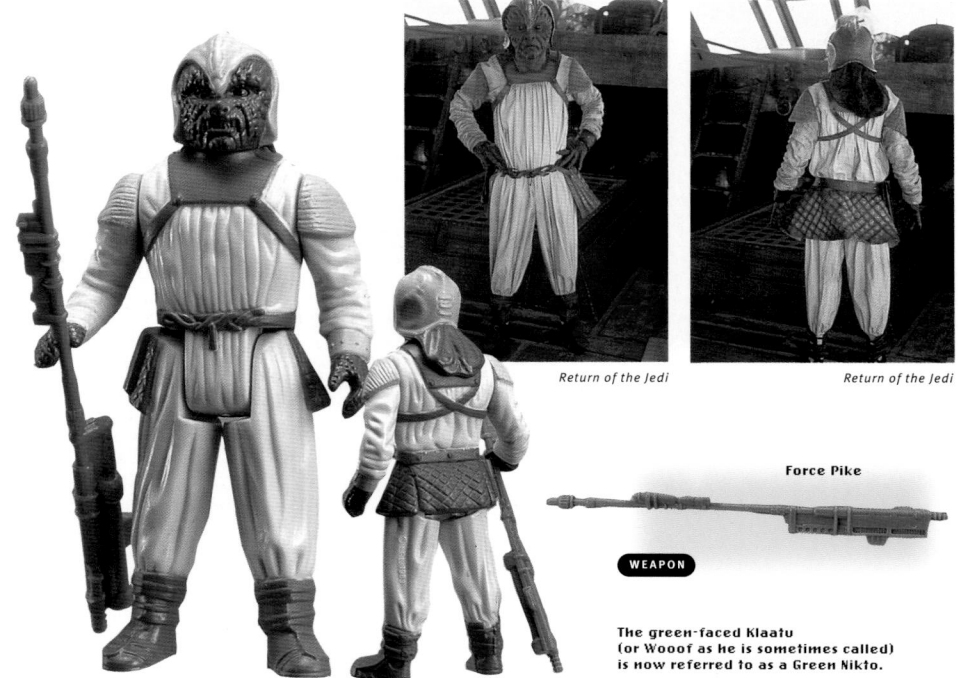

Return of the Jedi

Return of the Jedi

Force Pike

WEAPON

The green-faced Klaatu
(or Wooof as he is sometimes called)
is now referred to as a Green Nikto.

B-WING PILOT

Heavily armed B-wings play a major role in the Battle of Endor.

The B-wing pilots seen in the Rebel briefing room don't appear again until the victory celebration at the end of *Return of the Jedi*, since a B-wing battle sequence was never done as part of the film.

Return of the Jedi

Below, a B-wing pilot joins in the celebration.

Return of the Jedi

Blaster Pistol

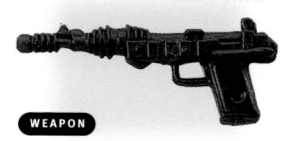

WEAPON

CARD VARIATIONS

JEDI CARD   POWER OF THE FORCE CARD

AT-ST DRIVER

It's not quite an AT-AT, but the scout walker is impressive.

The driver figure has realistic sculpting of the folds and creases of his suit. Many troop figures were made in the ongoing *Star Wars* line so that children could build armies of different armored or uniformed soldiers.

In the end, their ungainly structure was used against the AT-STs as the Ewoks used primitive techniques to trip them up and destroy them.

WEAPON

Blaster Pistol

CARD VARIATIONS

JEDI CARD   POWER OF THE FORCE CARD

HAN SOLO
(Trench Coat)

Not exactly the height of Coruscant fashion!

Han Solo, wearing his oversized camouflage trench coat, commands the moon of Endor strike team. The fourth sculpting of the Han action figure takes into account the maturing of actor Harrison Ford.

No. 71580

The action figure's trench coat comes with two different collars. One is the same camouflage material as the rest of the coat and the other is plain.

WEAPON

Blaster Pistol

CARD VARIATIONS

JEDI CARD   *JEDI* CARD   POWER OF THE FORCE CARD

TEEBO

Teebo is one of the bravest of the Ewok tribe.

With his striped fur and half-skull helmet, Teebo is a frightening visage as he approaches foes with his stone ax drawn.

Return of the Jedi

In order to hide seams on the Ewok costumes, appliances and paraphernalia were strategically placed.

CARD VARIATIONS

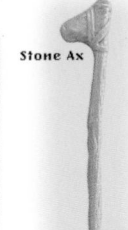

Stone Ax

JEDI CARD   POWER OF THE FORCE CARD   **WEAPON**

PRUNE FACE

Three "Prune Faces" are at the Rebel briefing.

Nicknamed "Prune Face" for their shriveled appearance, the actual species name of the characters is Dresselian.

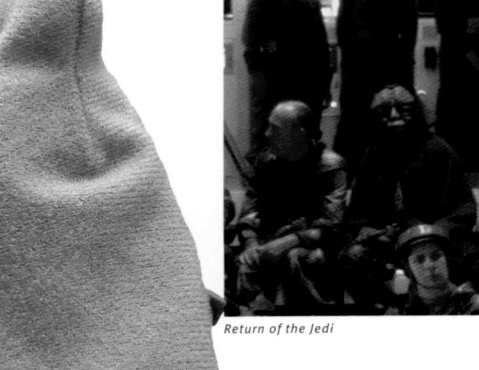

Return of the Jedi

Rifle

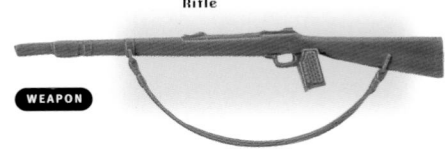

WEAPON

Return of the Jedi

No. 71320   Ages 4 and up

Prune Face

JEDI CARD

The variant Prune Face with an eye-patch became an action figure although his time on screen is infinitesimal.

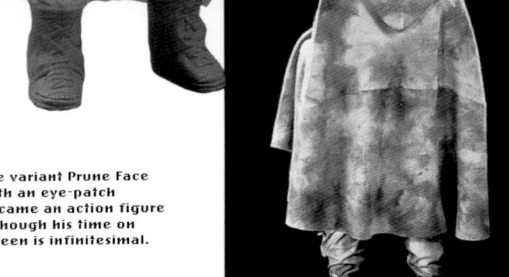

Return of the Jedi

Return of the Jedi

Seen here are two other Dresselians.

LUMAT

"Yub-nub echak yub-nub....
tobe tobe cheeki..."

(Ewok celebration song)

The Ewoks, moved by the story told by C-3PO, agree to join the battle against the Empire and help protect their own moon. Lumat, an Ewok warrior, is also the tribe's chief woodcutter.

Return of the Jedi

Return of the Jedi

Many figures released near the end of the *Jedi* logo card run were also released on cards with the Power of the Force logo.

CARD VARIATIONS

JEDI CARD

POWER OF THE FORCE CARD

Return of the Jedi

WEAPON

Bow

PAPLOO

For him, stealing a bike is an act of heroism.

"Our furry companion has gone and done something rather rash."

Paploo steals a speeder bike and takes off in order to lure Imperial troopers away from the shield bunker. The figure card shows a photo of the Ewok Romba from *Return of the Jedi,* but a European release of Romba has a photo of Paploo.

Return of the Jedi

Many different Ewoks were made into action figures. Ultimately there were eight in the line.

WEAPON

CARD VARIATIONS

JEDI CARD

POWER OF THE FORCE CARD

Battle
Staff

RANCOR KEEPER

Best friend of a monster?

The rancor keeper Malakili is the only one the rancor won't attack and eat. He is terribly upset when one of his pet's intended meals, Luke Skywalker, kills the beast instead. The action figure's headdress, along with those of the Ewoks, introduced a new, more pliable material to the Kenner line.

JEDI CARD

WEAPON

The rancor keeper figure was produced only after the separate rancor toy was released.

Vibroblade

promotions and foreign packaging

Nien Nunb
Jedi mail-in offers were abundant.

The mail-in Nien Nunb offer included a small sheet that told of the character's role in the film.

The Nien Nunb offer was first printed on never-released *Revenge of the Jedi* cards. During the release of the actual *Jedi* forty-eight-back cards, three layout variations could be found.

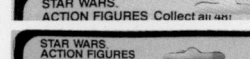

The Emperor
The long-awaited Emperor came first as a mail-in offer.

There were mail-in promotions nearly every year. The Emperor was the figure for 1983. All mail-aways came in plain white boxes.

Anakin Skywalker

At one with the Force.
Anakin Skywalker was the last promotional figure in the eight-year run of the Kenner *Star Wars* line. The figure was based on the spirit form of Anakin at the very end of *Jedi*.

The Power of the Force coin offer

The only way to get nearly half of the sixty-two Power of the Force coins was through this mail-in offer. Kenner also

sold full sets of coins to customers who wrote in and sent $29, but the company didn't publicly announce their availability.

Jedi Two-pack

Dwindling popularity led to unusual offers.

Overstocked figures were repacked in inexpensive two-packs, but not by Kenner itself, even though Kenner's logo appears on the package.

Foreign Cards
Figures are sold all over the world on different cards.

BRITISH
Kenner took over much worldwide distribution itself, such as in England.

JAPANESE
From 1983 to 1985, Tsukuda distributed the Kenner toys in Japan.

FRENCH

SPANISH

MEXICAN

Foreign cards are interesting for their wording and design, which is often different than the U.S. cards.

Spanish Top Toys cards had backs that looked more like the earliest *Star Wars* cards.

Mexican Lily Ledy cards had simple black-and-white printed card backs.

Luke Starkiller

What if he had remained the Starkiller?

Luke was intended to be a much different character.

Skywalker or Starkiller?

In *Star Wars: A New Hope*, the character of Luke Skywalker, as seen in actor Mark Hamill's portrayal, is a good-natured farm boy from a planet far from the center of the galaxy. As the story develops and we find out more about Luke—and he finds out more about himself—the character deepens and grows.

But the nature of the character who became Luke was originally intended to be much darker. One early version of the script by George Lucas was titled "The Adventures of the Star Killer." A Rebel ship is chased, captured, and boarded by the crew of an Imperial Star Destroyer. The Rebel Deak Starkiller engages in a laser sword battle with the ominous Imperial High Commander Darth Vader. Deak is defeated and lays dying, but he is able to get a message to the robot R2-D2, and it must be delivered to his brother, Luke, on the planet below.

The "chubby" Luke inherits his brother's spirit and begins his adventure in space. Luke as we see him in the final film was an amalgam of both Luke and Deak from the early script. An early Ralph McQuarrie preproduction painting depicts a slim man with a laser sword dueling with Vader. This is the early image of Captain Deak Starkiller. Early costume-fitting photos show Mark Hamill dressed in an early design of Ralph McQuarrie. It is this black shirt and pants that he wears beneath the yellow flight jacket at the award ceremony that brings *Star Wars* to its upbeat conclusion.

Luke Skywalker at the awards ceremony.

McQuarrie's early concept.

Mark Hamill in early costume.

Kenner Toys

the power of the force

1985

Two years after *Return of the Jedi,* and after seven years of high popularity, the *Star Wars* line was fading with no new movies in sight. So Kenner introduced a new overall brand concept, The Power of the Force. And with each figure came an aluminum character coin designed to spark renewed interest in the toys.

ROMBA

Ewoks come in many sizes, shapes, and colors.

Ewoks are short, and their fur is black, white, gray, brown, or a combination of colors. Their coats are solid, striped, or mottled. Each Ewok is different. Most didn't have much screen time and are known by name only from books, games, or action figures.

Return of the Jedi

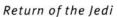

Return of the Jedi

Return of the Jedi

WEAPON

Romba's Spear

POWER OF THE FORCE CARD

LUKE SKYWALKER

(Battle Poncho)

Jumping onto an Imperial bike, Luke begins the chase.

Luke and Leia chase after scout troopers to try to prevent them from reporting that Rebels have landed on Endor's forest moon. The speeder bike chase in *Return of the Jedi* tops just about any thrill ride in an amusement park.

The figure's helmet is not removable, and under the poncho is Luke's Jedi outfit.

WEAPON

Blaster Pistol

POWER OF THE FORCE CARD

R2-D2

with Pop-up Lightsaber

Looking for storage? Try an R2 unit.

R2-D2, a captive aboard Jabba's sail barge, fires Luke Skywalker's hidden lightsaber high into the Tatooine sky and right into Luke's waiting hands. That evens up the battle against Jabba and his henchmen.

POWER OF THE FORCE CARD

Any firing of small objects was considered dangerous, so the pop-up lightsaber rises slowly as Artoo's head is turned, rather than popping out using a spring-loaded device.

AMANAMAN

A strange creature
nicknamed "Headhunter."

In a corner of Jabba's palace stands
a giant alien known as Amanaman.
He proudly displays his collection
of skulls on his staff.

The creature is not very visible in the film; the accuracy
of the toy can be seen alongside this reference photo from
Lucasfilm's archives. The species is now called "Amanin."

POWER OF THE FORCE CARD

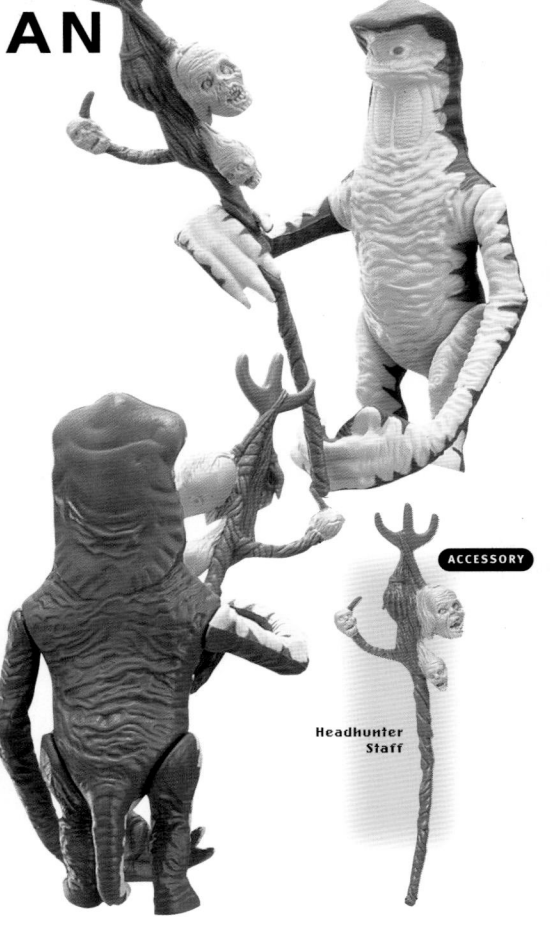

ACCESSORY

Headhunter
Staff

Return of the Jedi

BARADA

Baradas are from the planet Klaatuin.

This Barada was on Luke's skiff wearing
a yellow shirt. The *Return of the Jedi Special Edition*
adds another Barada to Jabba's palace band.

POWER OF THE FORCE CARD

Return of the Jedi

The sculpting of the figure was based on this
white-shirted Barada, but the shirt color was
changed to match the alien aboard Luke's skiff.

WEAPON

Battle Staff

Return of the Jedi

IMPERIAL GUNNER

The gunner appears fearsome even without his weapon.

This gunner is from *Return of the Jedi*. The figure was modeled after the troops standing in the docking bay for the Emperor's arrival at the second Death Star.

POWER OF THE FORCE CARD

Blaster Pistol

There is no body armor on the figure, so this is not a gunner from *Star Wars*.

LUKE SKYWALKER
(Imperial Stormtrooper Outfit)

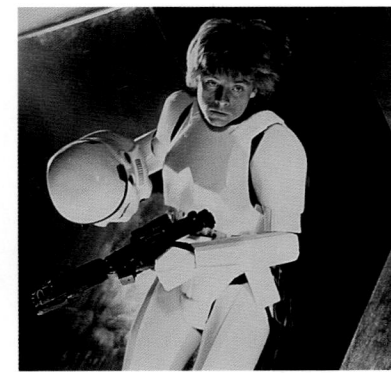

Star Wars

The Power of the Force line returned to characters that hadn't yet been done from all three of the films. Luke in his stormtrooper disguise was from *Star Wars*, yet it was one of the last figures to be released.

Unlike the original stormtrooper, this figure's head can rotate.

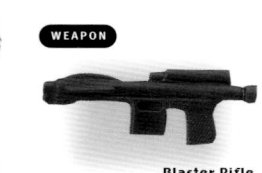

WEAPON

Blaster Rifle

POWER OF THE FORCE CARD

HAN SOLO
in Carbonite Chamber

"Chewie listen....
The princess,
you have to take care of her."

A smaller Han Solo in carbonite was originally included with the *Slave I* toy vehicle. This figure with its carbonite chamber is much more to scale than the earlier toy cargo.

The Empire Strikes Back

POWER OF THE FORCE CARD

The bull-necked Solo, with sculpting that makes him look somewhat like the Incredible Hulk, was due to molding limitations at the time.

EV-9D9

Torture is her game.

The tall droid EV-9D9 is a supervisor in Jabba the Hutt's droid and cyborg center. The only way she knows to accomplish her goals is through torture. Besides, she really enjoys it.

SPECIAL COLLECTORS COIN

POWER OF THE FORCE CARD

The jaw movement in the figure was an unusual feature that was dropped from the new Hasbro design.

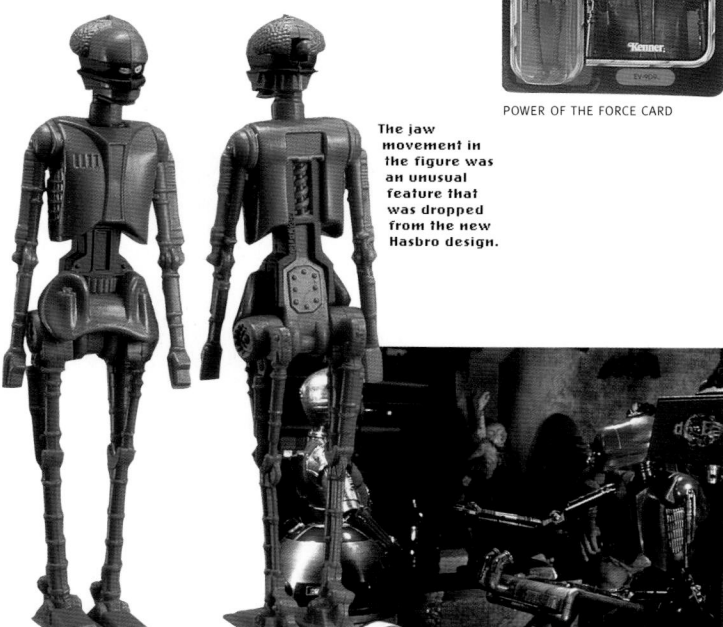

Return of the Jedi

WAROK

He helps hijack an AT-ST.

Warok is one of the Ewoks who helps Chewbacca take over an Imperial AT-ST at a crucial point in the fight for control of the shield bunker. He was said to be the hang glider flyer in *Jedi*, but reference photos seem to indicate that a different Ewok was the glider pilot.

Return of the Jedi

Return of the Jedi

Return of the Jedi

As with other Ewok figures, the sculpting is precise, but the fur color is different from the actual costume.

ANAKIN SKYWALKER

For Anakin, redemption comes at last.

Although Darth Vader denies it mightily, his son, Luke, senses that there is still some goodness buried deep within the dark heart of his father, who had once been Anakin Skywalker. And at a crucial moment, just when his son is about to die, Vader turns from the dark side to kill Emperor Palpatine and rescue Luke. Anakin soon becomes one with the Force.

Return of the Jedi

Anakin was first available through a mail-in offer, then was later available on the Power of the Force card.

SPECIAL COLLECTORS COIN

POWER OF THE FORCE CARD

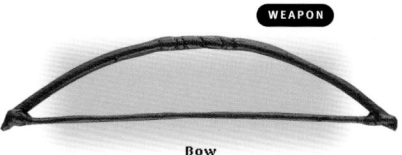

WEAPON

Bow

SPECIAL COLLECTORS COIN

POWER OF THE FORCE CARD

A-WING PILOT

"Green leader, standing by!"

Not many A-wing fighter pilot photos exist. In the Rebel briefing, many A-wing pilots are shown holding Y-wing pilot helmets.

POWER OF THE FORCE CARD

WEAPON

Blaster Pistol

Return of the Jedi

A-wing pilots are distinguishable in the film, including at least one female pilot.

Return of the Jedi

Return of the Jedi

LANDO CALRISSIAN

General Pilot

You have my promise: not a scratch.

"All right, old buddy. You know I know what she means to you. I'll take good care of her. She—she won't get a scratch. All right?"

Lando knows what the *Millennium Falcon* means to Han Solo.

WEAPON

Blaster Pistol

POWER OF THE FORCE CARD

The sculpting of Lando figures is always very accurate, as this figure shows with the introduction of the new cape material for General Calrissian.

Yak Face was the scarcest figure.

YAK FACE

Return of the Jedi

CANADIAN POWER OF THE FORCE CARD

The Power of the Force-carded Yak Face came with a weapon, while the Tri-logo version did not.

WEAPON

Intended to be the ninety-third figure in a line that stopped at ninety-two, Yak Face was never sold in American stores. Tri-logo versions were sold in Europe and carded Power of the Force coin cards were sold only in Canada and Australia.

Battle Staff

IMPERIAL DIGNITARY

The Emperor is our puppet, the dignitaries thought.

The hangers-on in the Emperor's court think they can control him, but they don't stand a chance. Several dignitaries and court officials are seen briefly in the background of *Jedi*, including this gaunt character whose skin was painted blue for the Kenner action figure version.

Return of the Jedi

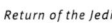

Return of the Jedi

Return of the Jedi

This group of court followers makes for an interesting picture, but there aren't many action possibilities for a kid interested in playing with his *Star Wars* toys.

Return of the Jedi

POWER OF THE FORCE CARD

Unproduced

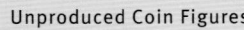
power of the force packaging

Unproduced Coin Figures

The Power of the Force line, according to Kenner's own catalog, was to include at least ninety-three figures—the largest figure assortment of all of the card types. Instead, it had the shortest life, only one year and scarcely three dozen figures. Among the rarest were the Gamorrean Guard, Nikto, and the AT-AT Driver (packed with a Warok coin). Below are some unissued proof cards.

Foreign packaging

EUROPEAN TRI-LOGO CARDS

Starting in 1984, European cards had logos in three languages (English, Spanish, and French) and other details in an additional three languages on both front and back.

Yak Face was widely available in Europe. The figure apparently was being saved in the United States for a mail-in promotion that never took place after the line lost steam.

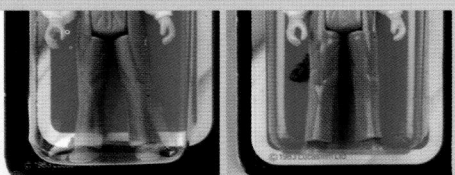

Lobot's photo is different from the U.S. version. As can be seen at left, the cards themselves were slightly different at the bottom.

An unusual variation found with the Tri-logo carded Luke Jedi: He can be found either with his cloak on or tucked behind him.

The Tri-logo R2-D2 came both in a sensorscope and a pop-up lightsaber version.

The card of Romba shows a photo of Paploo.

The IG-88 photo is reversed from that of the U.S. version.

In the photo, notice the absence of the life-support box from the AT-AT driver's chest.

A different photo is found on the Hoth Leia card.

The TIE pilot's photo is also different from the U.S. card.

The commando's outfit is much greener on the Tri-logo card.

The U.S. AT-ST driver's card shows the full-size prop while the Tri-logo depicts the small-scale effects miniature.

Here, Han is packaged on top of the carbonite block while in the United States, he is packaged underneath.

This photo was retouched after appearing on the U.S. card.

droids

Animated characters join the *Star Wars* galaxy.

In 1985, two *Star Wars*–based animated series began. One was *Droids: The Adventures of R2-D2 and C-3PO*. As the title says, the stories center on the Laurel and Hardy of the droid world and their adventures before they met Luke Skywalker. From the old figure line, an A-wing pilot and Boba Fett were included. Kenner released twelve figures as well as three vehicles in the *Droids* line. The 1986 Kenner catalog showed figures for a second series, but they were never released.

Above are prototypes for the unproduced second series. Among them was Vlix (fourth from right), a figure that was actually produced and sold carded in Brazil several years later.

At first, the C-3PO figure came with the same Power of the Force coin as the earlier release, only in a gold tone. The figure itself used the same mold as earlier releases.

The revised coin showed the animated version of the golden droid.

Aside from the two vehicles shown on the card backs, an A-wing fighter also was released.

A-WING PILOT

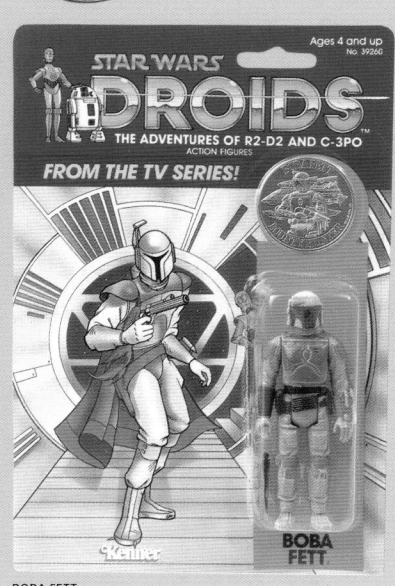

BOBA FETT

Canadian cards are all identical regardless of the figure included.

THALL JOBEN

JORD DUSAT

KEA MOLL

KEZ IBAN

UNCLE GUNDY

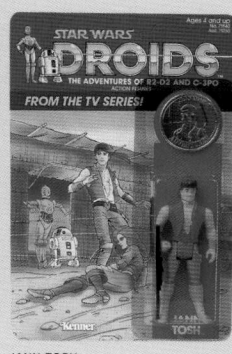

JANN TOSH

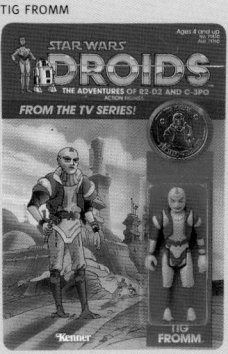

TIG FROMM

SISE FROMM

Tig and Sise Fromm were released after the other six figures.
All the cards had rounded corners at the bottom except for the
Boba Fett figure, whose card was squared off (opposite page).

ewoks

Ewok toys
were more popular
in Europe.

The *Ewoks* line was more successful
than *Droids*, especially in Europe. Their
animated series, which went into a second season of new episodes, is about
the Ewoks and their foes, the Duloks,
who share the forest moon of Endor.

CANADIAN CARD

KING GORNEESH

URGAH LADY GORNEESH

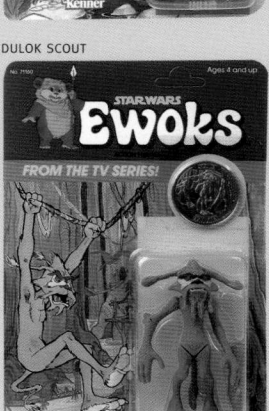

DULOK SCOUT

DULOK SHAMAN

LOGRAY

WICKET W. WARRICK

Principal characters Wicket and Logray
were released in a second wave after the Duloks.
Below are the unproduced prototypes for
a proposed second series.

prototypes

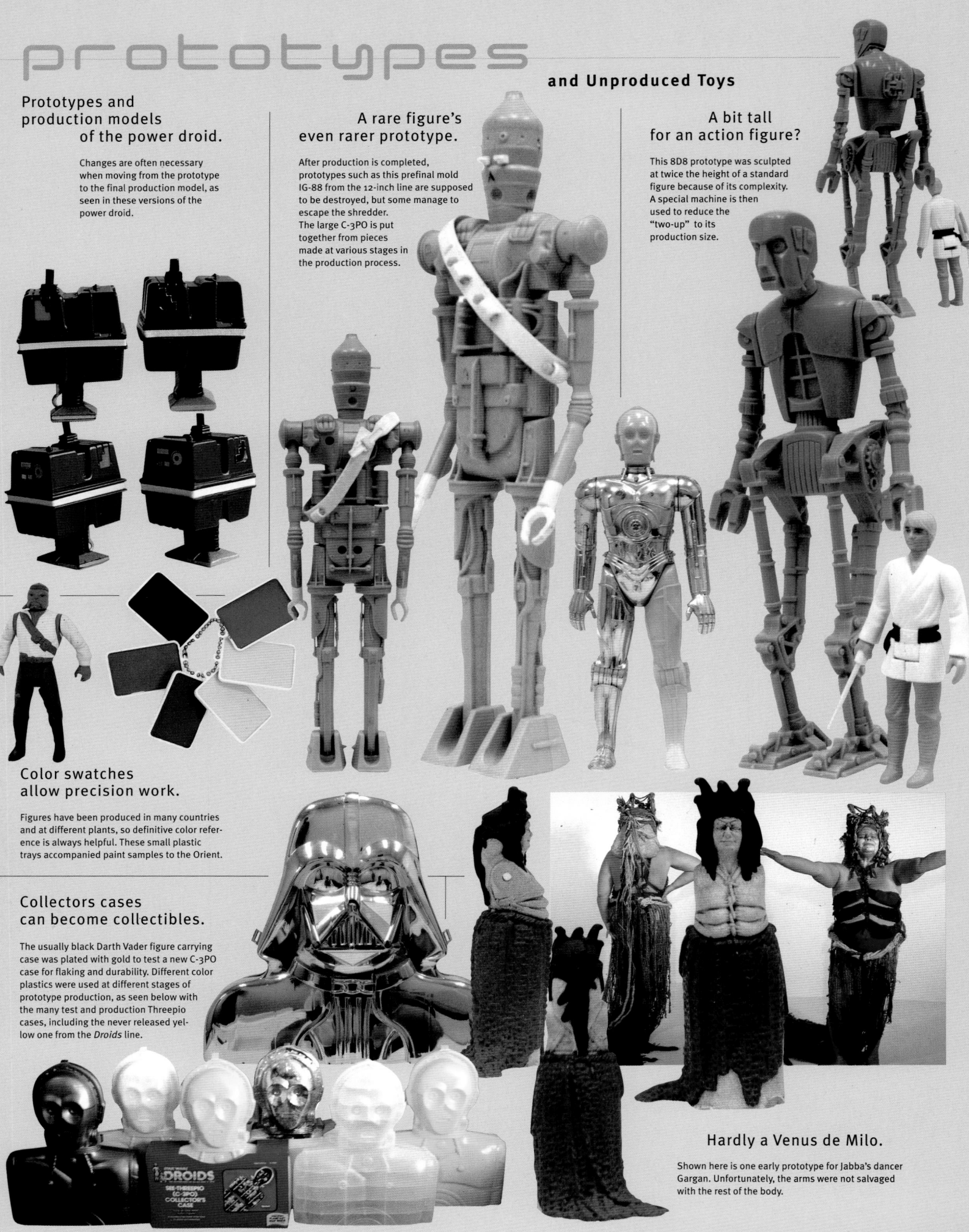

Prototypes and production models of the power droid.

Changes are often necessary when moving from the prototype to the final production model, as seen in these versions of the power droid.

A rare figure's even rarer prototype.

After production is completed, prototypes such as this prefinal mold IG-88 from the 12-inch line are supposed to be destroyed, but some manage to escape the shredder. The large C-3PO is put together from pieces made at various stages in the production process.

A bit tall for an action figure?

This 8D8 prototype was sculpted at twice the height of a standard figure because of its complexity. A special machine is then used to reduce the "two-up" to its production size.

Color swatches allow precision work.

Figures have been produced in many countries and at different plants, so definitive color reference is always helpful. These small plastic trays accompanied paint samples to the Orient.

Collectors cases can become collectibles.

The usually black Darth Vader figure carrying case was plated with gold to test a new C-3PO case for flaking and durability. Different color plastics were used at different stages of prototype production, as seen below with the many test and production Threepio cases, including the never released yellow one from the *Droids* line.

Hardly a Venus de Milo.

Shown here is one early prototype for Jabba's dancer Gargan. Unfortunately, the arms were not salvaged with the rest of the body.

58-84

135

Vehicles and playsets enhance the playability and enjoyment—and coincidentally, the sales—of action figures. Kenner tried hard to provide enough auxiliary pieces so that children could recreate nearly every event that occurred in the *Star Wars* trilogy.

LANDSPEEDER

COLLECTOR SERIES

The landspeeder was first released in 1978, with a reissue in a Collector Series box in 1983. The British version of the landspeeder has an engine hood that cannot be opened.

X-WING FIGHTER

The X-wing fighter released for *Star Wars* was molded in white. It was later molded in gray and released with "battle damage" stickers for *The Empire Strikes Back* and *Return of the Jedi*.

STAR WARS BOX

JEDI BOX

TIE FIGHTER

The TIE fighter was originally molded in white, then later changed to blue.

STAR WARS BOX

EMPIRE BOX

JEDI BOX

Above are the "battle damage" stickers that were included with later releases.

DARTH VADER TIE FIGHTER

STAR WARS BOX

COLLECTOR SERIES

DARTH VADER TIE FIGHTER

DARTH VADER TIE FIGHTER

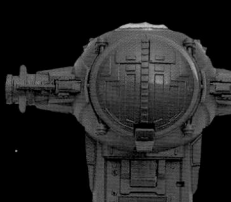

The central cockpit module for the standard TIE fighter was used for Darth Vader's TIE fighter as well. The modified cockpit with the open window hatch is from the *Jedi* reissue TIE fight and was also used for the TIE interceptor.

MILLENNIUM FALCON

The *Millennium Falcon* didn't undergo any mold changes during the entire first trilogy toy run, although the boxes changed for each film.

DROID FACTORY

The Jawa droid factory
includes interchangeable
droid parts that can be assembled
in many different ways. A special R2-D2
with a third leg was also included in this set.
The British version comes with either a blue
or yellow vacuformed base.

IMPERIAL TROOP TRANSPORTER

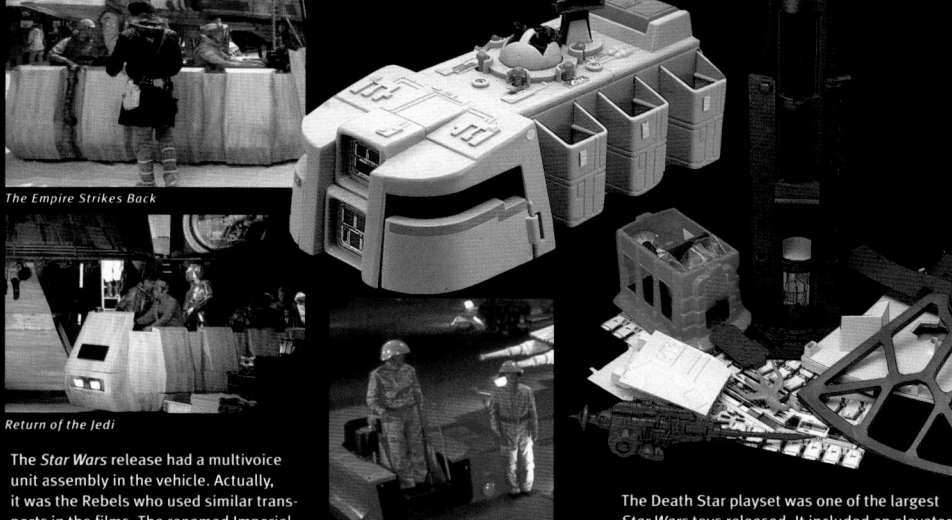

The Empire Strikes Back

Return of the Jedi

The *Star Wars* release had a multivoice
unit assembly in the vehicle. Actually,
it was the Rebels who used similar trans-
ports in the films. The renamed Imperial
Cruiser for *The Empire Strikes Back*
release was a Sears exclusive;
it had no electronics.

Star Wars

DEATH STAR SPACE STATION

The Death Star playset was one of the largest
Star Wars toys released. It included an elevator, multilevel
play areas, a trash compactor, and the dianoga trash monster.
British, European, and Australian Death Star playsets were
constructed of cardboard and were of a totally different design
(not shown).

No. 39290   Ages 4 and up

IMPERIAL TROOP
TRANSPORTER

STAR WARS BOX

No. 9399   Ages 4 and up!

IMPERIAL
CRUISER

EMPIRE BOX

Star Wars

Star Wars

RADIO-CONTROLLED JAWA SANDCRAWLER

The desert ark is on the horizon.

The immense Jawa sandcrawler is a combination apartment house, droid warehouse, and workshop on wheels. With its remote control, children can command the toy version of the vehicle to move straight ahead or in a curved backward motion. It is one of the most accurate toys in the trilogy, and it truly matches the details and proportions of the movie prop model.

Star Wars Special Edition

The side door of the sandcrawler lowers to provide access to action figures. R2-D2 and other droids can be hauled up by a hand-activated "elevator." There's also a control area where the Jawas steer the juggernaut.

Star Wars

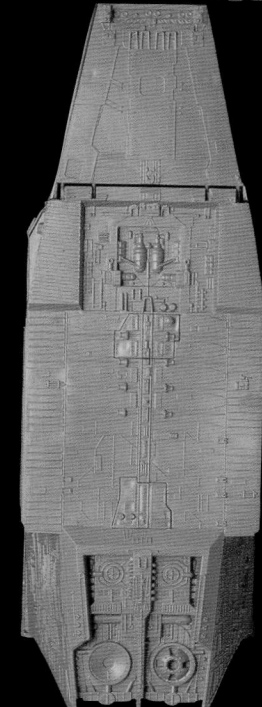

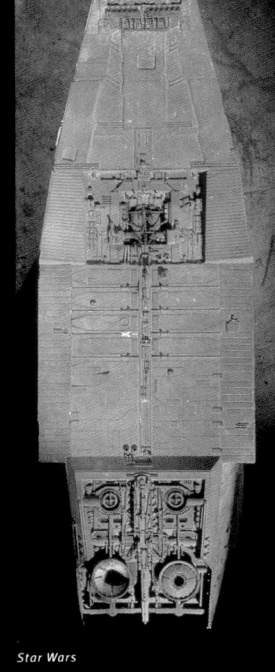

Star Wars

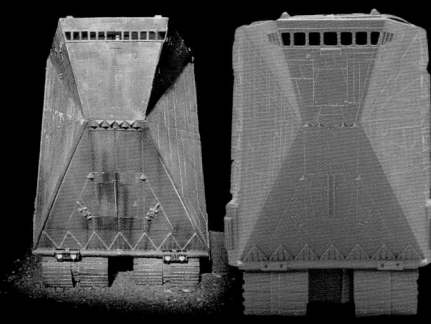

Star Wars

Droid "elevator"

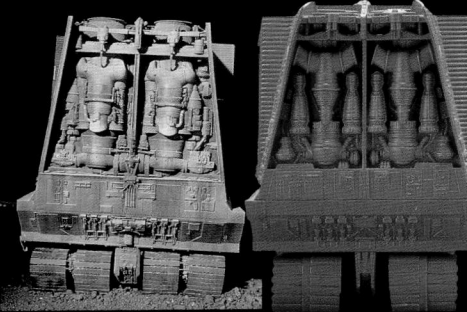

Star Wars

Star Wars

LAND OF THE JAWAS

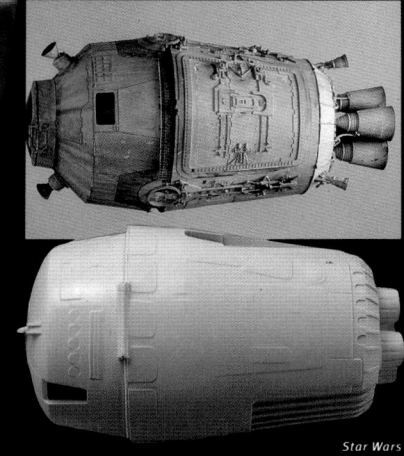

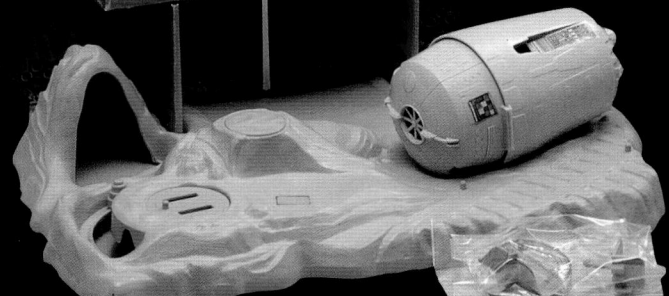

As a replacement for his broken Treadwell droid and to increase the number of farm workers, Owen Lars decides to make a purchase from the local Jawa merchants. The toy diorama combines this scene with the escape pod landing site and the Jawa capture of R2-D2.

Star Wars

Star Wars

The European version of the toy doesn't include a lifepod.

The background sandcrawler is cardboard while the Tatooine dunes base is plastic. The plastic escape pod can hold the droids.

Star Wars

PATROL DEWBACK

The giant green lizard of the desert.

Swing its tail and the dewback's head moves from side to side. The creature got very little screen time in the original *Star Wars*, but the toy was popular enough for it to be reissued in 1983 in a special collector's box.

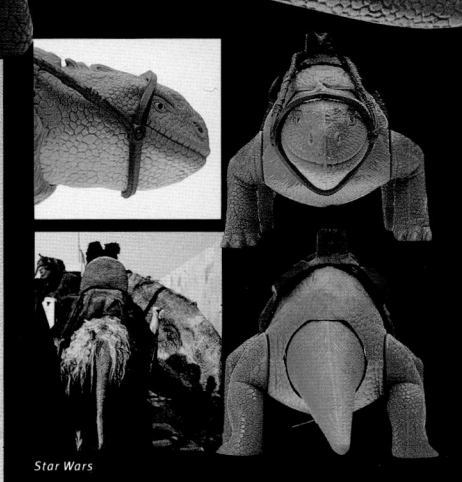

A trap door on the top of the dewback allowed action figures to "sit" atop their reptilian transport.

Star Wars

Star Wars

Star Wars

Star Wars

CREATURE CANTINA

Star Wars

Based on the interior of the cantina, the playset includes a bar, spring-loaded entrance doors, and an action figure showdown trigger and action lever that was common in many of the playsets at the time.

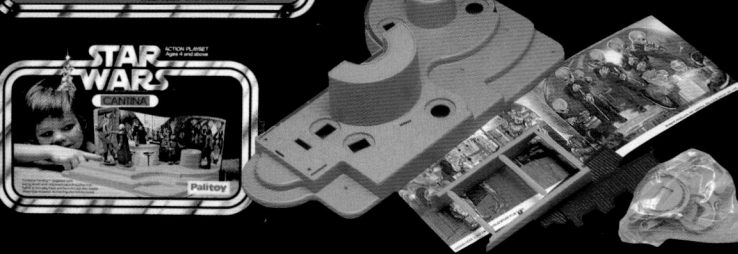

CANTINA ADVENTURE SET

A simple pop-up cardboard model recreates the streets of Mos Eisley.

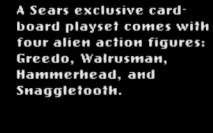

A Sears exclusive cardboard playset comes with four alien action figures: Greedo, Walrusman, Hammerhead, and Snaggletooth.

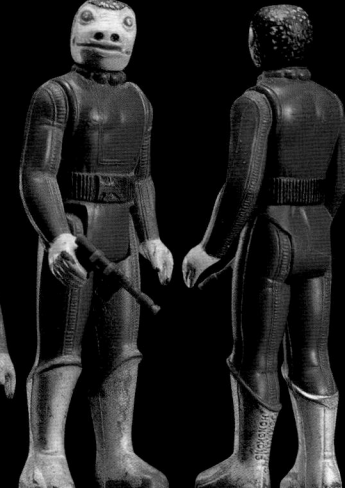

What is so special about this simple playset? It came with the tall blue Snaggletooth, which was soon replaced by a short one dressed in a red jumpsuit.

SONIC-CONTROLLED LANDSPEEDER

Responding to a clicking sonic transmitter in the shape of R2-D2, the sonic landspeeder moved forward or in a backward curved direction. The vehicle was exclusive to J.C. Penney stores.

Above is a comparison of the "Sonic-Controlled Landspeeder" and the standard landspeeder (right).

HOTH ICE PLANET

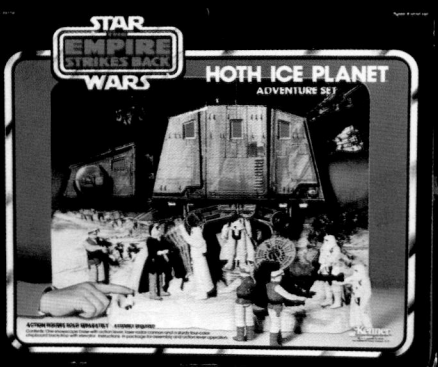

Using the same form from the Land of the Jawas base (but molded in white), the Hoth Ice Planet playset included a new Imperial walker cardboard backdrop, which was similar to the sandcrawler backdrop included with the Jawas set.

IMPERIAL ATTACK BASE

The Empire Strikes Back

In this playset, the ice bridge collapses and the laser cannon clicks as it rotates. But while the toy resembles the Rebels' Echo Base and the trench from the Hoth battle, the box photo shows toy Rebels attacking an Imperial station.

The Empire Strikes Back

"I thought they smelled bad on the *outside*."
TAUNTAUN

The Empire Strikes Back

Original release

Open-belly feature

Very similar to the Patrol Dewback toy, the tauntaun has a trap door in the creature's top to let riders "sit" upon its back.

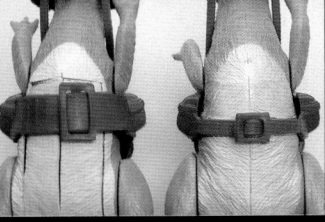

The original-issue tauntaun came with a closed belly. Later it was released with a pliable membrane dubbed an "open belly" feature.

The Empire Strikes Back

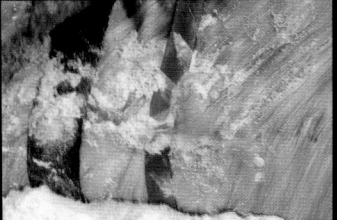

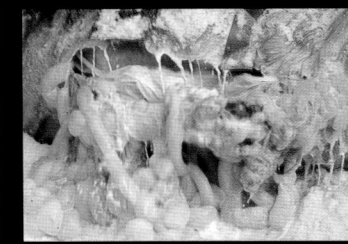

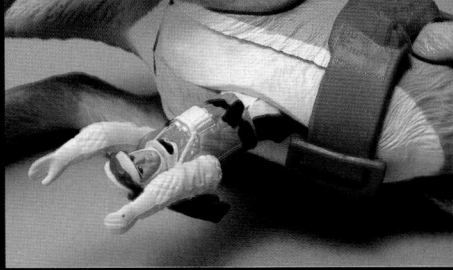

The only thing that would have excited kids more than the open belly feature would have been having the tauntaun's innards spill out!

The Empire Strikes Back

DARTH VADER'S STAR DESTROYER

EMPIRE BOX The box shows the various features of the vehicle.

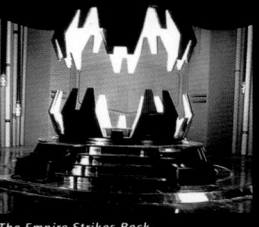

The Empire Strikes Back

Darth Vader's Star Destroyer playset recreates his meditation chamber as well as the control pit area. A transparent pink plastic plate can be lowered for Vader's "holographic" communication with the Emperor.

The Empire Strikes Back

Like many of the playsets, this one came in pieces with instructions for "easy" assembly.

The Empire Strikes Back

The Empire Strikes Back Special Edition

TWIN-POD CLOUD CAR

The twin-pod cloud car patrols the city.

The cloud car pilots intercept the *Millennium Falcon* as it makes its approach to Cloud City high over Bespin. Firing a shot across the *Falcon*'s bow, the pilots make it clear they are not to be ignored.

EMPIRE BOX

Each pod of the cloud car could hold one action figure, and the struts at its base could be in the up position for flying and lowered for a smooth landing.

The Empire Strikes Back

TURRET & PROBOT

The Imperial probe droid discovers Echo Base.

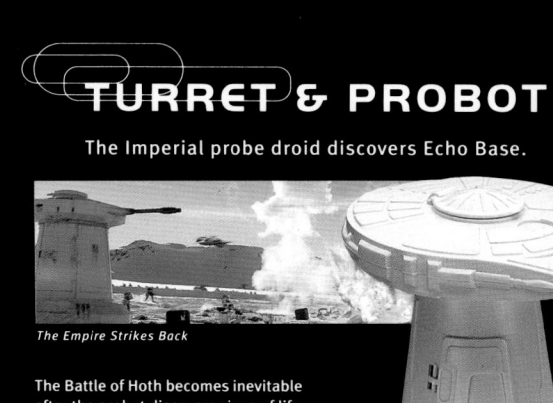

The Empire Strikes Back

The Empire Strikes Back

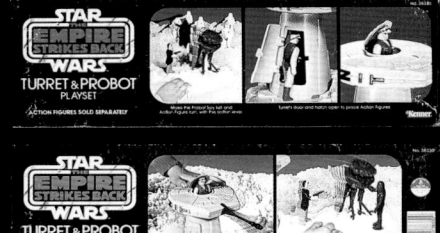

EMPIRE BOX

The Battle of Hoth becomes inevitable after the probot discovers signs of life on the frozen planet. The box printing for the playset changed from "Turret/Probot" to "Turret & Probot."

The design of the probot came from a sketch by Joe Johnston.

REBEL ARMORED SNOWSPEEDER

The Empire Strikes Back

"Rogue Group, use your harpoons and tow cables."

The snowspeeder underwent several design changes for its release in 1996. For one thing, the size of the original harpoon gun is smaller and more accurate to the original prop than is the new one.

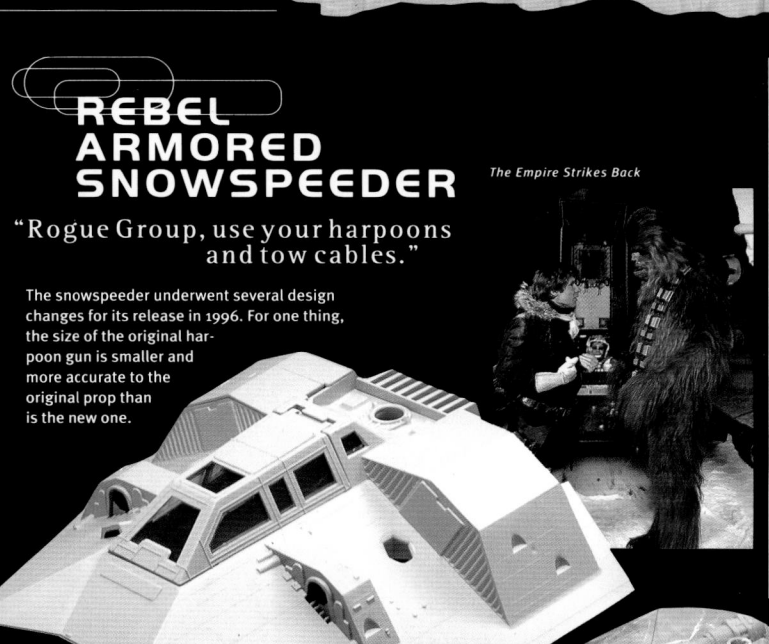

Empire boxes have a pink background in the toy photo. *Jedi* boxes (here in a bilingual format) have a blue background and different photo on the front.

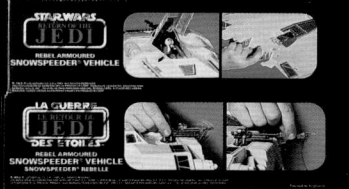

EMPIRE BOX

JEDI BOX

AT-AT

A thundering sound on the frozen Hoth plains.

The Empire's largest surface vehicle became a must-have toy. About twenty inches tall, it is the biggest and most expensive single *Star Wars* toy in the line.

EMPIRE BOX

Unlike the newer electronic version from the current toy line, the original AT-AT walker had a button inside the body that controlled the "motorized" movement and illumination of the chin guns.

SLAVE I

Boba Fett's vehicle of choice.

Boba Fett uses *Slave I* to track the *Millennium Falcon* and later to spirit away Han Solo, frozen in carbonite, in order to collect the bounty from Jabba the Hutt.

The original mold was used again for the current release. The only difference is that the original vehicle included decorative stickers and the newer version comes prepainted.

EMPIRE BOX

SCOUT WALKER

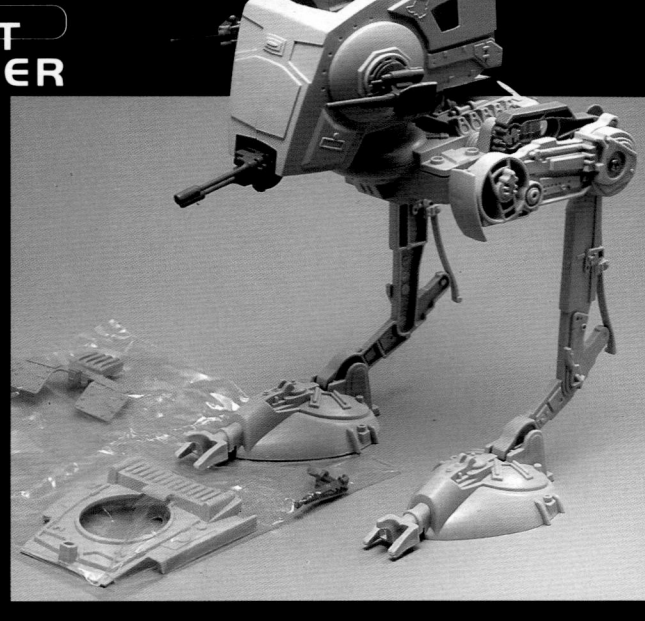

The AT-ST has not gone through any changes from its release for *The Empire Strikes Back* and *Return of the Jedi.*

Nickname: Chicken Walker.

The AT-ST is seen for only a few seconds in *Empire*, but it's featured in the final battle scene in *Jedi*. The AT-ST has an awkward movement — somewhat like a pecking chicken — and is a vulnerable target.

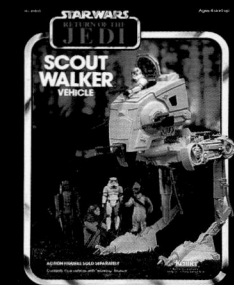

EMPIRE BOX

JEDI BOX

REBEL TRANSPORT

Rebel Transport or giant tuna?

The transport, seen briefly on Hoth, is used to evacuate many Rebels from Echo Base. The black tower, which in the film prop was farther to the rear, is used as a locking bolt.

EMPIRE BOX

EMPIRE BOX

The ship can also be used as an action figure storage case for real transport purposes.

The Empire Strikes Back

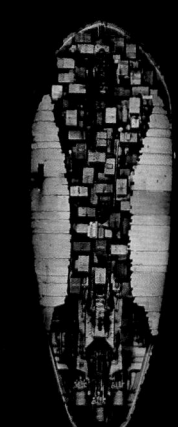

The Empire Strikes Back

DAGOBAH ACTION PLAYSET

This swamp houses a Jedi.

The set contains a precise replica of the exterior and interior of Yoda's house. It also includes spongy material that simulates the Dagobah swamp and lets R2-D2 start to drown. Later releases include a Jedi training backpack accessory so Luke can carry Yoda on his back.

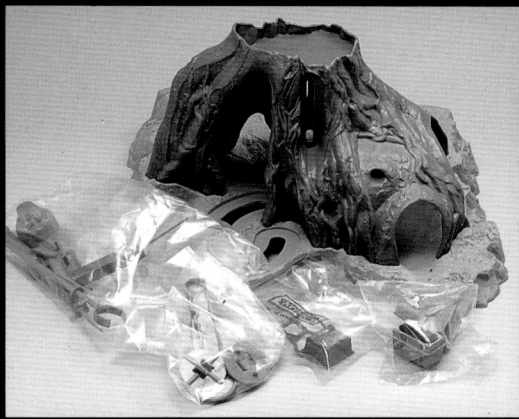

The Empire Strikes Back

The Empire Strikes Back

Figure Factoids
WAMPA, WAMPA, WAMPA

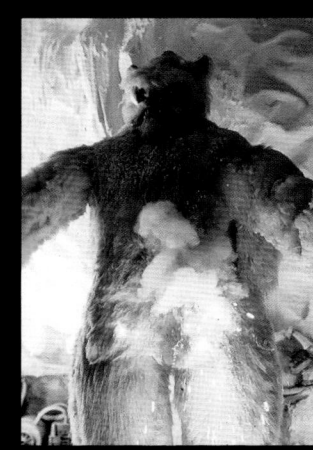

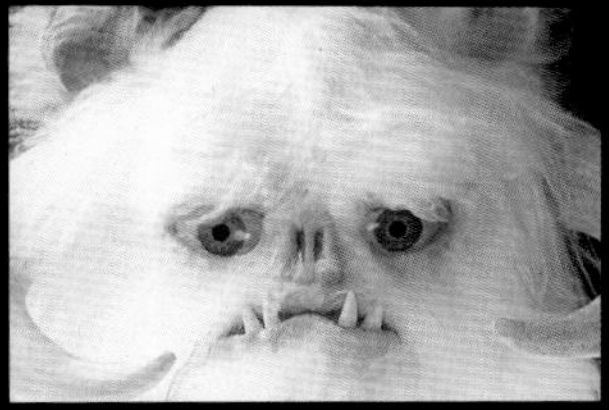

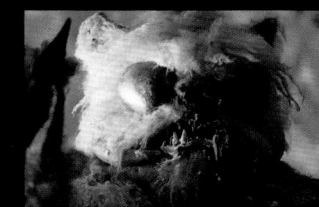

The original *Empire* doesn't have full-body shots of the wampa, since the three-meter tall suit used in filming just didn't work. Seen here are four different wampa designs that were used to some extent for *Empire*. Top left is the full-body costume for location shooting in Norway. Top right is for shooting inside Echo Base, a segment cut from the film. Middle photos are close-ups of the above. Bottom left is the hand puppet (operated by Phil Tippett) for the attack on Luke. Bottom right is the full-body costume made for *The Empire Strikes Back Special Edition*.

As ferocious as it looks!

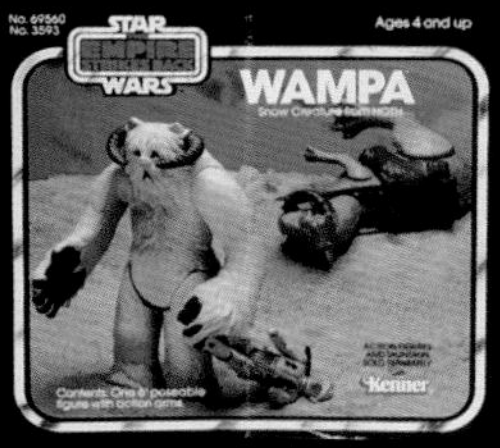

HOTH WAMPA

The original release box was printed simply "Wampa," while later versions called it "Hoth Wampa."

The toy wampa's arms are spring loaded and his face is modeled after the hand puppet prop.

ACCESSORIES

RADAR LASER CANNON™

TRI-POD LASER CANNON™

VEHICLE MAINTENANCE ENERGIZER™

Star Wars

Tri-Pod Laser Cannon

A precisely designed replica of the tripod laser cannon from the film includes a power unit that can hold smaller figure accessories such as blasters and rifles.

The Empire Strikes Back

Larger than figures but smaller than vehicles or playsets, these action figure accessories, which did appear in the trilogy, opened the way for the unusual and unique minirigs, which never had screen time.

Vehicle Maintenance Energizer

Released during *The Empire Strikes Back*, the vehicle maintenance energizer was actually seen in the Rebels' base on Yavin.

Radar Laser Cannon

As with many Kenner toys, a secret button caused the cannon to "explode."

Minirigs

Not appearing in any of the films, the minirigs were fairly inexpensive vehicles made to carry one character. They were done to provide more play value at a lower price than the larger vehicles.

REBEL COMMAND CENTER

Evacuate all personnel!

This Sears exclusive playset again reused the plastic base originally designed for the Land of the Jawas playset and included a painted cardboard backdrop.

Three figur
were included
AT-AT Commander
Luke in Hoth gear,
and R2-D2 with sensorsco

"I saw a city in the clouds."

CLOUD CITY PLAYSET

nds you have there."

"They were in pain."

Kenner began to make many of the larger film settings into Micro Collection line playsets. Apparently because of this, no Cloud City playsets were produced except for this Sears cardboard exclusive, which was more a vehicle to sell four action figures.

e set includes figures of Ugnaught, Lobot, Bespin
n Solo, and Dengar (who never visited Cloud City).

SPEEDER BIKE

Basically the vehicle is the same as the newly reissued version except for its decoration. A T-bar was incorporated to hold action figures on the seat; that seems unnecessary in the new line, but it was still left in the design.

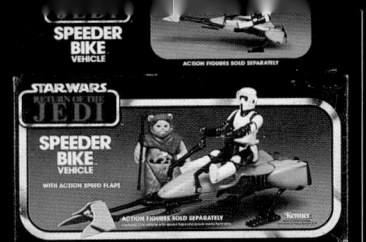

EWOK VILLAGE

All of the events that occurred around the Ewok village can be recreated with this fairly large plastic playset that contains such things as C-3PO's "flying" chair and the net that trapped Chewbacca and his friends.

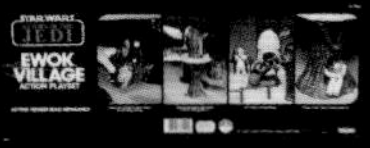

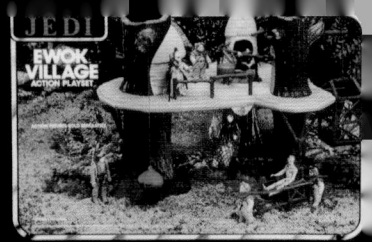

JABBA THE HUTT

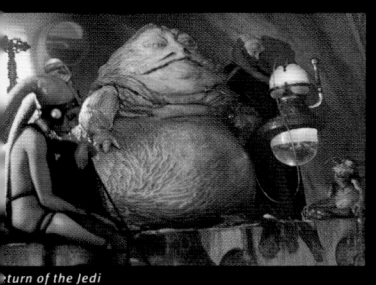

ᵉturn of the Jedi

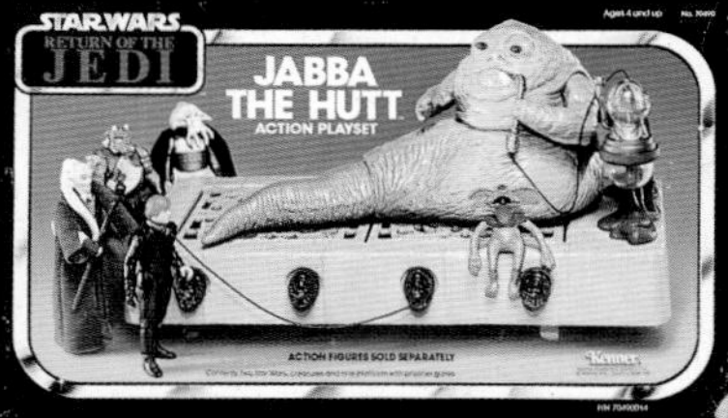

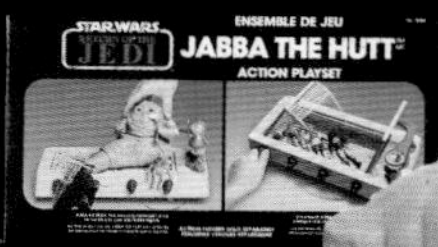

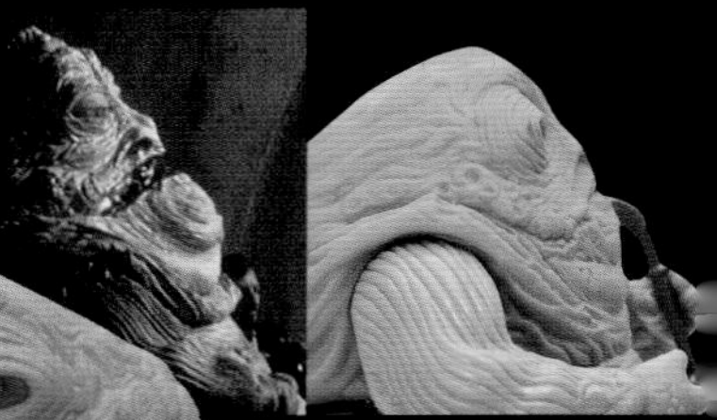

Return of the Jedi

"There will be
o bargain, young Jedi.
I shall enjoy
watching you die."

ıs Ugliness, Jabba the Hutt, would sooner squash a eature than talk with him. He has been in control for › long that he thinks he can handle an impudent Jedi st like others who have challenged him before.

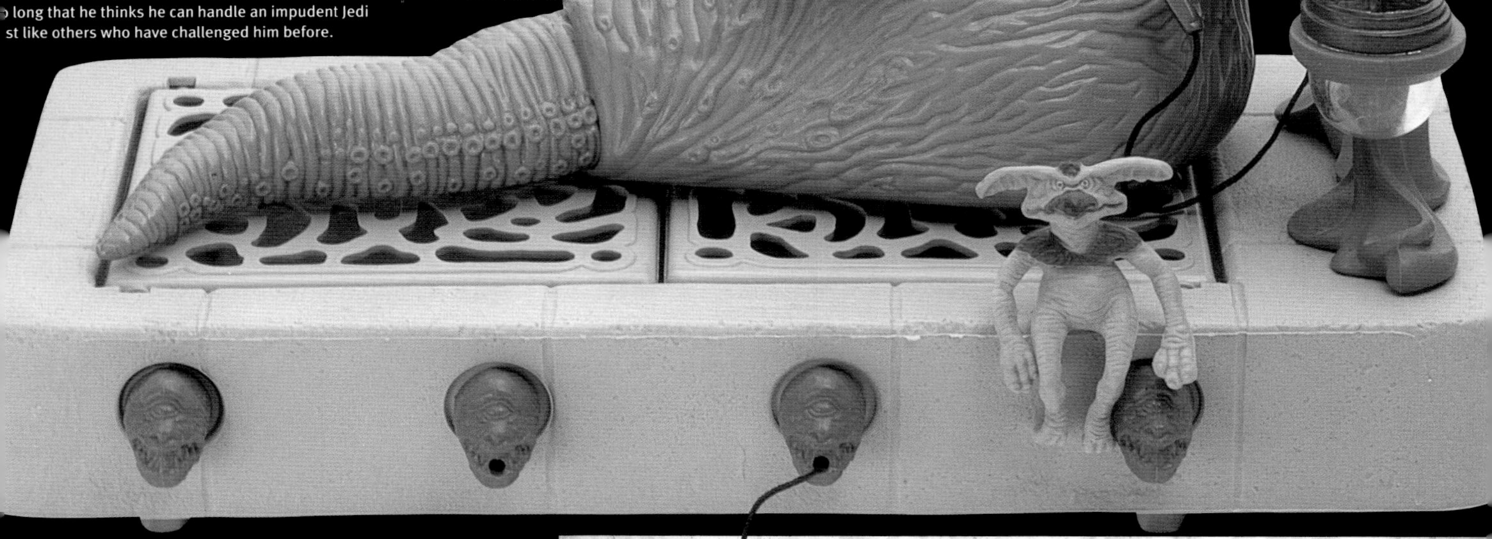

ıe set comes with Jabba, ıs throne, water pipe, risoner rope, and ıs cackling companion alacious Crumb.

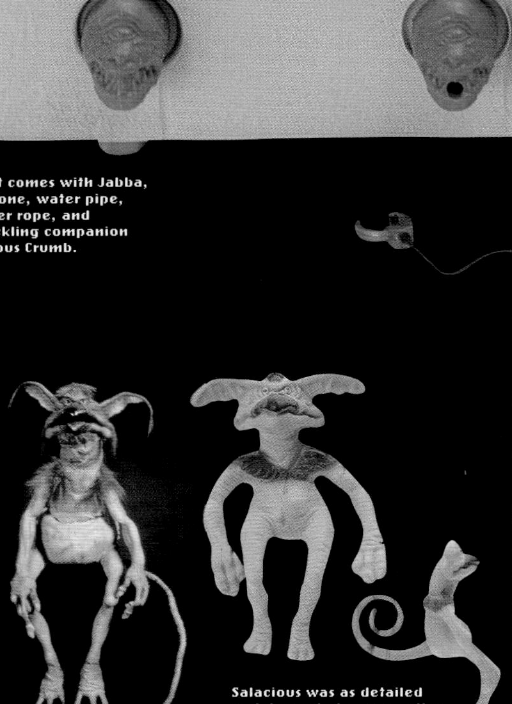

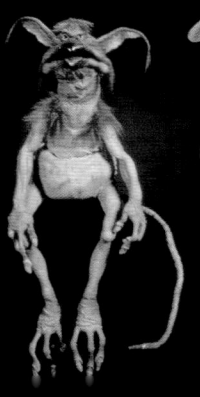

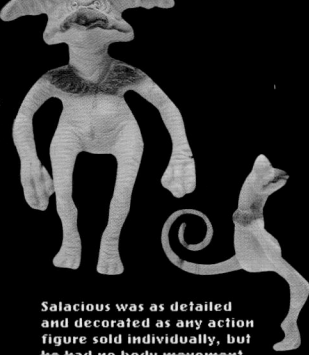

Salacious was as detailed and decorated as any action figure sold individually, but he had no body movement.

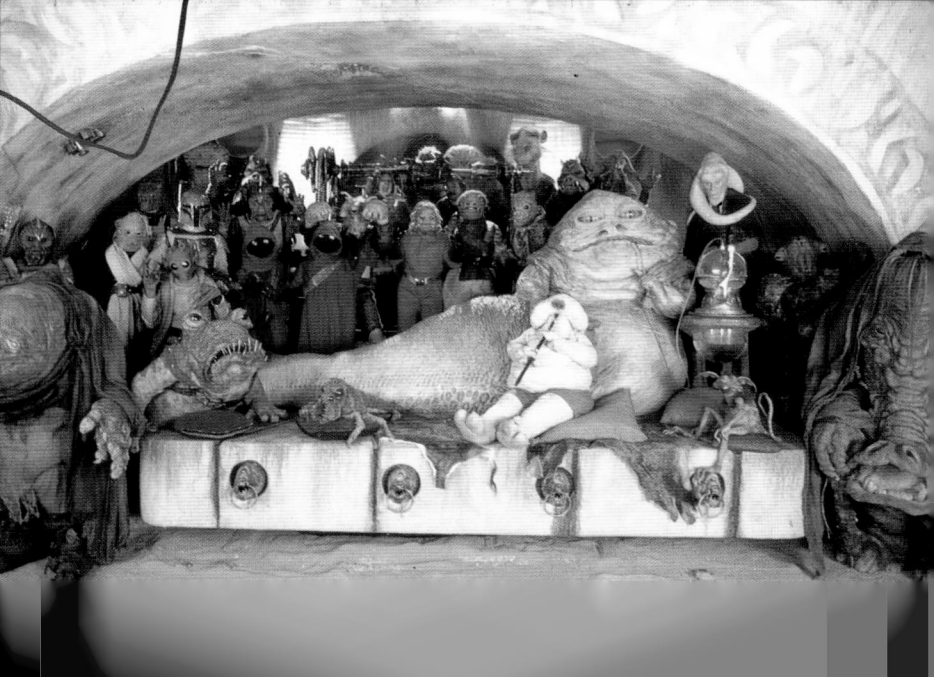

TIE INTERCEPTOR

Defending the second Death Star.

Vader's TIE fighter was the prototype for the TIE Interceptor starfighter. Changes in the cockpit, the shape of the wings, and the addition of wing-tipped cannons led to the final design.

Details in the base of the wing pylons were added to make the toy as accurate as possible when compared to the prop model.

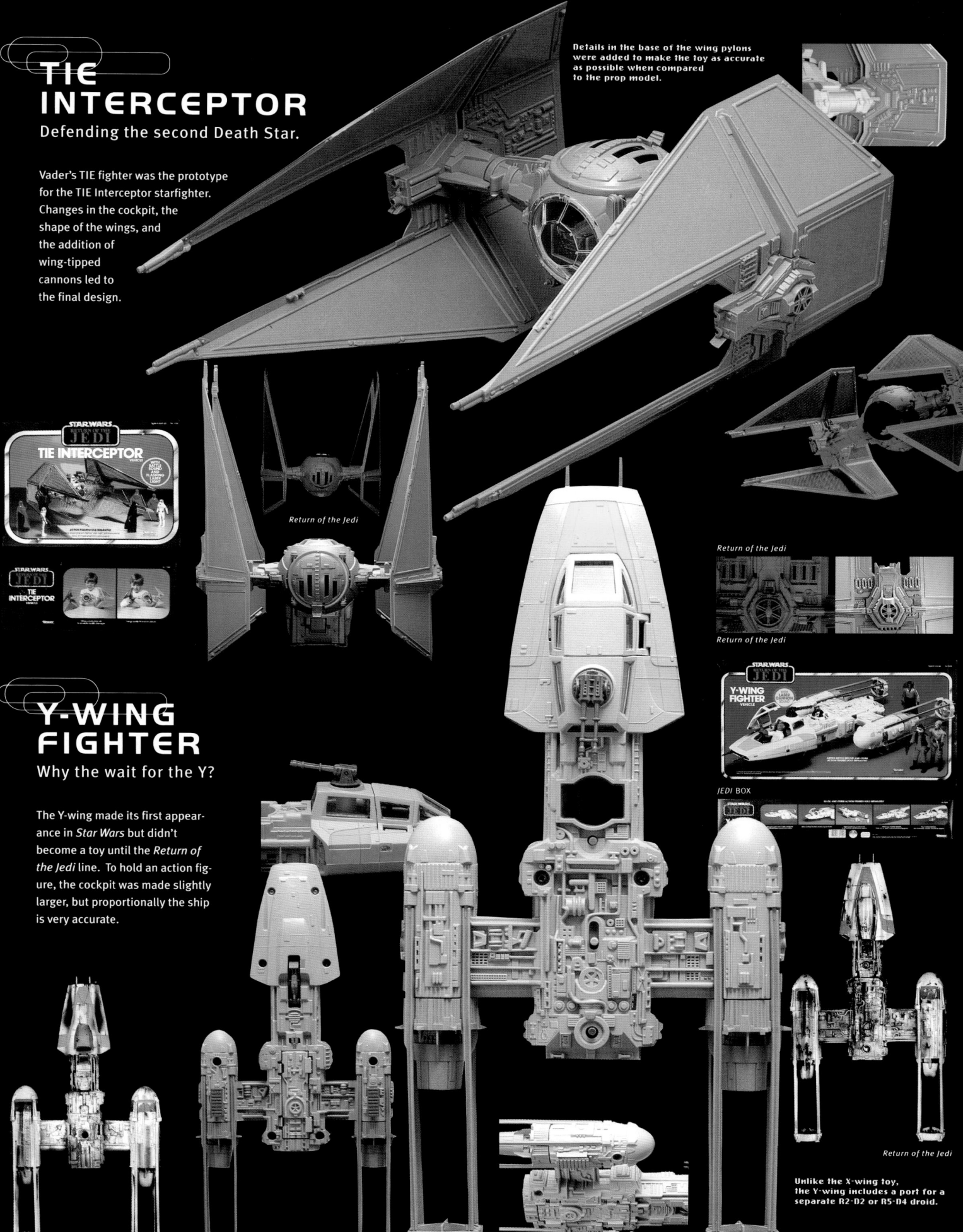

Return of the Jedi

Return of the Jedi

Return of the Jedi

Y-WING FIGHTER

Why the wait for the Y?

The Y-wing made its first appearance in *Star Wars* but didn't become a toy until the *Return of the Jedi* line. To hold an action figure, the cockpit was made slightly larger, but proportionally the ship is very accurate.

JEDI BOX

Return of the Jedi

Unlike the X-wing toy, the Y-wing includes a port for a separate R2-D2 or R5-D4 droid.

Return of the Jedi

B-WING FIGHTER

A heavily armed Rebel starfighter.

The B-wing in effect is one long, flat wing with an unusual "floating" cockpit at one end and one of the ship's three ion cannons at the other. About midway on the wing are two airfoils that extend out during combat, giving the ship the appearance of a cross or, with some imagination, the letter B.

JEDI BOX

TRILINGUAL BOX

Pressing the square button on the side of the ship creates an alert sound.

Return of the Jedi

Return of the Jedi

The wing can be opened by turning one of the engines on the back of the ship. The cockpit is isolated so that it will remain in the upright position no matter what the orientation of the rest of the ship.

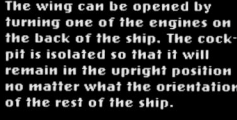

Return of the Jedi

Minirigs

Four more vehicles were added to the minirig line for *Jedi.*

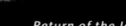

EWOK COMBAT GLIDER

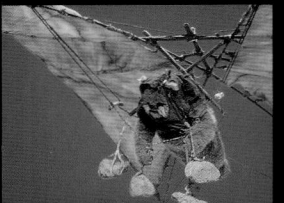

JEDI BOX

This combat hang glider comes with "boulders." But the Ewok in the photo doesn't appear to be Warok.

EWOK ASSAULT CATAPULT

Another Ewok weapon, the catapult also comes with plastic "boulders" to shoot at enemies.

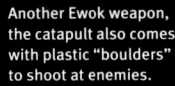

JEDI BOX

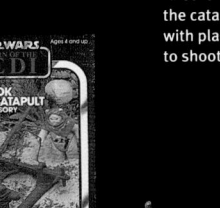

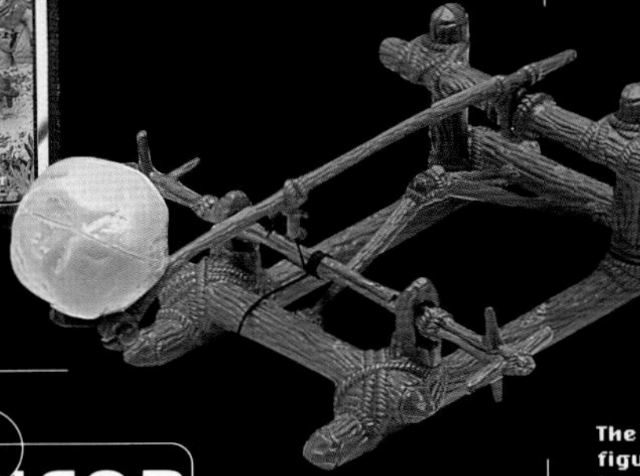

RANCOR MONSTER

JEDI BOX

Jabba the Hutt's gigantic pet is kept in a cave beneath Jabba's throne room. A lever on the rancor's back opens and closes his mouth.

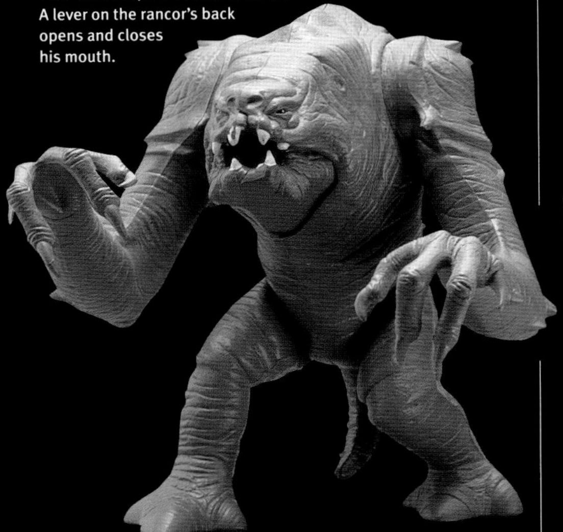

IMPERIAL SHUTTLE

A hyperdrive equipped transport.

This beautifully designed vehicle, which bears some resemblance to Luke's skyhopper, first appeared in *Return of the Jedi*. Later it made a brief appearance in *The Empire Strikes Back Special Edition*. The Emperor's shuttle has a gray stripe on its nose.

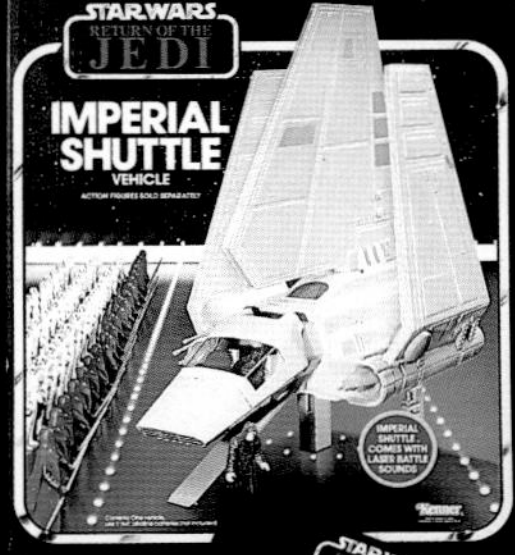

JEDI BOX

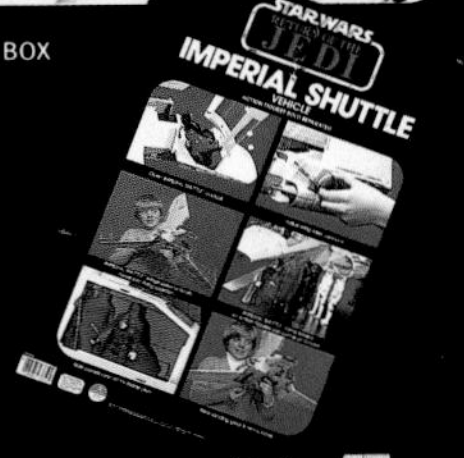

IMPERIAL SHUTTLE

Return of the Jedi

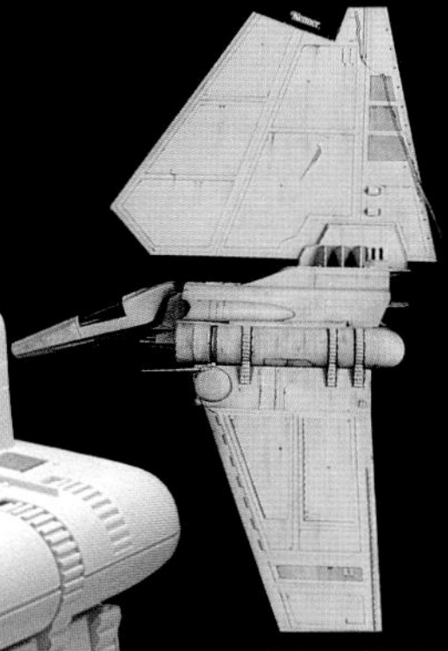

Return of the Jedi

The shuttle cockpit opens to hold two action figures. The ship's side panel can be removed to carry a brigade of troops.

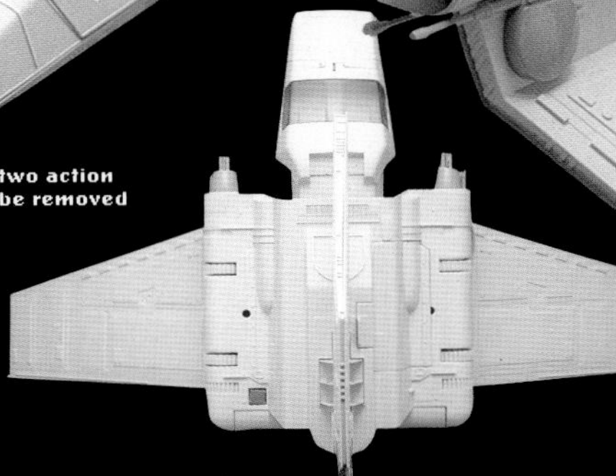

Return of the Jedi

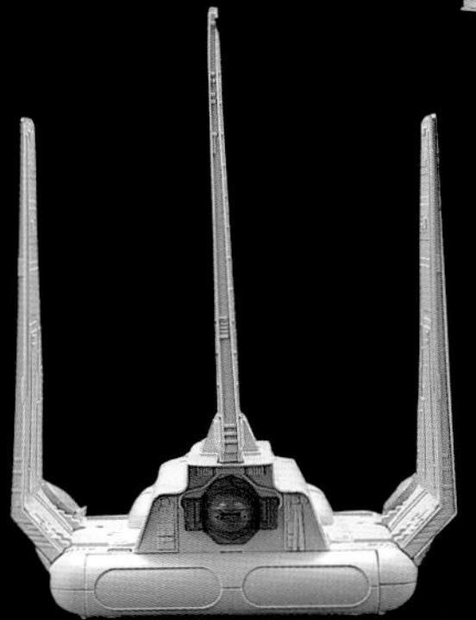

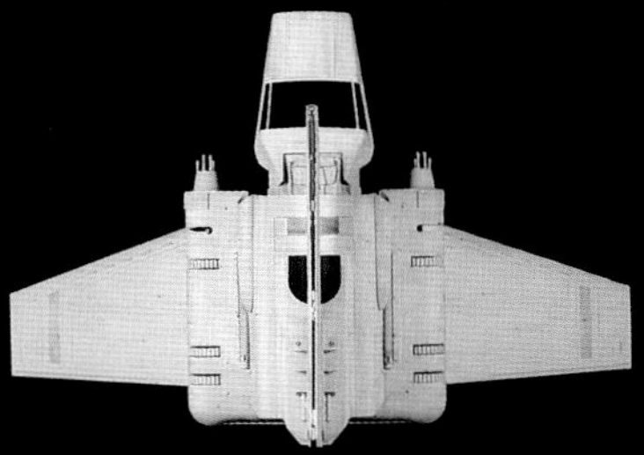

Return of the Jedi

Return of the Jedi

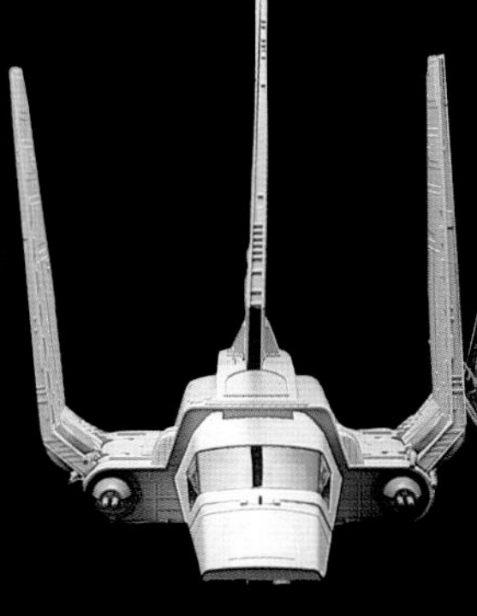

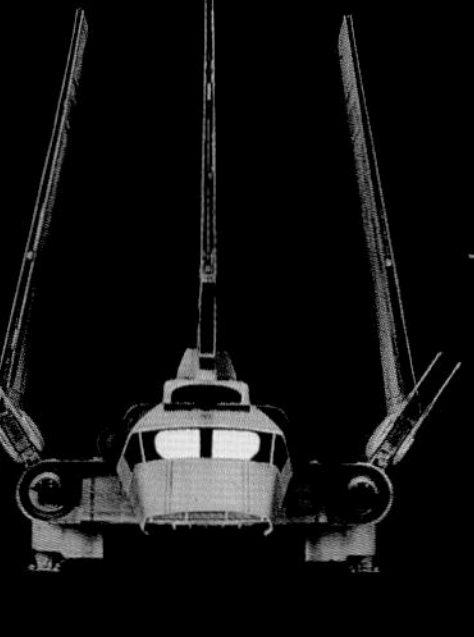

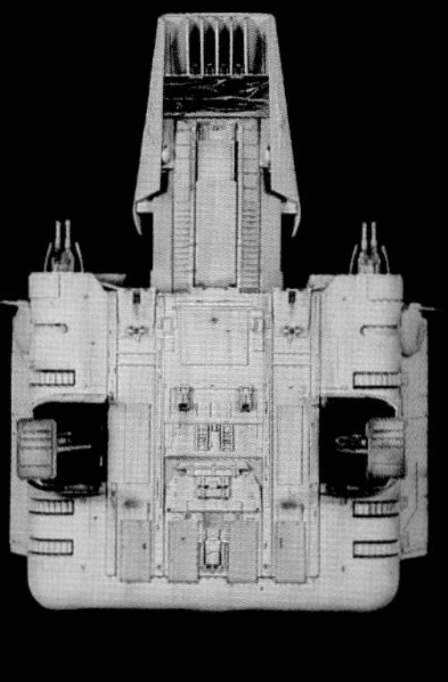

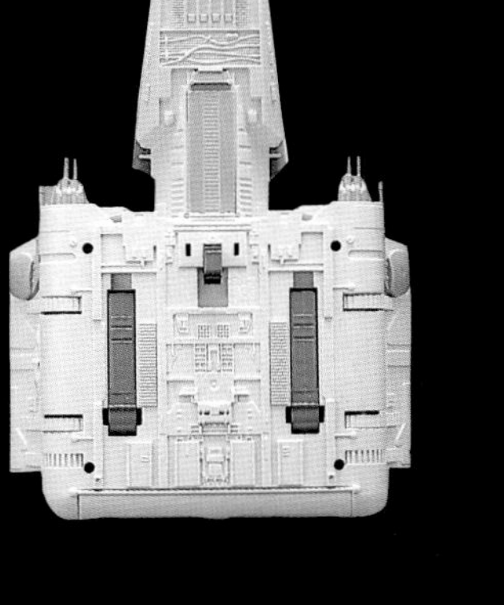

THE JABBA THE HUTT DUNGEON

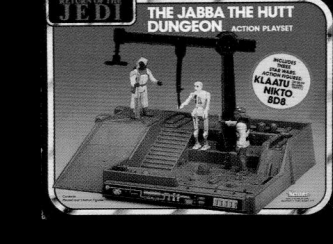

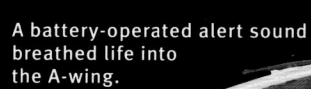

Return of the Jedi

This Sears exclusive playset, using a version of the much earlier Droid Factory base, was released in two consecutive years. The earlier version is shown here and came with 8D8, Klaatu in skiff guard outfit, and Nikto. The later version came with a brown base and action figures of EV-9D9, Barada, and Amanaman.

A-WING FIGHTER

A battery-operated alert sound breathed life into the A-wing.

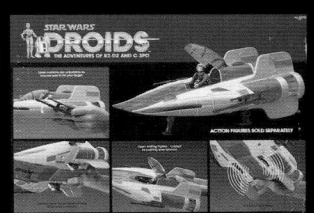

The fastest fighter in the Rebel fleet was the last to be released by Kenner.

Only available in the *Droids* box, the A-wing completed the Rebel fighter armada. It is accurate in proportion to the prop, although the cockpit was scaled up to accommodate an action figure pilot. As with the Y-wing fighter, the decoration was painted on, not applied with stickers like the X-wing.

TATOOINE SKIFF

Off to see the Sarlacc. . . .

One of the last toys released, the skiff was packaged in a Power of the Force box. Positioning vanes, retractable landing gear, and a working prisoner plank create many play possibilities.

POWER OF THE FORCE BOX

Return of the Jedi Special Edition

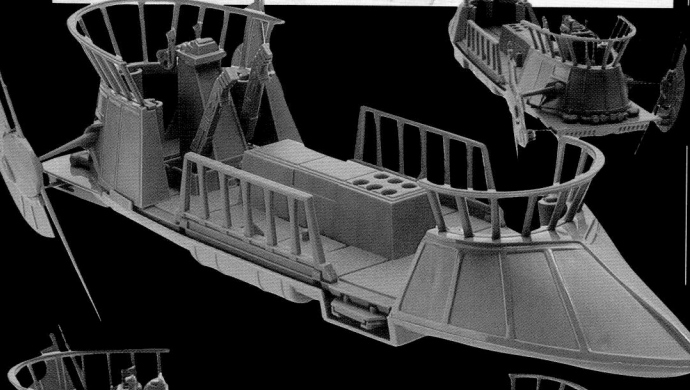

SY SNOOTLES
and the Rebo Band

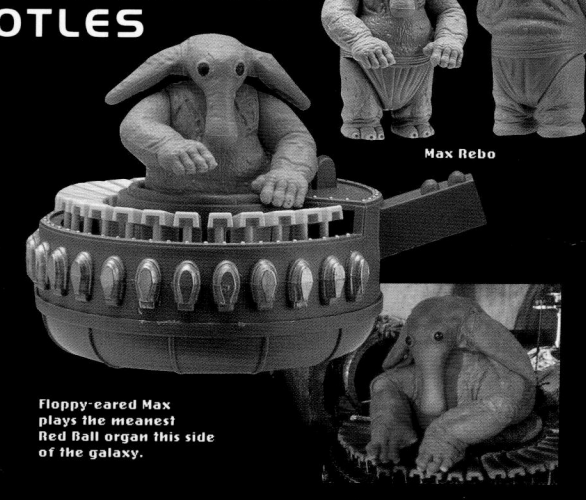

Max Rebo

Floppy-eared Max plays the meanest Red Ball organ this side of the galaxy.

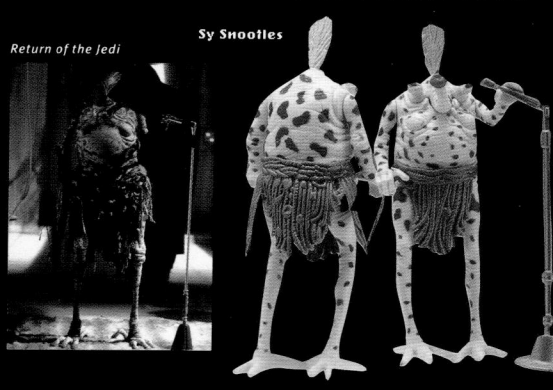

Play it again, Max.

Although never released on individual cards, the Max Rebo band members are considered true action figures. The figures came in a blister attached to the cardboard behind them.

Max Rebo is an Ortolan. Droopy McCool is a Kitonak. Sy Snootles is from a still-unknown species.

Return of the Jedi

Sy Snootles

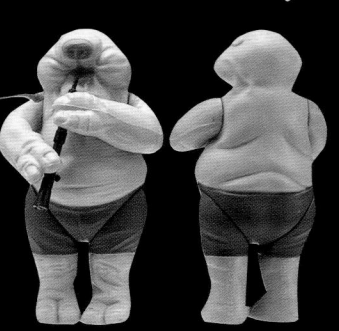

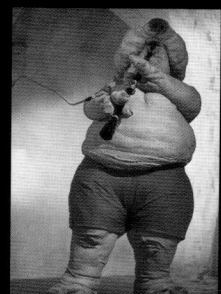

Droopy McCool

Return of the Jedi

EWOK BATTLE WAGON

This Ewok chariot has what appears to be a bantha skull attached to the front, raising the question of how banthas, thought indigenous to Tatooine, got to the forest moon of Endor.

Not considered minirigs, these three minivehicles were some of the last toys produced in the *Star Wars* line and are difficult to find.

Along with the A-wing, two other small *Droids* vehicles were produced.

ACCESSORY SETS
European Sets

In Europe three different playpacks were sold. Each contained several figures and one or two larger accessories.

The Hoth Rescue playpack included two creatures—a tauntaun and a wampa—along with Luke and Han.

The Ewok Combat playpack provided a catapult, two Ewoks, and two storm-troopers as targets for the boulders.

The Endor Chase playpack came with two biker scouts, one speeder bike, Princess Leia, and Wicket the Ewok.

ACTION FIGURE COLLECTOR CASES

The Darth Vader collector case was available in at least three different packaging designs and, in limited quantities, with three action figures included.

LASER RIFLE CARRY CASE

The laser rifle case could also be used as a toy weapon.

CHEWBACCA BANDOLIER STRAP

For the collector who wants to wear the figures, there is the Chewbacca bandolier strap (above). The C-3PO collector case (below) was reissued for the current line with an added voice chip and flashing eye lights.

The simple box-shaped figure cases were carried through all three films. Case fronts changed artwork according to the current film. The rarest of all is the *Return of the Jedi* collector case.

12-inch Figures

A short life for the 12-inch line.

Kenner released a line of 12-inch figures in 1978 and 1979. But most buyers preferred the smaller figures, and there weren't any vehicles or accessories for the larger ones, so the line was canceled in 1980.

LUKE SKYWALKER

PRINCESS LEIA ORGANA

HAN SOLO

BEN (OBI-WAN) KENOBI

STORMTROOPER

SEE-THREEPIO (C-3PO)

ARTOO-DETOO (R2-D2)

JAWA

DARTH VADER

CHEWBACCA

IG-88

BOBA FETT (*STAR WARS* BOX)

There were plans to produce new *Empire* clothing for Han, Luke and Leia, and *Empire* boxes were printed up for the entire line. But only Boba Fett was issued in both *Star Wars* and *Empire* boxes, and IG-88 was the only figure in just an *Empire* box.

BOBA FETT (*EMPIRE* BOX)

1998 update

WAVE 13
COLLECTION 1 · QTR 1998
LUKE SKYWALKER
(Bespin Outfit)

The Empire Strikes Back

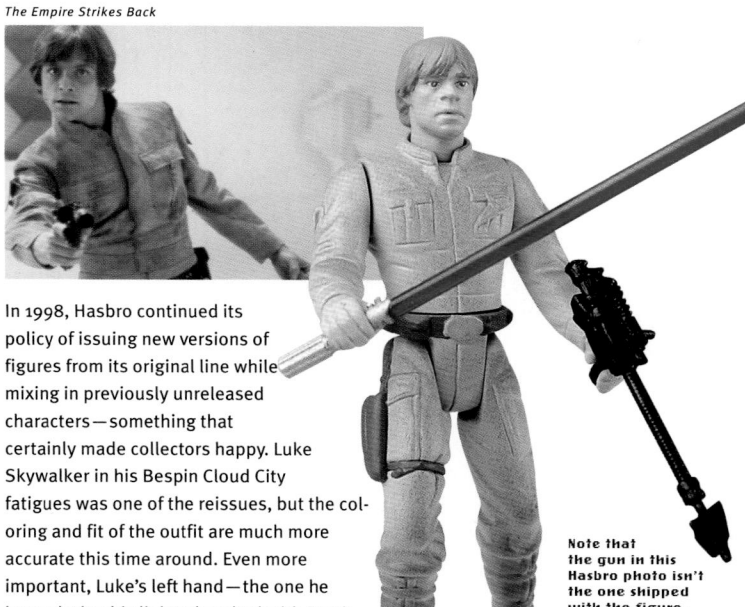

In 1998, Hasbro continued its policy of issuing new versions of figures from its original line while mixing in previously unreleased characters—something that certainly made collectors happy. Luke Skywalker in his Bespin Cloud City fatigues was one of the reissues, but the coloring and fit of the outfit are much more accurate this time around. Even more important, Luke's left hand—the one he loses during his lightsaber duel with Darth Vader—can be detached.
This Luke also benefits from a torso slimmed down from the new line's initial Luke release in 1995.

Note that the gun in this Hasbro photo isn't the one shipped with the figure.

WAVE 13
COLLECTION 1 · QTR 1998
PRINCESS LEIA ORGANA
(Ewok Celebration Outfit)

Princess Leia, in the outfit she wore at the Ewok celebration ceremony in *Return of the Jedi*, is a first-time release. To mark the occasion, Hasbro has resculpted the standard Leia face and come up with a beautiful princess wearing a primitive but attractive dress and unique hairstyle.

Return of the Jedi

Unlike the Leia released in the two-pack, the dress is all plastic. She also is shown with an incorrect weapon.

WAVE 13
COLLECTION 1 · QTR 1998
ENDOR
REBEL SOLDIER

The Endor Rebel Soldier is a replacement for the original line's Rebel Commando. The look is very different because of the advent of new toy-making techniques, such as tampo printing (where the design is, in effect, stamped onto irregular surfaces) and much smaller and more delicate paint masks. The detail can be seen in the camouflage outfit, which in the original was solid green.

The soldier also comes with a large, realistic-looking backpack.

Return of the Jedi

WAVE 13
COLLECTION 1 · QTR 1998
LANDO CALRISSIAN
in General's Gear

Return of the Jedi

The Lando sculpt doesn't differ much from the earlier Lando figures in the line. But a toy line can't have too many dashing knaves-turned-heroes. Lando got his instant commission because of his exploits in the off-screen Battle of Tanaab. Pliable new plastic material allows the sculptor to give Lando's cape some "attitude" of its own, a far cry from the limp piece of fabric draped around the neck of the original line's version.

The gun in this Hasbro photo isn't the one shipped with the figure.

LAK SIVRAK

BIGGS DARKLIGHTER

Star Wars

Lak Sivrak was an interesting choice for a figure. The "wolfman" mask that George Lucas used in the cantina scene wasn't one of the director's favorites because he thought it looked too much like the off-the-shelf mask that it was. So in 1997's *Star Wars Special Edition*, Lak and another wolfman were replaced in two shots, although a wolfman can still be seen fleetingly in the background.

Sivrak and his species also live on in the literature of the expanded *Star Wars* universe.

Star Wars

Another first-time entry, Biggs Darklighter has an almost mystical appeal to die-hard *Star Wars* fans. Here, the dashing, mustachioed Biggs wears his X-wing pilot outfit, the only way he was seen in the original film. Now some fans are hoping for a Biggs variation, dressed in the spiffy togs he wore in the cut scene.

Biggs originally had a bigger role in the film, but an early scene between Biggs and his buddy Luke was cut by George Lucas; it wasn't seen by the general public until the release of LucasArts' "Behind the Magic" CD-ROM set in fall 1998.

EWOKS: WICKET AND LOGRAY

While some fans don't like the Ewoks at all, many adore them. But it wasn't until 1998 that Hasbro released the first Ewok in its new line—and then it released two of them in one pack, just as it released two small Jawas together. But in this case, the Ewoks have distinct personalities: Wicket, the young hero who befriends Princess Leia, and Logray, the fierce medicine man who wears the half skull of a great forest bird on his head.

Advances in sculpting and materials show in these new and improved versions of Wicket and Logray.

Logray comes with his medicine pouch and his staff, which is much sharper and more detailed in this version. Wicket comes with his spear. Both Ewoks have removable cowls.

Logray

Wicket

Return of the Jedi

Return of the Jedi

DARTH VADER
with Removable Helmet

ISHI TIB

Return of the Jedi

Ishi Tib (also called Birdlizzard), the bulbous-eyed biped with a beaklike mouth, is a first-timer in the action figure line; he was most notable as one of Jabba the Hutt's subordinates. The alien's features are a very good copy of the movie version. The surprise is that this Ishi Tib is one of the good guys, taken from a brief sighting in the Rebel briefing room. In creating his believable galaxy, George Lucas often used the same species as both good and evil.

Ishi Tib is actually the name of his species, who hail from the planet Tibrin.

Of all the figures that fans and collectors lusted after in the 1980s, none was higher on the list than a Darth Vader figure whose mask and helmet could be removed to reveal the scarred face of Anakin Skywalker, just as happened in *Return of the Jedi*.

Kenner made several early attempts, but it took the technology of the 1990s to allow Hasbro to carry off the removable helmet trick without any compromises in the sculpt or the final toy. For added play value, the figure has a removable hand—Luke Skywalker's payback—and a jointed elbow so the arm wielding the lightsaber can move in and out.

Return of the Jedi

CAPTAIN PIETT

Human faces are the hardest to replicate in this scale, but Piett is a passable likeness.

The Empire Strikes Back

After Grand Moff Tarkin, perhaps the best-known Imperial officer is Captain Piett, who not only survived the harsh controlling tactics of Lord Vader but received a battlefield promotion to admiral after his predecessor, Admiral Ozzel, made a fatal mistake during the Empire assault on the Hoth Rebel base.

ZUCKUSS

The Empire Strikes Back

Another entry in the "is it 4-LOM or is it Zuckuss?" sweepstakes, the bounty hunter's new sculpting is even closer to the mark than the original Zuckuss (then called 4-LOM).

In the expanded mythos, Zuckuss has been described as a native of the gaseous planet Gand. He has to wear his special breathing mask on Tatooine to protect him from "harmful" oxygen.

PRINCESS LEIA ORGANA

All New Likeness!

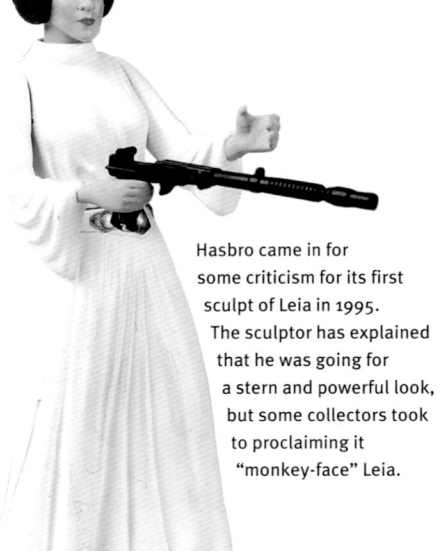

Star Wars

Hasbro came in for some criticism for its first sculpt of Leia in 1995. The sculptor has explained that he was going for a stern and powerful look, but some collectors took to proclaiming it "monkey-face" Leia.

The "all new likeness" Leia retains the double Danish buns hairstyle and the long white gown, but her facial features have been softened and her body isn't quite as Amazonian as the first release. Unlike the first release, however, none of Leia's clothing detaches.

LUKE SKYWALKER

with Blast Shield Helmet

One of the first signs that Luke Skywalker does indeed have undeveloped Force powers is a scene in the *Millennium Falcon* where, deliberately blinded by the solid faceplate of a blast shield helmet, he practices his lightsaber skills with a floating training remote.

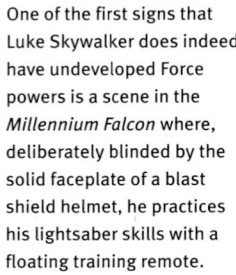

This figure, another first in the line, includes a very accurate reproduction of the helmet, which fits Luke quite well.

R2-D2

with Datalink and Periscope

Star Wars

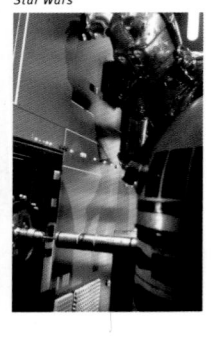

Droids don't wear clothing—well, not usually—so it's difficult to come up with new versions of such major characters as R2-D2 and C-3PO. But taking a cue from the initial Kenner line, Hasbro has provided Artoo with a periscope, like the one he used in the Dagobah swamp, and a scomp or data link, which the trusty droid used several times during the trilogy to help the Rebel heroes. Neither are detachable, but the droid also comes with removable buzz saw and claw appliances.

C-3PO

with Removable Limbs and Backpack

Since C-3PO doesn't have any pop-out or add-on devices that we know of, the designers simply replicated a feature from the original line.

The Empire Strikes Back

Kids will once again be able to remove Threepio's limbs and stick them in a net backpack, recreating the scene in *The Empire Strikes Back* where Chewbacca carries the broken golden droid. For the first time, the golden one's head can be removed, and any of the removable parts can be stuck in any of the slots, creating a very mixed-up droid.

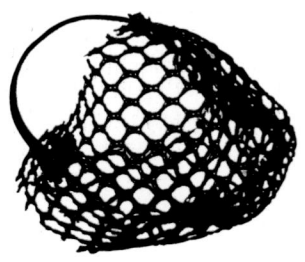

UGNAUGHTS

The Empire Strikes Back

Another two-pack due to their small size, the Ugnaughts are incredibly well sculpted characters from *The Empire Strikes Back*. These diminutive workers, half-human but also piglike, are from the planet Gentes, but they virtually run Cloud City on Bespin, doing much of the manual labor. While small, they are very hard working, especially in the Tibanna gas-processing operations.

8D8 DROID

Return of the Jedi

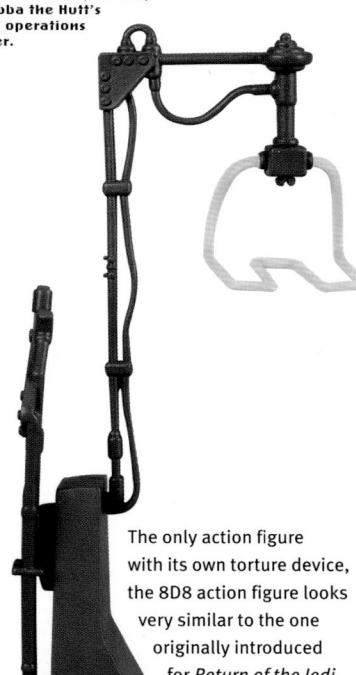

The thin-faced droid has almost humanoid features and worked under the real torturer, EV-9D9, in Jabba the Hutt's droid operations center.

The only action figure with its own torture device, the 8D8 action figure looks very similar to the one originally introduced for *Return of the Jedi*.

DEATH STAR TROOPER

Star Wars

Similar in some respects to the first line's early Death Squad Commander (later changed to the less gruesome Star Destroyer Commander), this figure has a lot more attitude, a great face sculpt, and an authentically styled helmet that can be removed.

REE-YEES

Another background alien in the group of hangers-on who swarmed around Jabba the Hutt, Ree-Yees really comes to life in this gunslinger pose.

Return of the Jedi

The three-eyed, goat-faced Gran is from the planet Kinyen. He was banished from his homeworld after murdering another Gran and ended up as a heavy-drinking petty thief on Tatooine—and an Imperial agent.

LOBOT

CHEWBACCA
as Boushh's Bounty

The Empire Strikes Back

Lando Calrissian's silent and mysterious chief assistant on Cloud City, Lobot used his implanted head bracket to communicate directly with the city's central computer. The advanced cyborg components also dramatically increased Lobot's intelligence.

Lobot has much more of an action stance the second time around.

He is said to have helped Lando win Cloud City from its nasty administrator in a sabacc game.

Besides the droids R2-D2 and C-3PO, Chewbacca is the only major character throughout the trilogy who doesn't have a costume change—mainly because he doesn't wear any clothes, except for accessories such as his bandolier strap with ammunition and his pouch. Chewie in chains is one of several sculptings of the Wookiee in the current line, including the original Chewbacca and the version of him as the flattop bounty hunter Snoova from the *Shadows of the Empire* multimedia project.

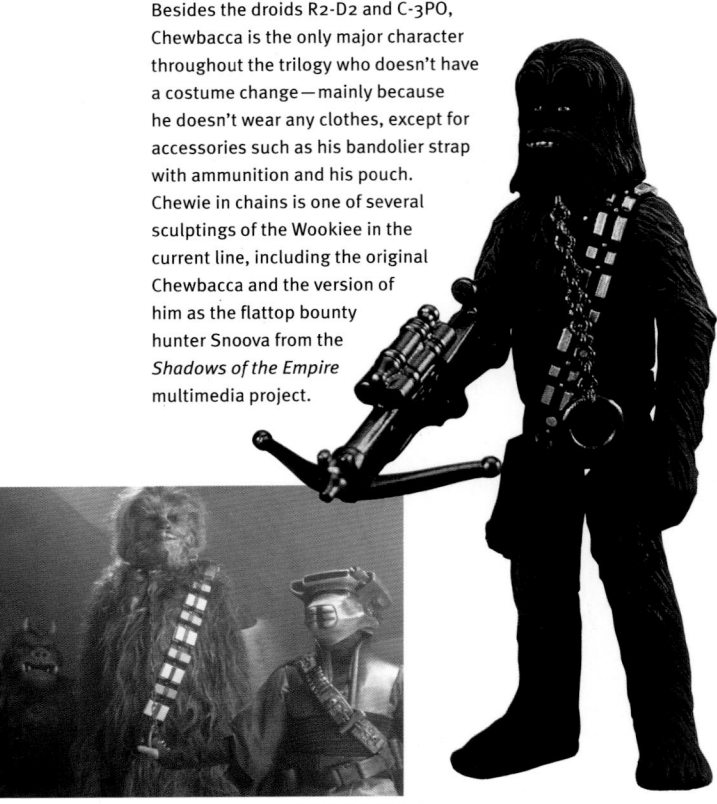

Return of the Jedi

ORRIMAARKO
(Prune Face)

MON MOTHMA

Called Prune Face in the original line, Orrimaarko and a few of his fellow Dresselians can be seen during the Rebel briefing prior to the Battle of Endor. The original Prune Face was covered by a plain tan cloth cloak.

Orrimaarko, distinguished by his eye patch, was a noted resistance fighter against the Empire and the first of his species to be given command of a SpecForce team.

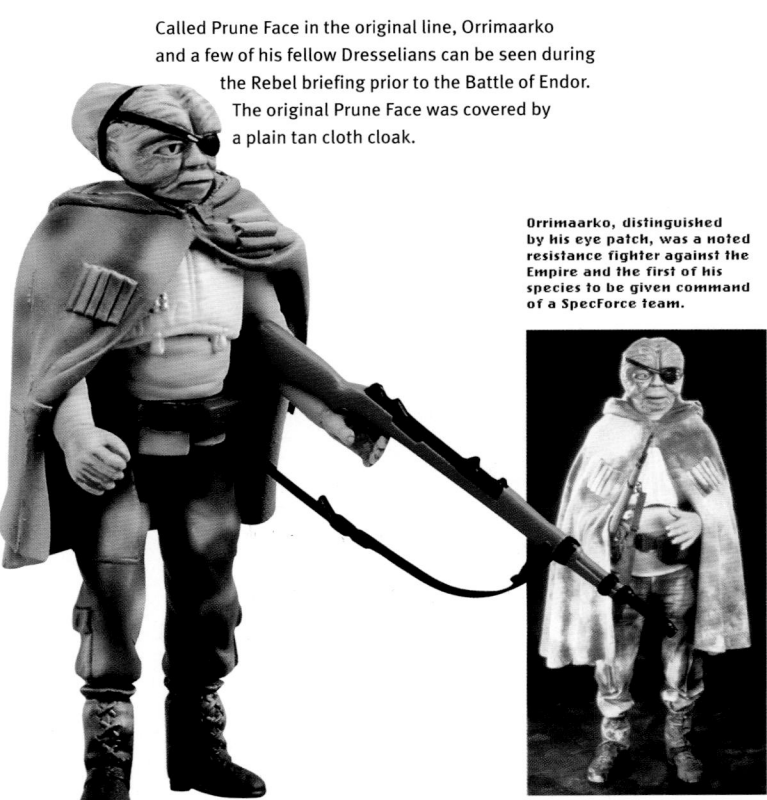

Looking more like a schoolteacher than a leading Rebel, Mon Mothma led by example and through her charismatic speeches.

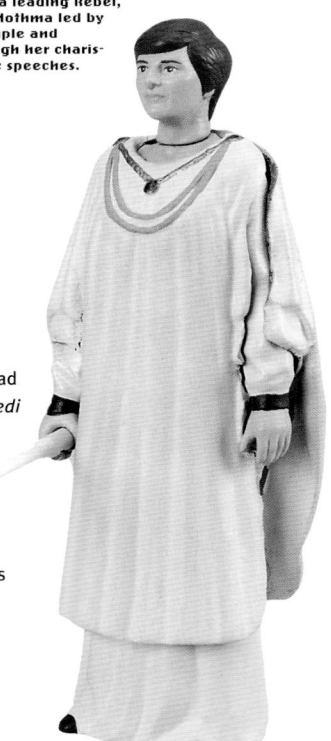

Return of the Jedi

Another of the most-requested figures by fans, Mon Mothma had very few lines in *Return of the Jedi* despite her position as leader of the Rebel Alliance. While the original line had only one female figure—Princess Leia in several versions—Hasbro has made a concerted attempt to produce more female action figures in the new *Star Wars* line.

Return of the Jedi

Kenner first attempted to create action figures of characters not directly taken from the first three *Star Wars* films in 1985 with the introduction of two small lines based on the *Ewoks* and *Droids* cartoon series. The line was a moderate success, although collectors today prize mainly two characters that were crossovers from the films: Boba Fett and an A-wing pilot.

Hasbro revisited the concept with a small line segment in 1996 devoted to figures from the *Shadows of the Empire* multimedia project, which included a novel, video game, "soundtrack" album, and toys. Again, the film-related characters sold best, and the main villain, Prince Xizor, was overproduced, warming pegs for quite a while before disappearing from store shelves.

In 1998, Hasbro returned to the expanded universe of novels, comics, and video games with a line segment that mixed well-known film-based characters with popular figures from other media. And to drive home the uniqueness of the line, Hasbro switched from its packages with slides from the films to cards whose backs could be slit to reveal a pop-open three-dimensional scene in which to place the characters.

WAVE 21 **3** QTR **1998**
COLLECTION 2
IMPERIAL SENTINEL
(From the *Dark Empire* comic book series)

WAVE 21 **3** QTR **1998**
COLLECTION 2
LUKE SKYWALKER
(From the *Dark Empire* comic book series)

From Dark Horse Comics' *Dark Empire* comic book series came four figures. The face sculpt on the new Luke Skywalker figure is chilling; it captures Luke as he strays closer than ever to the dark side of the Force. He is dressed in the cloak of a Dark Jedi, mirroring the taste in clothing of the clone Emperor.

The mysterious and frightful Imperial Sentinels were large guards used to protect the reborn clone Emperor's citadel on the planet Byss. Their origins are unknown, but some believe that the majestic crimson Sentinels were giant cyborgs or droids.

The Sentinels bear a resemblance to a 1986 unproduced Kenner figure, Atha Prime, which was part of an attempt to extend the original Power of the Force line with nonfilm characters.

The ysalamiri should be on a rack, but the Hasbro sculptor used a little creative license.

Many fans believe that the *Star Wars* "renaissance" of the 1990s was spurred by novelist Timothy Zahn's Thrawn trilogy of books, starting with *Heir to the Empire*, which soared to number one on the *New York Times* hardcover bestseller list when it was released in 1991. Dark Horse later translated the books into a comic series, from which this figure is sculpted. So it was fitting that Hasbro introduced figures of the series' two most popular characters.

Grand Admiral Thrawn himself, resplendent in a starched white uniform that makes his blue skin and red eyes stand out even more, nearly succeeded in carrying out the task that the Emperor had failed to complete: destroying the Rebel Alliance. Around his neck is one of the rodentlike Force-blocking creatures—the ysalamiri—that he used to neutralize the power of the Jedi.

WAVE 21 **3** QTR **1998**
COLLECTION 2
GRAND ADMIRAL THRAWN
(From the Thrawn novels)

LEIA ORGANA SOLO

(From the *Dark Empire* comic book series)

The figure for Luke Skywalker's now-married sister, Leia Organa Solo, is the first time that an action figure of Leia has been portrayed as a Jedi. She wears a Jedi cape and has her own lightsaber.

CLONE EMPEROR

(From the *Dark Empire* comic book series)

The clone Emperor—a plot device that split the fan community, especially after the clone was killed and then resurfaced in a following series—is a very close match to the two-dimensional character that inhabited the comic pages.

MARA JADE

(From the Thrawn novels)

Even more popular than Thrawn among fans is Mara Jade, who has been borrowed by other *Star Wars* authors as part of a grand continuity; she has become a very important part of the expanded galaxy.

Mara, who has some Force powers (and thus comes with a lightsaber), started out as a villain, the "Emperor's Hand," with a blood oath to kill Luke Skywalker. She failed in that mission and eventually played a vital role in the New Republic and in the lives of its leaders.

KYLE KATARN

(From the Dark Forces video game)

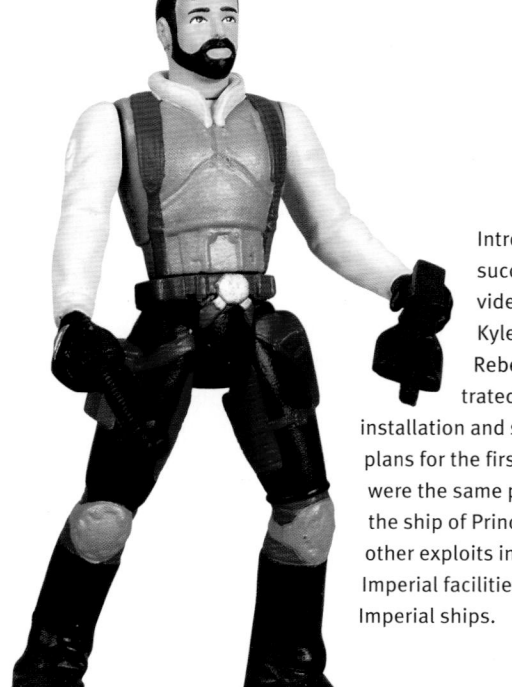

Introduced in the highly successful LucasArts video game Dark Forces, Kyle Katarn is a topflight Rebel agent who infiltrated a top secret Imperial installation and stole the technical plans for the first Death Star. These were the same plans later beamed to the ship of Princess Leia Organa. His other exploits include blowing up Imperial facilities and infiltrating Imperial ships.

DEATH STAR DROID

with Mouse Droid

A C-3PO look-alike, except for its face and silver color, this Death Star Droid was one of many aboard the Empire's huge battle station. It is similar to the droid in the first Kenner line, except for the way its arms and legs are positioned. The droid comes with another Death Star worker, a small Mouse Droid, or MSE-6. These ubiquitous droids do everything from cleaning ships to delivering orders and sensitive documents. This is the first time a Mouse Droid has been made in the action figure line.

Star Wars

POTE SNITKIN

For those fans who say they want every alien in the films, Hasbro came up with this incredible hulk, Pote Snitkin, seen only briefly in *Return of the Jedi*.

According to expanded universe lore, Snitkin is a member of a species called the Skrilling, about whom almost nothing is known. He was the helmsman, or pilot, on one of Jabba the Hutt's skiffs and was among those killed during Luke Skywalker's rescue of Han Solo and Princess Leia. He looks like he could be a one-man band—or at least lead a parade.

Return of the Jedi

AT-AT DRIVER

This is the second AT-AT driver in Hasbro's new line, although it is the first one on a card. The company packaged a similar AT-AT driver along with the commander, General Veers, in the giant Imperial walker that was released in 1997, which was the most expensive item in the *Star Wars* line. This driver is decorated like the first but seems more comfortable standing than sitting.

The Empire Strikes Back

SPACETROOPER

(From the Thrawn novels)

Spacetroopers, or elite Zero-G stormtroopers, are used to launch assaults in space on another ship. Each trooper comes equipped with armor and equipment that enables him to function almost like an independent spacecraft. They can withstand the vacuum of space, propel themselves through space, and attack and breach nearly any target.

Another figure from the expanded universe segment, this buffed-up stormtrooper first appeared in Timothy Zahn's Thrawn trilogy.

DARKTROOPER

(from the Dark Forces video game)

Developed in secret by the Empire, this fighting force comprised the next generation of stormtroopers. Their armor is made of the nearly impervious metal phrik, and they are so well equipped that they are, in effect, powerful self-contained weapons platforms.

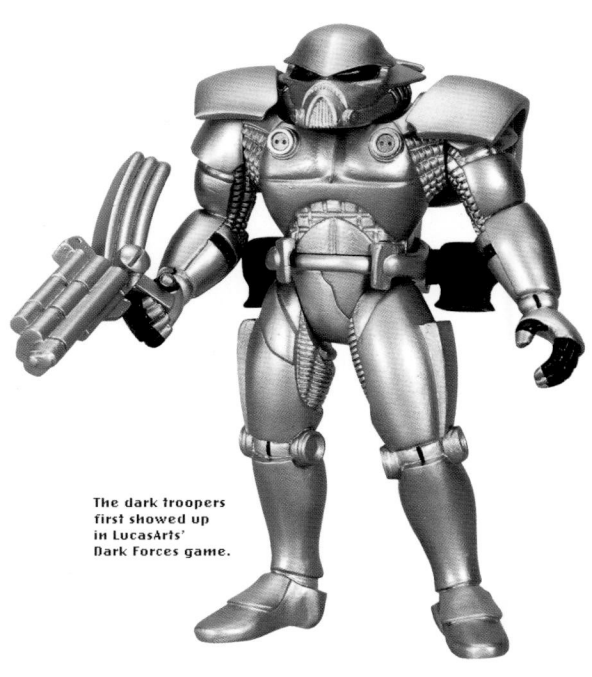

The dark troopers first showed up in LucasArts' Dark Forces game.

princess Leia collection

Hasbro decided to make a small-scale fashion statement with the Princess Leia Collection. Reminiscent of the original Kenner line, it released two-packs twinning a cloth-covered Leia with another character. All the Leia figures use a new, far prettier face sculpt than the original Hasbro Leia. And the quality and fit of the clothing is light-years removed from the original line. Two of the fig-

ures, Ceremonial Leia (with a cloth-jacketed Luke Skywalker) and Endor Leia (with Wicket the Ewok) even have hairpieces made out of pliable material, not plastic. The line marked the first release of a Leia figure as the Princess appeared at the medal ceremony at the end of *Star Wars*.

I QTR 1998
PRINCESS LEIA
and R2-D2

This is the Princess that first greeted us at the beginning of *Star Wars,* with that unusual "Danish pastry" hairstyle. She bends to load R2-D2 with vital, top secret information.

Star Wars

I QTR 1998
PRINCESS LEIA
and Luke Skywalker

This marks the first time that a figure has been made of Luke or Leia at the awards ceremony that ends *Star Wars*.

Star Wars

Leia is elegant in her billowing white gown with a special belt and a stunning necklace. Luke comes with a cloth jacket and a medal around his neck.

I QTR 1998
PRINCESS LEIA
and Han Solo

When she arrives on Bespin's Cloud City, Leia has a reason to wear something more than fatigues.

The Empire Strikes Back

In the original Kenner line, the lounge jacket over her dress was made from printed vinyl. Here it is patterned, sheer cloth.

I QTR 1998
PRINCESS LEIA
and Wicket the Ewok

Even though it is a somewhat primitive look, Leia's outfit as an honored guest in the Ewok village is an attractive one. In this case, the blouse is part of the plastic figure while the skirt is cloth.

Return of the Jedi

12-inch figures

I QTR 1998
TRILOGY ASSORTMENT

Hasbro was surprised but delighted that its 12-inch figures were so popular the second time around, widely sought by collectors who sometimes got frustrated while trying to find chain-store exclusives or even regular-line figures made in relatively small quantities. In 1998 it released assortments tagged to the individual films as seen on this page, except for the late-arriving *Return of the Jedi* assortment. But it also introduced eighteen store exclusives, a staggering number, keeping collectors on the prowl. Hasbro wasn't able to provide photographs of any of the exclusives in time for this book's deadline.

Yoda

R2-D2

Jawa

I QTR 1998
THE EMPIRE STRIKES BACK ASSORTMENT

AT-AT Driver

Snowtrooper

Han Solo
in Hoth Gear

Luke Skywalker
in Hoth Gear

2 QTR 1998
A NEW HOPE ASSORTMENT

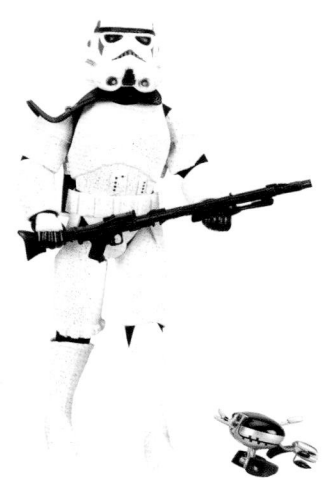

Sandtrooper with
white shoulder pouldron
and probe droid

Luke Skywalker
in Ceremonial Clothing

Grand Moff Tarkin
and interrogator droid

Greedo

CINEMA SCENE THREE-PACKS

I QTR 1998
FINAL JEDI DUEL

Darth Vader, Luke Skywalker, Emperor Palpatine

Hasbro continued its popular three-packs depicting scenes from the first trilogy with this Final Jedi Duel pack that contains Emperor Palpatine seated on his throne and a Jedi Luke and Darth Vader in dueling poses.

Return of the Jedi

I QTR 1998
PURCHASE OF THE DROIDS

Uncle Owen, Luke Skywalker, C-3PO

For the first time in any line, Hasbro introduced an Uncle Owen Lars figure—a character that collectors have long been seeking. C-3PO has a restraining bolt and a properly worn appearance for a droid that has just trekked through the Jundland Wastes, and Luke carries his macrobinoculars on his belt.

Star Wars

2 QTR 1998
JABBA THE HUTT'S DANCERS

Rystáll, Greeata, Lyn Me

This is probably the most eagerly awaited of the three-packs because it contains three completely new figures, Jabba's dancers, who were added to the *Return of the Jedi Special Edition*. The sculpting of the three dancers—Rystáll, Greeata, and Lyn Me—are incredibly true-to-life and impeccably decorated.

Return of the Jedi Special Edition

3 QTR 1998
MYNOCK HUNT

Han Solo, Princess Leia, Chewbacca

It only slowly dawns on the intrepid trio of Chewbacca, Princess Leia, and Han Solo that the cave they are in after fleeing Imperial forces is more than it seems to be. Here, they leave the relative safety of the *Millennium Falcon*, don breathing masks, and chase away the pesky mynocks before the energy-feeding, silicon-based flying parasites can damage the ship. The set comes with the first mynock figure ever produced.

The Empire Strikes Back

The Empire Strikes Back

multipacks

TWO-PACKS

George Lucas thought it would be fun to have an up-tempo musical interlude "interrupt" his third *Star Wars* film, just as the cantina number did in the first. His artists and technicians created a group of funny aliens to be members of the Max Rebo Band—and then they did it again years later to increase the size of the band for the *Return of the Jedi Special Edition.* Kenner's original Max Rebo Band set came with Max, Sy Snootles, and Droopy McCool.

Max Rebo Band Pairs
(At selected Wal-Mart stores)

These two-packs were a Wal-Mart exclusive, and each paired a band member first seen in 1983 with one first seen in 1997. Sy Snootles, who was a puppet in the original film, and new singer Joh Yowza were both computer-generated in the *Special Edition.* Max Rebo comes with his Red Ball Jett organ.

Droopy McCool

Barquin D'an

1 QTR 1998
DROOPY MCCOOL AND BARQUIN D'AN

Droopy McCool, the chubby Kitonak musician, is a specialist on the chidinaklu, a flutelike instrument made by hollowing out the chidinka plant. Barquin D'an, a Bith, follows in the musical tradition of his species by blowing cool notes on a kloo horn.

Return of the Jedi   *Return of the Jedi Special Edition*

Return of the Jedi

Sy Snootles

3 QTR 1998
SY SNOOTLES AND JOH YOWZAH

The two lead singers in the Max Rebo Band are, by turns, sultry and bluesy. Sy Snootles, a longtime jizz wailer, has a reedy voice that is due, in large part, to her unusual facial anatomy. Joh Yowzah, a long-legged Yuzzum from the forest moon of Endor, has the pipes and mouth to really blast out a song.

Return of the Jedi Special Edition

Joh Yowzah

4 QTR 1998
MAX REBO AND DODA BODONAWIEEDO

Max Rebo, a squat blue Ortolan, leads the jizz-wailer band that has his name, and also plays the keyboards on his Red Ball Jett organ. Doda Bodonawieedo, a Rodian horn player, favors a modified fanfar.

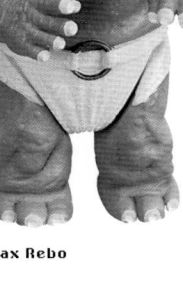

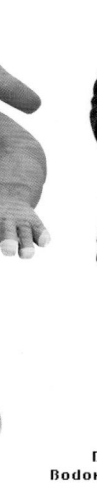

Return of the Jedi Special Edition

Max Rebo

Doda Bodonawieedo

Return of the Jedi

promotions

OOLA AND SALACIOUS CRUMB—

SW Insider 7/98

Return of the Jedi

Return of the Jedi

This 1998 exclusive from the *Star Wars Insider*/Official *Star Wars* Fan Club marks the first time that the Twi'lek dancer Oola has been transformed into an action figure. Her role was expanded a bit in the *Return of the Jedi Special Edition*. Hasbro did an amazing job with Oola's fishnetlike costume, sculpting and painting most of it but using real cloth where it billows on her lower legs. An earlier Salacious figure was released with a Jabba the Hutt playset after *Jedi* opened in 1983.

Oola comes packaged in an open window box with Jabba the Hutt's court jester, Salacious Crumb.

SLIDE VIEWER MACROBINOCULARS

The Empire Strikes Back

With the vast majority of Hasbro's 1998 carded figures coming with a "Freeze Frame Action Slide" showing the character as it appeared in one of the *Star Wars* films, collectors needed some place to store the slides and a way to look at them. The company's first mail-away promotion was for a plastic slide sheet with an inserted paper label. But later in the year collectors could send away for this nifty slide viewer in the shape of Luke Skywalker's macrobinoculars, along with two exclusive slides.

BESPIN HAN SOLO

The Empire Strikes Back

CHEWBACCA

The Empire Strikes Back

SNOWTROOPER

The Empire Strikes Back

millennium minted coin collection

The original Kenner Power of the Force carded figure line came with sculpted coins that have become highly collectible. Hasbro decided to tap into the nostalgia and collectibility angles with a small line segment in 1998 exclusively for Toys "Я" Us. The coins use the fronts of the original coins but have a different back. The figures seem to vary only slightly from the regular carded figures, mainly in their decoration. The first wave of the first three figures released had the words Millennium Minted Coin printed on an inside card, but this was quickly removed.

The Bespin Han Solo figure comes with a gun whose muzzle is painted silver, not black. Chewbacca has an additional paint color—gray—for highlights. The snowtrooper's waist pouches are painted a different shade. The Luke and Leia figures have normal legs instead of the jointed ones that came with the figures when they were sold with speeder bikes.

WAVE 2 · 2 QTR 1998
LUKE SKYWALKER
in Endor Gear

Return of the Jedi

WAVE 3 · 2 QTR 1998
PRINCESS LEIA
in Endor Gear

Return of the Jedi

WAVE 4 · 2 QTR 1998
EMPEROR PALPATINE

Return of the Jedi

WAVE 5 · 3 QTR 1998
C-3PO

Star Wars

epic Force Figures

As an experiment, and to provide even more detail in its sculpting and decoration, Hasbro introduced its 6-inch line of Epic Force figures. Made more to admire and display than to play with, these really are more figurines than action figures, since they aren't jointed and are attached to their bases.

Part of the fun of the limited line of Epic Force figures is the action base, which rotates 360 degrees with the push of a thumbwheel. And the package doesn't even have to be opened, since the wheel is accessible from outside the large plastic bubble that covers the toy. Each of the figures is a completely new sculpt, and all are in action poses.

WAVE 1 | QTR **1998**

LUKE SKYWALKER

Luke Skywalker doesn't have time for a clothing change. He's wearing his Bespin fatigues and wielding a lightsaber as he darts through Cloud City, straight toward the carbonite freezing chamber in *The Empire Strikes Back*.

WAVE 1 | QTR **1998**

DARTH VADER

Darth Vader never has to worry about what to wear. He's making a point, but he's ready to strike in a pose from the ferocious duel with his son Luke in *The Empire Strikes Back*.

WAVE 1 | QTR **1998**

BOBA FETT

Boba Fett fires his rifle in an attempt to bring a chaotic situation under control when the Rebel prisoners get the upper hand on Jabba the Hutt's sail skiff in *Return of the Jedi*.

WAVE 2 | QTR **1998**

C-3PO

C-3PO holds his left leg high when R2-D2 is forced to temporarily abandon repair work on the golden droid in favor of a more pressing matter—a broken hyperdrive on the *Millennium Falcon*.

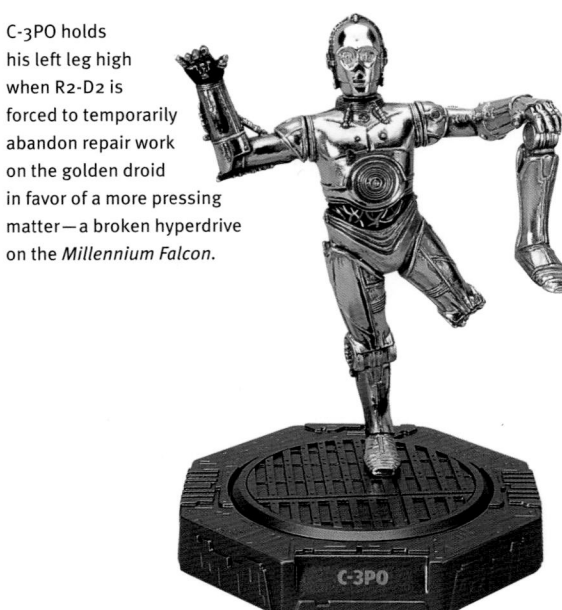

STORMTROOPER

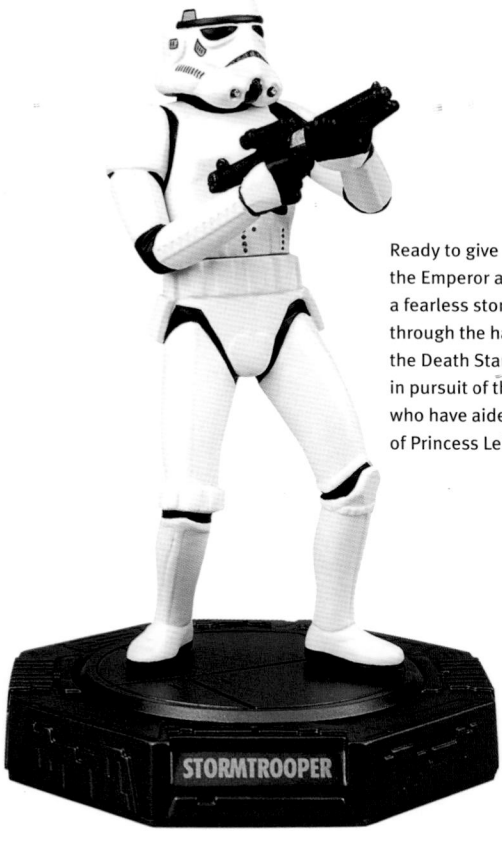

Ready to give his life for the Emperor and Darth Vader, a fearless stormtrooper rushes through the hallways of the Death Star in *Star Wars* in pursuit of the Rebels who have aided the escape of Princess Leia.

PRINCESS LEIA

Princess Leia Organa escapes Bespin's Cloud City in her white jumpsuit, her hair still styled as it was when she wore her diaphanous Bespin gown in *The Empire Strikes Back*.

HAN SOLO

Smuggler Han Solo fires his blaster pistol at hordes of stormtroopers aboard the Death Star in *Star Wars*. By necessity, Han has recently been a stormtrooper himself— or at least disguised as one—as evidenced by the stormtrooper belt around his waist.

OBI-WAN KENOBI

Obi-Wan Kenobi strikes a pose with his lightsaber as he does battle with Darth Vader aboard the Death Star in *Star Wars*. His selfless actions divert attention from his escaping friends, and he soon becomes one with the Force.

CHEWBACCA

Chewbacca, moments after the rescue of Princess Leia Organa from the Death Star in *Star Wars*, still wears broken Imperial binders on one wrist and carries a "borrowed" Imperial rifle that helped in the escape.

vehicles and GUNNER STATIONS

Continuing with its simple and relatively low-cost mini-playsets or environments with figures, Hasbro released three gunner stations to recreate action from *Star Wars*. Both Han Solo and Luke Skywalker are sculpted with their communications equipment on their heads and are able to sit down to operate the "rapid fire quad laser" cannons. A Darth Vader that can sit comes in what is essentially his TIE fighter cockpit.

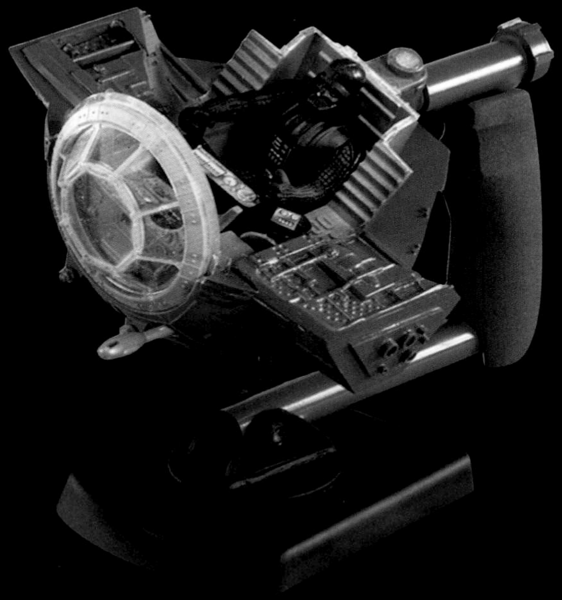

WAVE 2 2 QTR 1998

DARTH VADER

with TIE Fighter Gunner Station

The Dark Lord of the Sith sits snugly in the cockpit of his one-person, experimental TIE fighter, in hot pursuit of the last remaining Rebel threat to the not-so-impervious Imperial Death Star.

WAVE 1 2 QTR 1998

HAN SOLO

with *Falcon* Gunner Station

In addition to his molded-on communications headgear, Han Solo is wearing his pilot gloves as he both controls the *Falcon* and fights the Imperial forces.

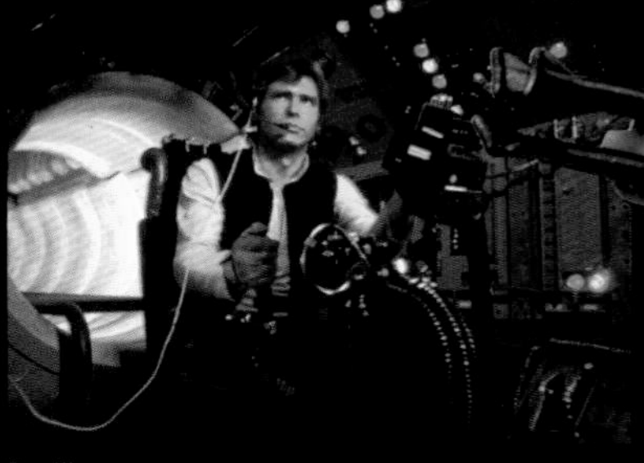

Star Wars

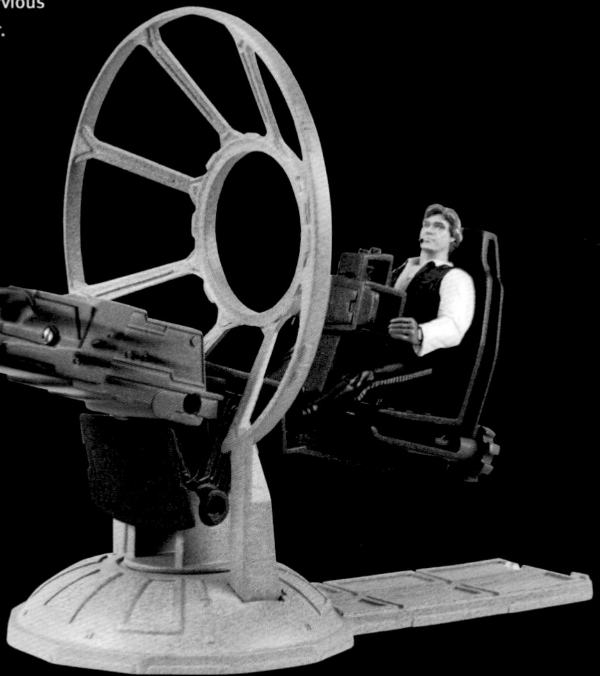

WAVE 1 2 QTR 1998

LUKE SKYWALKER

with *Falcon* Gunner Station

Seated in a gunner station of the *Millennium Falcon*, Luke Skywalker is wearing a stormtrooper belt and gun holster, evidence of his small band's recent escape from the Death Star. The two gunner stations attach to each other. A dial on the back of each operates a quad laser cannon. When the knob is rotated, the projectiles fire one at a time. The faster it is turned, the faster the gun fires.

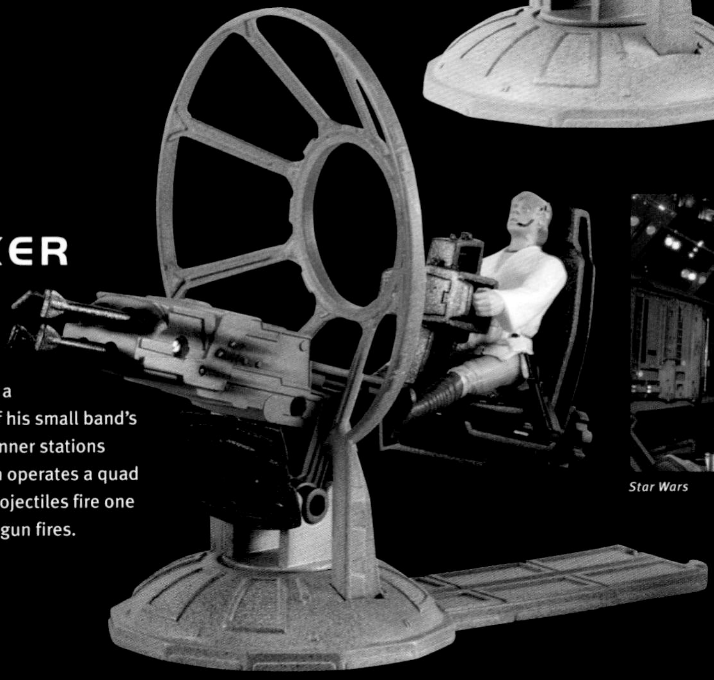

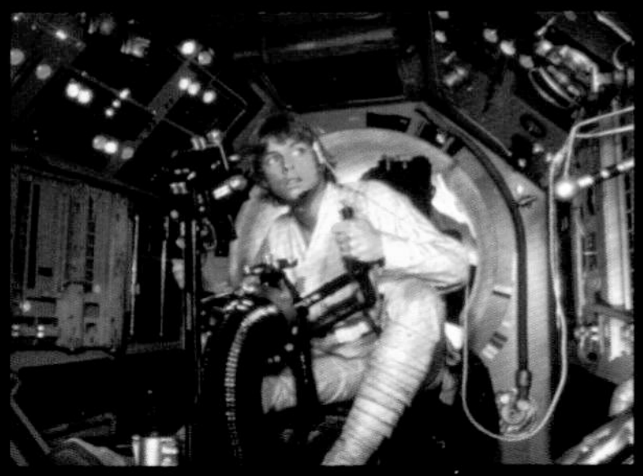

Star Wars

COMPLETE GALAXY

In yet another variation on a theme, Hasbro's Complete Galaxy line segment provides action figures inside planetary domes. A poseable Darth Vader figure has a removable helmet dome and sits in his meditation chamber, which has an apparatus to hold the helmet. Closed, the toy becomes the Death Star, with various printed captions identifying such things as the "superlaser focus lens." Yoda comes inside the planet Dagobah and includes an attached flying predator that is glimpsed only briefly in *The Empire Strikes Back*. A Luke Jedi figure comes with the planet Tatooine. When opened, the globe contains the Great Pit of Carkoon and the Sarlacc monster as reconceived in the *Return of the Jedi Special Edition*. The forest moon of Endor comes with a high-flying Ewok and a hang glider whose "wings" fold out when the globe is opened.

WAVE 1 · 2 QTR 1998
DEATH STAR
with Darth Vader

Darth Vader's knees bend so that he can sit in his meditation chamber inside the Death Star dome. Only the helmet part of his mask is removable, revealing the scarred back of his head. His cape is made of cloth rather than the standard plastic.

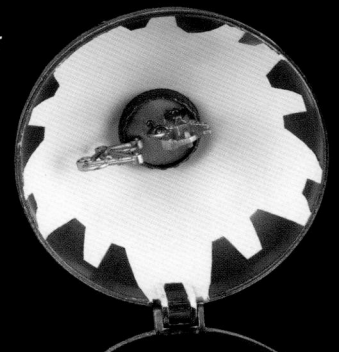

DEATH STAR

WAVE 2 · 3 QTR 1998
ENDOR
with Ewok

A hang glider extends its wings as the Endor moon dome is opened. The Ewok is actually a Wicket repaint, although it is meant to be a different Ewok. The Ewok comes with a sling-shot for dropping "boulders" on Imperial forces below.

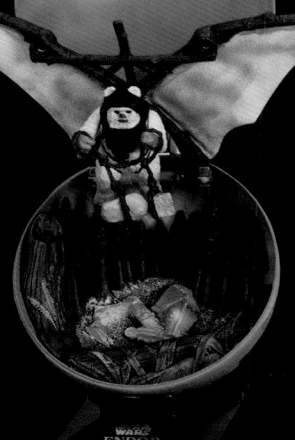

ENDOR

WAVE 2 · 3 QTR 1998
TATOOINE
with Luke Skywalker

Inside the Tatooine dome, Luke Skywalker is at a perilous moment. Jabba the Hutt's henchmen are just about to force him off a short gangplank into the Sarlacc's mouth, when R2-D2 flips him his lightsaber. The figure is the Luke Jedi Knight version, without a cloak. The dome is marked with familiar Tatooine sites.

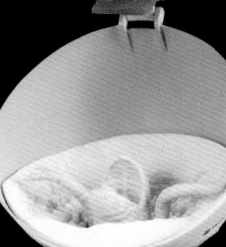

TATOOINE

TATOOINE

WAVE 1 · 2 QTR 1998
DAGOBAH
with Yoda and Flying Creature

The planet of swamps and bogs comes complete with a flying predator, which is easy to miss if you blink during *The Empire Strikes Back*. The Yoda figure is a somewhat more detailed likeness than the first Yoda in the Hasbro/Kenner line.

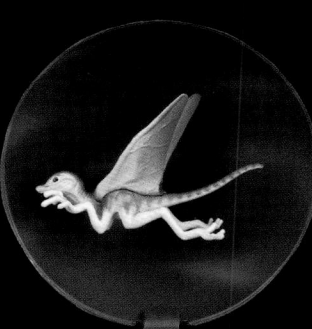

DAGOBAH

CREATURE ASSORTMENT

To enable fans to recreate the opening of *The Empire Strikes Back*, Hasbro released figures of tauntauns and a wampa as Kenner had done years earlier. But both creatures are far more realistically sculpted and painted this time around, and each comes with special figures.

The tauntaun with Luke in Hoth gear allows the figure to sit on the noble beast. While the Luke/Hoth figure with the wampa may look identical at a distance, it has a scarred face from the wampa attack, and the scarf on the hat can turn upside down when Luke is hanging from his legs in the wampa's cave. The Han Solo in Hoth gear figure can also sit, and unlike the previous Han/Hoth, his fur-lined hood is sculpted up over his head.

WAVE 2 | 1QTR 1998
TAUNTAUN
with Luke Skywalker in Hoth Gear

The Luke Skywalker figure has a knee joint so that he can be properly placed astride his faithful tauntaun.

The Empire Strikes Back

WAVE 3 | 2QTR 1998
WAMPA
with Luke Skywalker in Hoth Gear

Luke's scarf rotates so that when he hangs upside down in the ice cave to await digestion by the wampa, the scarf can be turned toward the ground. One of the wampa's arms has swinging arm action, while the other can be removed—or sliced off with a lightsaber.

The Empire Strikes Back

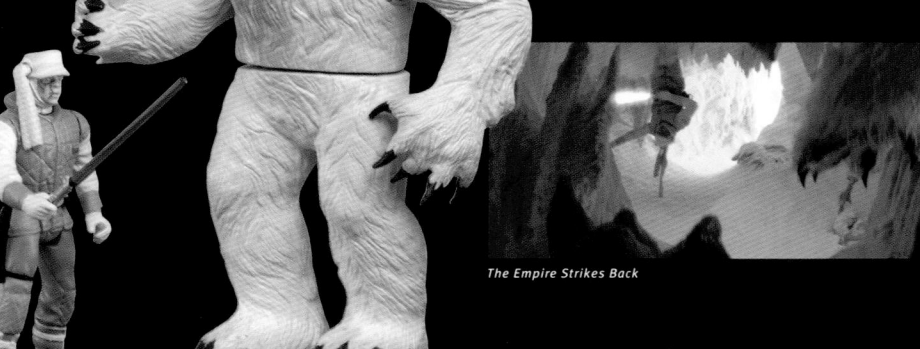

WAVE 4 | 3QTR 1998
TAUNTAUN
with Han Solo

The Empire Strikes Back

Han comes with knee joints so that he can ride his tauntaun to rescue his missing comrade. Unlike the carded Han in Hoth gear figure, this one has the hood of his snowsuit up to ward off the frigid Hoth night.

DELUXE CREATURE ASSORTMENT

Perhaps the most eagerly awaited creature release was that of the bantha, the stolid beast of burden that appears fleetingly in *Star Wars* and, with the *Special Edition, Return of the Jedi*. It has never been released as a toy before, and the Hasbro *Star Wars* team seemed to take extra care to make it special. The creature is beautifully sculpted, has long artificial hair, and comes with a huge saddle. The creature is packaged with a Tusken Raider in a partial cloth outfit.

While Kenner had released a rancor in the initial line, this one is sculpted and detailed to look much more like the film version. It has soft, pliable skin and comes with a Luke Jedi figure with a new head sculpt. The set also comes with the bone that Luke uses to jam the beast's mouth open to avoid becoming its next meal.

BANTHA
and Tusken Raider

The much-requested bantha met most fans' expectations, with a true-to-the-film sculpt and lifelike hair. The Tusken Raider's knees bend, and his lower front covering—a sort of extended loincloth—is made of fabric.

Star Wars

RANCOR
and Luke Skywalker

The rancor has what the toy industry calls "lifelike skin," a rubbery plastic that has texture and pliability similar to an animal's outer covering. Jedi Luke is dressed in black but without his Jedi cape or black glove that he wears in his battle with Jabba's minions. He comes with a handy bone, better to prop open the rancor's mouth—at least for an instant.

Return of the Jedi

VEHICLES

Unlike most film production companies, Lucasfilm prides itself on keeping nearly all of the working material that leads up to a film. Besides the actual props and matte paintings, its archives house thousands of early concept drawings of creatures, characters, vehicles, and environments that were modified, refined, and finally winnowed down to the chosen few. But with such a vast treasure trove available, it's fun to explore what might have been.

For its expanded universe vehicles segment, Hasbro has gone back to earlier concept drawings that eventually led to the twin-pod cloud car (single-pod cloud car), snowspeeder (airspeeder), and speeder bike. It has also included figures dressed in prototype costumes that later developed in a different way.

1 QTR 1998
EXPANDED UNIVERSE CLOUD CAR
with Pilot

The single-pod cloud car is based on a sketch by Joe Johnston, while the cloud car pilot is based on some design work from artist Ralph McQuarrie. The final design of the vehicle became more rounded, previewing the Art Moderne/Nouveau lines of Cloud City itself.

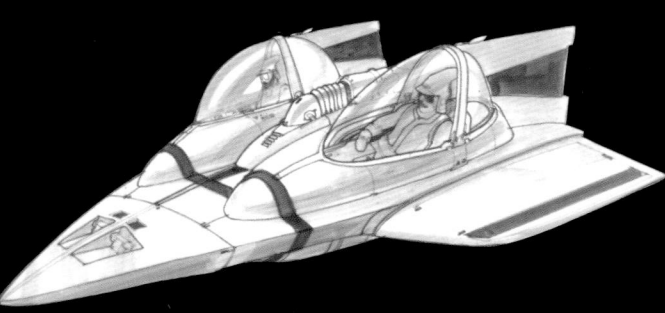

1 QTR 1998
EXPANDED UNIVERSE SPEEDER BIKE
with Pilot

Both this version of the speeder bike and its pilot are based on a sketch by Joe Johnston. Sometimes a design is discarded, only to surface later, such as the one for Luke's skyhopper, which became an Imperial shuttle. And often it can take dozens of preliminary sketches to get all the elements that George Lucas seeks.

EXPANDED UNIVERSE AIRSPEEDER

with Pilot

Both the airspeeder and its pilot are based on sketches by concept artist Ralph McQuarrie. The vehicle design was later turned into a snowspeeder and modified to hold two in the cockpit, a forward-facing pilot and a rear-facing gunner.

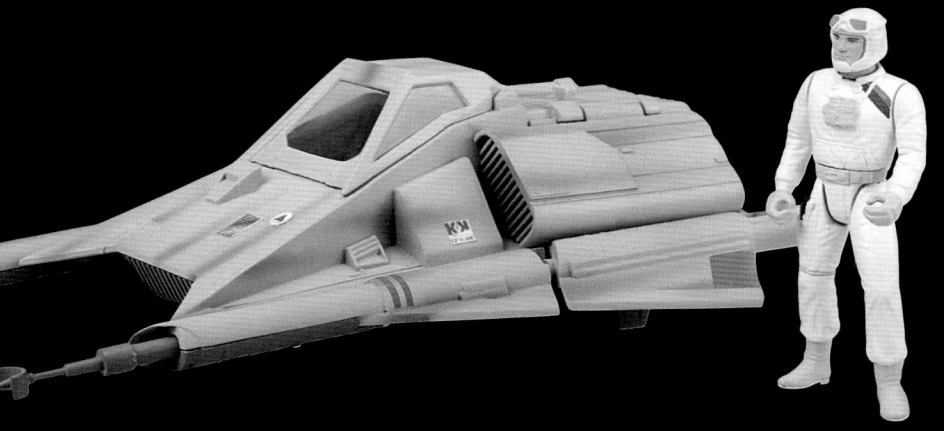

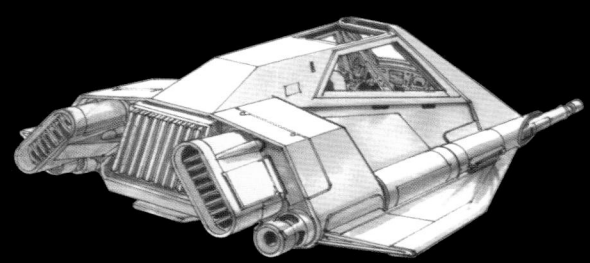

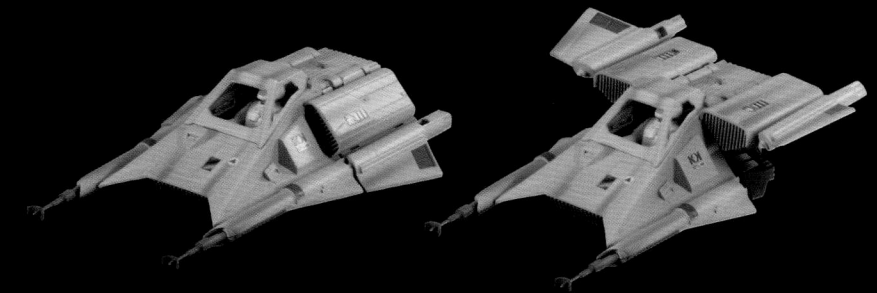

ELECTRONIC POWER FX X-WING FIGHTER

Perhaps the ultimate Hasbro vehicle, this X-wing fighter really rocks! Its size and lines are much closer to the original models used in *Star Wars* than the company's earlier X-wing fighter. It comes with the torso of Luke Skywalker and the top of R2-D2, both of which turn and make sounds or talk when pushed or pulled with a lever. The electronics recreate not only the sound and lights of the X-wing's engines but all the dialogue between Luke, Artoo, and the spirit of Obi-Wan Kenobi as Luke heads down the Death Star trench in one last attempt to save the Rebel Alliance. The wings can separate or close together, and the ship can launch a large red proton torpedo. There's also a targeting computer that lights up. All in all, this is one of the best *Star Wars* toys ever made, seen here in a pre-production version.

CHARACTER	CARD TYPE	CARD PHOTO VARIATION/FIGURE VARIATION

ORIGINAL *STAR WARS* LINE (1978–85)

CHARACTER	CARD TYPE	CARD PHOTO VARIATION/FIGURE VARIATION
Luke Skywalker	SW 12-back	Photo: on Tatooine/telescoping saber - yellow hair
	SW 12-back	Photo: on Tatooine/yellow hair
	other SW card	Photo: on Tatooine/yellow hair
	ESB card	Photo: on Tatooine/yellow or brown hair
	ROTJ card	Photo: on Tatooine/yellow or brown hair
	ROTJ card	Photo: in gunport/yellow or brown hair
	Trilogo card	Photo: in gunport/yellow or brown hair
Princess Leia Organa	SW 12-back	
	other SW card	
	ESB card	
	ROTJ card	
	Trilogo card	
Chewbacca	SW 12-back	Photo: combed back hair
	other SW card	Photo: combed back hair
	ESB card	Photo: combed back hair
	ROTJ card	Photo: combed back hair
	ROTJ card	Photo: frizzy hair
	POTF card	Photo: frizzy hair
	Trilogo card	Photo: frizzy hair
Han Solo	SW 12-back	Photo: holding gun w/ one hand/small head
	SW 12-back	Photo: holding gun w/ one hand/large head
	other SW card	Photo: holding gun w/ one hand/large head
	other SW card	Photo: holding gun w/ one hand/small head
	ESB card	Photo: holding gun w/ one hand/small head
	ESB card	Photo: holding gun w/ one hand/large head
	ROTJ card	Photo: holding gun w/ one hand/large head
	ROTJ card	Photo: holding gun w/ both hands/large head
	Trilogo card	Photo: holding gun w/ both hands/large head
Artoo-Detoo (R2-D2)	SW 12-back	
	other SW card	
	ESB card	
See-Threepio (C-3PO)	SW 12-back	
	SW 12-back	Takara head/torso sculpt
	other SW card	
	ESB card	
Ben (Obi-Wan) Kenobi	SW 12-back	Photo: hood down/telescoping lightsaber, white or gray hair
	SW 12-back	Photo: hood down/white or gray hair
	other SW card	Photo: hood down/white or gray hair
	ESB card	Photo: hood down/white or gray hair
	ROTJ card	Photo: hood down/white or gray hair
	ROTJ card	Photo: hood up/white or gray hair
	POTF card	Photo: hood up /white or gray hair
	Trilogo card	Photo: hood up /white or gray hair
Darth Vader	SW 12-back	Photo: w/ lightsaber/telescoping lightsaber
	SW 12-back	Photo: w/ lightsaber/Takara head sculpt
	SW 12-back	Photo: w/ lightsaber
	other SW card	Photo: w/ lightsaber
	ESB card	Photo: w/ lightsaber
	ROTJ card	Photo: w/ lightsaber
	ROTJ card	Photo: pointing
	POTF card	Photo: w/ lightsaber
	Trilogo card	Photo: w/ lightsaber
Stormtrooper	SW 12-back	Photo: two stormtroopers
	other SW card	Photo: two stormtroopers
	ESB card	Photo: two stormtroopers/may be packed with larger than normal gun
	ROTJ card	Photo: two stormtroopers
Imperial Stormtrooper	POTF card	Photo: two stormtroopers
Stormtrooper (Garde Imperial)	Trilogo card	Photo: one stormtrooper
Jawa	SW 12-back	Photo: Jawa shooting right/vinyl cape
	SW 12-back	Photo: Jawa shooting right/cloth cape
	other SW card	Photo: Jawa shooting right/cloth cape
	ESB card	Photo: Jawa shooting right/cloth cape
	ROTJ card	Photo: Jawa shooting right/cloth cape
	POTF card	Photo: Jawa shooting right/cloth cape
	Trilogo card	Photo: Jawa shooting left/cloth cape
Sand People	SW 12-back	solid cheek tubes
	other SW card	solid cheek tubes
	ESB card	solid cheek tubes

CHARACTER	CARD TYPE	CARD PHOTO VARIATION/FIGURE VARIATION
Tusken Raider (Sand People)	ROTJ card	solid or hollow cheek tubes
Tusken Raider (Sand People) (Homme des Sables)	Trilogo card	solid or hollow cheek tubes
Death Squad Commander	SW 12-back	
	other SW card	
	ESB card	
Star Destroyer Commander	ESB card	
	ROTJ card	
Luke Skywalker: X-wing Pilot	SW card	
Luke Skywalker (X-wing Pilot)	ESB card	
Luke Skywalker (X-wing Fighter Pilot)	ROTJ card	
	POTF card	
	Trilogo card	
Greedo	SW card	
	ESB card	
	ROTJ card	
	Trilogo card	(note: card front is not trilogo but card back is)
Hammerhead	SW card	
	ESB card	
	ROTJ card	
	Trilogo card	(note: card front is not trilogo but card back is)
Snaggletooth	SW card	red/short
	ESB card	red/short
	ROTJ card	red/short
	Trilogo card	(note: card front is not trilogo but card back is) red/short
Walrusman	SW card	
	ESB card	
	ROTJ card	
	Trilogo card	(note: card front is not trilogo but card back is)
Power Droid	SW card	
	ESB card	
	ROTJ card	
Death Star Droid	SW card	
	ESB card	
	ROTJ card	
	Trilogo card	
R5-D4	SW card	
	ESB card	
Arfive-Defour (R5-D4)	ROTJ card	
	Trilogo card	
Boba Fett	white mailer box with Kenner paper insert	
	SW card	Photo: painting of Fett shooting flame thrower
	ESB card	Photo: painting of Fett shooting flame thrower
	ROTJ card	Photo: painting of Fett shooting flame thrower
	ROTJ card	Photo: Fett against blue sky background
	Trilogo card	Photo: Fett against blue sky background/figure made of light blue plastic
Leia Organa (Bespin Gown)	ESB card	Photo: 3/4 angle/turtle neck or crew neck dress
	ESB card	Photo: front/turtle neck or crew neck dress
Princess Leia Organa (Bespin Gown)	ROTJ card	Photo: front/turtle neck or crew neck dress
	Trilogo card	Photo: front/turtle neck or crew neck dress
Luke Skywalker (Bespin Fatigues)	ESB card	Photo: knees up/yellow or brown hair
	ESB card	Photo: waist up holding gun in right hand/yellow or brown hair
	ROTJ card	Photo: waist up holding gun in right hand/yellow or brown hair
	Trilogo card	Photo: waist up holding gun in left hand/yellow or brown hair
Han Solo (Hoth Outfit)	ESB card	
Han Solo (Hoth Battle Gear)	ROTJ card	
	Trilogo card	
Lando Calrissian	ESB card	Photo: looking right/teeth not painted
	ESB card	Photo: looking right/teeth painted
	ROTJ card	Photo: looking right/teeth painted
	Trilogo card	Photo: looking left/teeth painted

ORIGINAL *STAR WARS* LINE (1978–85)

CHARACTER	CARD TYPE	CARD PHOTO VARIATION/FIGURE VARIATION
Imperial Stormtrooper (Hoth Battle Gear)	ESB card ROTJ card Trilogo card	
Rebel Soldier (Hoth Battle Gear)	ESB card ROTJ card Trilogo card	
Bespin Security Guard	ESB card ROTJ card	white guard - short or long mustache white guard - short or long mustache
Bossk (Bounty Hunter)	white mailer box ESB card ROTJ card Trilogo card	gun may have silver accents
FX-7 Medical Droid FX-7 (Medical Droid) FX-7	ESB card ESB card ESB card ROTJ card Trilogo card	Photo: reversed
IG-88 (Bounty Hunter) IG-88	ESB card ROTJ card Trilogo card	gray or silver figure silver figure Photo: background is matted out/silver figure
Yoda Yoda, The Jedi Master	ESB card ESB card ESB card ROTJ card ROTJ card POTF card Trilogo card	Photo: sitting/light green skin, orange snake Photo: sitting/dark green skin, orange snake Photo: sitting/dark green skin, brown snake Photo: sitting/dark green skin, brown snake Photo: standing/dark green skin, brown snake Photo: standing/dark green skin, brown snake Photo: standing/dark green skin, brown snake
2-1B Two-Onebee (2-1B)	ESB card ROTJ card Trilogo card	
Ugnaught	ESB card ROTJ card Trilogo card	blue smock purple smock purple smock
Dengar	ESB card ROTJ card Trilogo card	
Lobot	ESB card ROTJ card Trilogo card	Photo: standing w/ stormtroopers Photo: standing w/ stormtroopers Photo: standing w/ Bespin guards
Han Solo (Bespin Outfit)	ESB card ROTJ card Trilogo card	
Leia (Hoth Outfit) Princess Leia Organa (Hoth Outfit)	ESB card ROTJ card Trilogo card	Photo: standing in doorway Photo: standing in doorway Photo: standing w/ hands on hips
Imperial Commander	ESB card ROTJ card Trilogo card	
AT-AT Driver AT-AT Driver (Conducteur du AT-AT)	ESB card ROTJ card POTF card Trilogo card	
Rebel Commander	ESB card ROTJ card Trilogo card	
Bespin Security Guard	ESB card ROTJ card Trilogo card	black guard black guard black guard

CHARACTER	CARD TYPE	CARD PHOTO VARIATION/FIGURE VARIATION
Luke (Hoth Battle Gear)	ESB card ROTJ card Trilogo card	
AT-AT Commander	ESB card ROTJ card Trilogo card	
Artoo-Detoo (R2-D2) Artoo-Detoo (R2-D2) (with sensorscope)	ESB card ESB card ROTJ card Trilogo card	has sensorscope although card doesn't say so
C-3PO (Removable limbs) See-Threepio (C-3PO) (with removable limbs) See-Threepio (C-3PO) See-Threepio (C-3PO) with removable limbs	ESB card ESB card ROTJ card POTF card Trilogo card	limbs are removable although card doesn't note it
(Twin Pod) Cloud Car Pilot Cloud Car Pilot	ESB card ESB card ROTJ card Trilogo card	
Imperial TIE Fighter Pilot	ESB card ROTJ card Trilogo card	Photo: 2 TIEs chasing Falcon Photo: 2 TIEs chasing Falcon Photo: 2 TIEs (no Falcon in photo)
Zuckuss	ESB card ROTJ card Trilogo card	
4-LOM	white mailer box ESB card ROTJ card	
Admiral Ackbar	white mailer box ROTJ card Trilogo card	
Luke Skywalker (Jedi Knight Outfit)	ROTJ card ROTJ card POTF card Trilogo card	blue lightsaber/snap or sewn cape closure green lightsaber/snap or sewn cape closure green lightsaber/snap or sewn cape closure green lightsaber/cape may be packaged on or off figure
Emperor's Royal Guard Emperor's Royal Guard (Garde Royal de L'Empereur)	ROTJ card Trilogo card	
Biker Scout	ROTJ card POTF card Trilogo card	short or long mouthpiece short mouthpiece short mouthpiece
Squid Head	ROTJ card Trilogo card	
Bib Fortuna	ROTJ card Trilogo card	
Princess Leia Organa (Boushh Disguise) Boushh	ROTJ card Trilogo card	
Nien Nunb	white mailer box ROTJ card Trilogo card	
Ree-Yees	ROTJ card Trilogo card	
Lando Calrissian (Skiff Guard Disguise)	ROTJ card Trilogo card	
Chief Chirpa	ROTJ card Trilogo card	
Klaatu	ROTJ card Trilogo card	tan or gray legs tan or gray legs

ORIGINAL *STAR WARS* LINE (1978–85)

CHARACTER	CARD TYPE	CARD PHOTO VARIATION/FIGURE VARIATION
Rebel Commando	ROTJ card Trilogo card	Photo: colors retouched
Gamorrean Guard	ROTJ card POTF card Trilogo card	silver or dark armor silver or dark armor silver or dark armor
Logray (Ewok Medicine Man)	ROTJ card Trilogo card	
General Madine	ROTJ card	gray or olive hair
Weequay	ROTJ card Trilogo card	
Klaatu (In Skiff Guard Outfit) Klaatu (Skiff Guard Outfit)	ROTJ card Trilogo card	
Nikto	ROTJ card POTF card Trilogo card	
8D8	ROTJ card Trilogo card	
Prune Face	ROTJ card Trilogo card	
AT-ST Driver	ROTJ card POTF card Trilogo card	Photo: full-size AT-ST Photo: full-size AT-ST Photo: model AT-ST
B-wing Pilot	ROTJ card POTF card Trilogo card	
Teebo	ROTJ card POTF card Trilogo card	
Wicket W. Warrick	ROTJ card POTF card Trilogo card	Spear packaged on left or right side of bubble Spear packaged on left side of bubble
Rancor Keeper Rancor Keeper (Gardien du Rancor Monster)	ROTJ card Trilogo card	
The Emperor	ROTJ card POTF card Trilogo card	
Han (In Trench Coat)	ROTJ card POTF card Trilogo card	w/ camo or gray collar w/ camo or gray collar w/ camo or gray collar
Princess Leia Organa (In Combat Poncho)	ROTJ card POTF card Trilogo card	
Paploo Paploo (Action Figure)	ROTJ card POTF card Trilogo card	
Lumat Lumat Ewok Warrior (Figurine Guerriere Ewok)	ROTJ card POTF card Trilogo card	
Anakin Skywalker **Anakin Skywalker Anakin Skywalker	white mailer box POTF card Trilogo card	
Amanaman	POTF card Trilogo card	
Barada	POTF card Trilogo card	

CHARACTER	CARD TYPE	CARD PHOTO VARIATION/FIGURE VARIATION
EV-9D9	POTF card Trilogo card	
A-wing Pilot	POTF card Trilogo card	Photo: reversed
Luke Skywalker (In Battle Poncho)	POTF card Trilogo card	
Imperial Gunner	POTF card Trilogo card	
Luke Skywalker (Imperial Stormtrooper Outfit) Luke Skywalker (Imperial Stormtrooper Outfit) Jenue de Soldat Imperial	POTF card Trilogo card	Photo: looking right Photo: looking left
Lando Calrissian (General Pilot)	POTF card Trilogo card	
Romba	POTF card Trilogo card	Photo: different Ewok than photo on POTF card
Imperial Dignitary Imperial Dignitary (Dignitaire Imperial)	POTF card Trilogo card	
Warok	POTF card Trilogo card	
Han Solo (In Carbonite Chamber) Han Solo (Emmuré)	POTF card Trilogo card	figure packaged under carbonite figure packaged on top of carbonite
Artoo-Detoo (R2-D2) with pop-up Lightsaber Artoo-Detoo (R2-D2) with pop-up Lightsaber (avec Sabre Laser)	POTF card Trilogo card	Photo: reversed
**Yak Face Yak Face	POTF card Trilogo card	

FIGURE MULTIPACKS

Early Bird 4 figure mail-in set
(Luke, Leia, Chewbacca, R2) in plastic tray in white mailer box

Star Wars Action Figure 3-packs

Android Set *(C-3PO, R2-D2, Chewbacca)*
Villain Set *(Stormtrooper, Vader, Death Squad Commander)*
Hero Set *(Han, Leia, Ben)*
Creature Set *(Hammerhead, Walrus Man, Greedo)*
Droid Set *(R5-D4, Death Star Droid, Power Droid)*
Hero Set *(Luke X-wing, Ben, Han)*
Villain Set *(Sand People, Boba Fett, Snaggletooth)*
Creature Set *(Hammerhead, Walrusman, Greedo)*

The Empire Strikes Back Action Figure 3-packs

Hoth Rebels *(Han Hoth, Rebel Soldier, FX-7)*
Bespin Alliance *(Bespin Security Guard [white], Lando, Luke Bespin)*
Imperial Forces *(Bossk, Snowtrooper, IG-88)*
Rebel Set *(2-1B, Leia Hoth, Rebel Commander)*
Bespin Set *(Han Bespin, Ugnaught, Lobot)*
Imperial Set *(Imperial Commander, Dengar, AT-AT Driver)*
Rebel Set *(Leia Hoth, R2-D2 w/sensorscope, Luke Hoth)*
Bespin Set *(C-3PO w/removable limbs, Ugnaught, Cloud Car Pilot)*
Imperial Set *(Zuckuss, AT-AT Driver, TIE Pilot)*

The Empire Strikes Back Boxed Multipacks

Darth Vader, Stormtrooper (Hoth Battle Gear), AT-AT Driver, Rebel Soldier (Hoth Battle Gear), IG-88, Yoda
Rebel Soldier (Hoth Battle Gear), C-3PO, R2-D2, Han Solo (Hoth Battle Gear), Darth Vader, Stormtrooper (Hoth Battle Gear)

Return of the Jedi Multipacks

Sy Snootles and the Rebo Band	ROTJ box	
Sy Snootles and the Rebo Band	Trilogo box	
Action figure 2-packs	ROTJ card	(2 figures randomly packed on generic ROTJ card)

ORIGINAL *STAR WARS* LINE (1978–85)

Playsets with Action Figures (All Sears Exclusives)

Cantina Adventure Set (Snaggletooth, Walrusman, Hammerhead, Greedo)	boxed
Cloud City Playset (Han Bespin, Lobot, Dengar, Ugnaught)	boxed
Rebel Command Center (Luke Hoth, AT-AT Commander, R2-D2 w/ sensorscope)	boxed
Jabba the Hutt Dungeon (Klaatu Skiff Guard, Nikto, 8D8)	boxed
Jabba the Hutt Dungeon (Amanaman, Barada, EV-9D9)	boxed

Vehicles or Playsets with Special Offer Figures Enclosed

Landspeeder w/ Luke Skywalker and C-3PO
TIE Fighter (SW box) w/ Darth Vader and Stormtrooper
X-wing Fighter (SW box) w/ Luke Skywalker and Han Solo
Millennium Falcon (SW box) w/ Han Solo and Chewbacca
Hoth Ice Planet Adventure Set w/ Imperial Stormtrooper (Hoth Battle Gear)
Twin Pod Cloud Card w/ Bespin Guard (white)
Rebel Armored Snowspeeder w/ Rebel Soldier (Hoth Battle Gear)
MTV-7 minirig w/ AT-AT Driver
MLC-3 minirig w/ Rebel Commander
PDT-8 minirig w/ 2-1B
CAP-2 minirig w/ Bossk
INT-4 minirig w/ AT-AT Commander
Darth Vader Collectors Case w/ Boba Fett, IG-88, and Bossk
Darth Vader Collectors Case w/ Yoda, Darth Vader, and Luke Skywalker (Bespin Fatigues)

Droids Action Figures

Artoo Detoo R2-D2	Droids card	
See-Threepio C-3PO	Droids card	w/ Droids coin
See-Threepio C-3PO	Droids card	w/ Protocol Droid coin
Thall Joben	Droids card	
Jord Dusat	Droids card	
Kea Moll	Droids card	
Tig Fromm	Droids card	
Sise Fromm	Droids card	
Uncle Gundy	Droids card	
Kez-Iban	Droids card	
Jann Tosh	Droids card	
Boba Fett	Droids card	
A-wing Pilot	Droids card	
**Vlix	Droids Glasslite card	(released only in Brazil)

Ewoks Action Figures

King Gorneesh	Ewoks card
Lady Urgah Gorneesh	Ewoks card
Dulok Shaman	Ewoks card
Dulok Scout	Ewoks card
Wicket W. Warrick	Ewoks card
Logray Ewok Medicine Man	Ewoks card

POWER OF THE FORCE SERIES 2 (1995–98)

CHARACTER	CARD VARIATION	MISC. VARIATION
Luke Skywalker	.00 (orange)	long saber
	.00 (orange)	short saber/short saber tray
Darth Vader	.00 (orange)	long saber
	.00 (orange)	short saber/long saber tray
	.00 (orange)	short saber/short saber tray
	.01 (green w/ or w/out foil sticker)	
	.02 (green w/ or w/out foil sticker)	
	.02 (green w/ or w/out foil sticker)	sculpt from SOTE 2-pack
	.03 (freeze frame)	
C-3PO	.00 (orange)	
	.01 (green w/ or w/out foil sticker)	
R2-D2	.00 (orange)	
	.01 (green w/ or w/out foil sticker)	
Stormtrooper	.00 (orange)	
	.00 (orange w/ foil sticker)	
	.01 (green w/ or w/out foil sticker)	
	.02 (freeze frame)	
Ben (Obi-Wan) Kenobi	.00 (orange)	long saber
	.01 (orange)	long saber
	.01 (orange)	short saber/short saber tray

CHARACTER	CARD VARIATION	MISC. VARIATION
Ben (Obi-Wan) Kenobi	.01 (orange w/ foil sticker)	
	.02 (green w/ or w/out foil sticker)	
	.03 (freeze frame)	
	.04 (freeze frame)	
Han Solo	.00 (orange)	
	.01 (green w/ or w/out foil sticker)	
	.02 (freeze frame)	
Chewbacca	.00 (orange)	
	.01 (green w/ or w/out foil sticker)	
Princess Leia Organa	.00 (orange)	three stripes on belt
	.00 (orange)	two stripes on belt
	.00 (orange w/ foil sticker)	two stripes on belt
	.01 (green w/ or w/out foil sticker)	two stripes on belt
Luke in X-wing Fighter Pilot Gear	.00 (orange)	long saber
	.00 (orange)	short saber/long tray
	.01 (orange)	long saber
	.01 (orange)	short saber/long tray
	.01 (orange)	short saber/short tray
	.02 (green w/ or w/out foil sticker)	
Boba Fett	.00 (orange)	half circles on hands
	.00 (orange)	half circles on hands
	.01 (orange)	half circles on hands
	.01 (orange)	full circles on hands
	.02 (green w/ or w/out foil sticker)	full circles on hands
	.03 (green w/ or w/out foil sticker)	full circles on hands
	.04 (freeze frame)	full circles on hands
Lando Calrissian	.00 (orange)	
	.01 (green w/ or w/out foil sticker)	available from club stores ESB 3-pack
TIE Fighter Pilot	.00 (orange)	
	.01 (orange)	
	.02 (orange)	
	.03 (green w/ or w/out foil sticker)	
	.04 (green w/ or w/out foil sticker)	
	.05 (freeze frame)	
Yoda	.00 (orange)	
	.00 (orange w/ foil sticker)	
	.01 (orange)	
	.02 (green w/ or w/out foil sticker)	
	.03 (green w/ or w/out foil sticker)	
Han Solo in Hoth Gear	.00 (orange)	open right hand
	.00 (orange)	closed right hand
Luke Skywalker in Dagobah Fatigues	.00 (orange)	long saber
	.00 (orange)	short saber/long tray
	.00 (orange)	short saber/short tray
Dash Rendar	.00 (SOTE)	
Chewbacca in Bounty Hunter Disguise	.00 (SOTE)	
Luke Skywalker in Imperial Guard Disguise	.00 (SOTE)	
Prince Xizor	.00 (SOTE)	
Leia in Boushh Disguise	.00 (SOTE)	
	.01 (SOTE)	
	.02 (green card)	
Jedi Knight Luke Skywalker	.00 (orange)	tan vest/in or out saber handle
	.00 (orange)	dark vest/in or out saber handle
	.00 (green theater edition)	dark vest/out saber handle
	.01 (green w/ or w/out foil sticker)	dark vest/out saber handle
	.02 (green w/ or w/out foil sticker)	dark vest/out saber handle
Han Solo (Carbonite)	.00 (orange)	
	.01 (orange)	
	.02 (green w/ or w/out foil sticker)	
	.03 (green w/ or w/out foil sticker)	
	.04 (freeze frame)	
	.05 (freeze frame)	

POWER OF THE FORCE SERIES 2 (1995–98)

CHARACTER	CARD VARIATION	MISC. VARIATION
Sandtrooper	.oo (orange) .o1 (green w/ or w/out foil sticker) .o2 (green w/ or w/out foil sticker) .o3 (freeze frame)	
Greedo	.oo (orange) .o1 (green w/ or w/out foil sticker)	
Death Star Gunner	.oo (orange) .o1 (green w/ or w/out foil sticker) .o2 (green w/ or w/out foil sticker)	
R5-D4	.oo (orange w/ and w/out warning sticker) .oo (orange w/ and w/out warning sticker) .o1 (green w/ or w/out foil or warning sticker) .o1 (green w/ or w/out foil or warning sticker)	straight button launcher L-shaped button launcher straight button launcher L-shaped button launcher
Tusken Raider	.oo (orange) .oo (orange) .o1 (green w/ or w/out foil sticker) .o1 (green w/ or w/out foil sticker)	closed left hand open left hand closed left hand open left hand
Luke Skywalker in Stormtrooper Disguise	.oo (orange) .o1 (green w/ or w/out foil sticker) .o2 (green w/ or w/out foil sticker) .o3 (freeze frame) .o4 (freeze frame)	
Jawas	.oo (orange) .o1 (green w/ or w/out foil sticker) .o2 (green w/ or w/out foil sticker)	
Momaw Nadon "Hammerhead"	.oo (orange) .o1 (green w/ or w/out foil sticker)	
Bossk	.oo (green w/ or w/out foil sticker) .o1 (green w/ or w/out foil sticker)	
2-1B Medic Droid	.oo (green w/ or w/out foil sticker) .o1 (green w/ or w/out foil sticker)	
Luke Skywalker in Hoth Gear	.oo (green w/ or w/out foil sticker) .o1 (green w/ or w/out foil sticker)	
Hoth Rebel Soldier	.oo (green w/ or w/out foil sticker) .o1 (green w/ or w/out foil sticker) .o2 (freeze frame) .o3 (freeze frame)	
AT-ST Driver	.oo (green w/ or w/out foil sticker) .o1 (green w/ or w/out foil sticker) .o2 (green w/ or w/out foil sticker) .o3 (freeze frame)	
Han Solo in Endor Gear	.oo (green w/ or w/out foil sticker) .oo (green w/ or w/out foil sticker) .o1 (freeze frame) .o2 (freeze frame)	blue pants brown pants brown pants brown pants
Lando Calrissian as Skiff Guard	.oo (green w/ or w/out foil sticker) .o1 (freeze frame) .o2 (freeze frame)	
Emperor Palpatine	.oo (green w/ or w/out foil sticker) .o1 (green w/ or w/out foil sticker) .o2 (freeze frame)	
Bib Fortuna	.oo (green w/ or w/out foil sticker) .o1 (green w/ or w/out foil sticker)	
Rebel Fleet Trooper	.oo (green w/ or w/out foil sticker) .o1 (green w/ or w/out foil sticker) .o2 under .o1 sticker (freeze frame) .o2 (freeze frame)	
Grand Moff Tarkin	.oo (green w/ or w/out foil sticker) .o1 (green w/ or w/out foil sticker) .o2 (freeze frame)	
Weequay Skiff Guard	.oo (green w/ or w/out foil sticker) .o1 (green w/ or w/out foil sticker) .o2 (freeze frame)	
ASP-7 Droid	.oo (green w/ or w/out foil sticker)	
Dengar	.oo (green w/ or w/out foil sticker)	
4-LOM	.oo (green w/ or w/out foil sticker)	
Admiral Ackbar	.oo (green w/ or w/out foil sticker) .o1 (freeze frame)	
Ponda Baba	.oo (green w/ or w/out foil sticker) .o1 (green w/ or w/out foil sticker)	
Garindan Long Snoot	.oo (green w/ or w/out foil sticker) .o1 (freeze frame)	
Princess Leia Organa as Jabba's Prisoner	.oo (green w/ or w/out foil sticker) .o1 (freeze frame) .o2 (freeze frame)	
Han Solo in Bespin Gear	.oo (green w/ or w/out foil sticker) .o1 (freeze frame) .o2 (freeze frame)	
Emperor's Royal Guard	.oo (green w/ or w/out foil sticker) .o1 (freeze frame)	
Snowtrooper	.oo (green w/ or w/out foil sticker) .o1 (freeze frame)	
Nien Nunb	.oo (green w/ or w/out foil sticker) .o1 (freeze frame)	
Saelt-Marae (Yak Face)	.oo (green w/ or w/out foil sticker) .o1 (freeze frame)	
EV-9D9 Droid	.oo (green w/ or w/out foil sticker) .o1 (freeze frame)	
Gamorrean Guard	.oo (green w/ or w/out foil sticker) .o1 (freeze frame)	
Malakili (Rancor Keeper)	.oo (green w/ or w/out foil sticker) .o1 (freeze frame)	
Luke Skywalker in Ceremonial Outfit	.oo (green w/ or w/out foil sticker) .o1 (green w/ or w/out foil sticker) .o1 (freeze frame)	
Princess Leia Organa in Ewok Celebration Outfit	.oo (freeze frame) .o1 (freeze frame)	
Bespin Luke Skywalker	.oo (freeze frame) .o1 (freeze frame)	
Endor Rebel Soldier	.oo (freeze frame) .o1 (freeze frame)	
Lando Calrissian in General's Gear	.oo (freeze frame) .o1 (freeze frame)	
Biggs Darklighter	.oo (freeze frame)	
Lak Sivrak	.oo (freeze frame)	
Ewoks: Wicket and Logray	.oo (freeze frame)	
Darth Vader with Removable Helmet	.oo (freeze frame)	
Captain Piett	.oo (freeze frame)	
Ishi Tib	.oo (freeze frame)	

CHARACTER	CARD TYPE	MISC. VARIATION

POWER OF THE FORCE SERIES 2 (1995–98)

CHARACTER	CARD TYPE	MISC. VARIATION
Zuckuss	.oo (freeze frame)	
Princess Leia Organa All New Likeness!	.oo (freeze frame)	
R2-D2 with Datalink and Periscope	.oo (freeze frame)	
C-3PO with Removable Limbs	.oo (freeze frame)	
Luke Skywalker with Blast Shield Helmet	.oo (freeze frame)	
Ugnaughts	.oo (freeze frame)	
8D8 Droid	.oo (freeze frame)	
Death Star Trooper	.oo (freeze frame)	
Ree-Yees	.oo (freeze frame)	
Lobot	.oo (freeze frame)	
Chewbacca as Boushh's Bounty	.oo (freeze frame)	
Orrimaarko (Prune Face)	.oo (freeze frame)	
Mon Mothma	.oo (freeze frame)	
Luke Skywalker (From *Dark Empire* Comic Book Series)	.oo–.02 (Expanded Universe fold out card)	
Imperial Sentinel (From *Dark Empire* Comic Book Series)	.oo–.02 (Expanded Universe fold out card)	
Grand Admiral Thrawn (From the *Heir to the Empire* Trilogy Novels)	.oo–.02 (Expanded Universe fold out card)	
Leia Organa Solo (From *Dark Empire* Comic Book Series)	.oo–.03 (Expanded Universe fold out card)	
Clone Emperor (From *Dark Empire* Comic Book Series)	.oo–.02 (Expanded Universe fold out card)	
Mara Jade (From the *Heir to the Empire* Trilogy Novels)	carded (Expanded Universe fold out card)	
Kyle Katarn (From the *Dark Forces* Video Game)	carded (Expanded Universe fold out card)	
Death Star Droid with Mouse Droid	.oo (freeze frame)	
Pote Snitkin	.oo (freeze frame)	
AT-AT Driver	.oo (freeze frame)	
Princess Leia in Hoth Gear	.oo (freeze frame)	
Spacetrooper (From the *Heir to the Empire* Trilogy Novels)	(Expanded Universe fold out card)	
Darktrooper (From the *Dark Forces* Video Game)	(Expanded Universe fold out card)	

CHARACTER	CARD TYPE
FIGURE MULTIPACKS	
Classic Edition 4-pack (Toys "Я" Us)	boxed
3-pack 1 (Sam's Club [*Luke, Ben, Vader*]) 3-pack 2 (Sam's Club [*Lando, Chewie, Han*]) 3-pack 3 (Sam's Club [*R2-D2, Stormtrooper, C-3PO*])	
Star Wars 3-pack (Club stores [*Luke Stormtrooper, Tusken Raider, Ben*]) The Empire Strikes Back 3-pack (Club stores [*Lando, Luke Dagobah, TIE Pilot*]) Return of the Jedi 3-pack (Club stores [*Luke Jedi, AT-ST Driver, Leia Boushh*])	
Boba Fett vs. IG-88	.oo .01
Darth Vader vs. Prince Xizor	.oo .01
Death Star Escape 3-pack (Han and Luke in Stormtrooper Disguises, Chewbacca)	.oo .01
Cantina Showdown 3-pack (Dr. Evazan, Ponda Baba, Ben Kenobi)	.oo .01
Final Jedi Duel 3-pack (Emperor, Vader, Luke)	.oo .01
Purchase of the Droids 3-pack (Uncle Owen, Luke, C-3PO)	.oo .01
Jabba the Hutt's Dancers (Rystáll, Greeata, Lyn Me)	.oo
Mynock Hunt (Han, Leia, Chewbacca)	.oo
Max Rebo Band Pairs (Wal-Mart) Droopy McCool and Barquin D'an	.oo .01
Sy Snootles and Joh Yowzah	.oo .01
Max Rebo and Doda Bodonawieedo	.oo
Deluxe Figures	
Deluxe Crowd Control Stormtrooper	.oo .01
Deluxe Luke Skywalker's Desert Sport Skiff	.oo
Deluxe Han Solo with Smuggler Flight Pack	.oo
Deluxe Boba Fett	.oo .01
Deluxe Probe Droid	.oo .01 .02
Deluxe Snowtrooper	.oo
Deluxe Hoth Rebel Soldier	.oo
Electronic Power F/X Figures	
Electronic Power F/X R2-D2	.oo .01 .02
Electronic Power F/X Darth Vader	.oo
Electronic Power F/X Ben (Obi-Wan) Kenobi	.oo
Electronic Power F/X Emperor Palpatine	.oo .01
Electronic Power F/X Luke Skywalker	.oo

POWER OF THE FORCE SERIES 2 (1995–98)

Beast Collections

Ronto and Jawa	.00
Dewback and Sandtrooper	.00
	.01
Jabba the Hutt and Han Solo	.00
	.01
	.02
Luke Skywalker and Tauntaun	.00
Wampa and Luke Skywalker	.00
Rancor and Luke Skywalker	.00
Bantha and Tusken Raider	.00
Han Solo and Tauntaun	.00

Princess Leia Collection

Princess Leia and Luke Skywalker	.00
	.01
Princess Leia and Han Solo	.00
	.01
Princess Leia and Wicket the Ewok	.00
	.01
Princess Leia and R2-D2	.00
	.01

Millennium Minted Coin Collection

Bespin Han Solo	.00 (w/ or w/out MMC on card)
Chewbacca	.00 (w/ or w/out MMC on card)
Snowtrooper	.00 (w/ or w/out MMC on card)
Luke Skywalker in Endor Gear	.00
Princess Leia in Endor Gear	.00
Emperor Palpatine	.00
C-3PO	.00

Gunner Stations

Millennium Falcon with Luke Skywalker	.00
	.01
Millennium Falcon with Han Solo	.00
	.01
TIE Fighter with Darth Vader	.00

Complete Galaxy

Death Star with Darth Vader	.00
Dagobah with Yoda and Flying Predator	.00
Tatooine with Luke Skywalker	.00
Endor with Ewok	.00

Vehicles or Accessories Packaged with Action Figures

Imperial Speeder Bike with Biker Scout	boxed
Swoop Vehicle with Swooptrooper	boxed
Speeder Bike with Luke Skywalker in Endor Gear	.00
	.01
Speeder Bike with Leia in Endor Gear	.00
	.01
A-wing with Pilot	.00
Millennium Falcon Carry Case with Wedge Antilles	boxed
Millennium Falcon Carry Case with Imperial Scanning Crew Trooper	boxed
Electronic Imperial AT-AT Walker with AT-AT Driver and AT-AT Commander	.00
	.01
Airspeeder with Airspeeder Pilot	.00
Cloud Car with Cloud Car Pilot	.00
Speeder Bike with Rebel Speeder Bike Pilot	.00
	.01
Intergalactic Battle Game with Luke Skywalker in Trash Compactor and Darth Vader with Removable Dome	boxed
Interactive PC Playset with Han Solo	boxed

Promotional Action Figures

Han Solo in Stormtrooper Disguise (Kellogg's Froot Loops premium)
Spirit of Obi-Wan Kenobi (Frito-Lay premium)
Cantina Band Member (*Star Wars Insider* exclusive)
B'omarr Monk (Internet/Redemption coupon included w/ select Spirit of Kenobi figures)
Oola with Salacious Crumb (*Star Wars Insider* exclusive)

NOTE: ** Vlix and POTF carded versions of Yak Face and Anakin Skywalker were not available in the U.S.

ACKNOWLEDGMENTS

Original Text
EIMEI TAKEDA
SEIJI TAKAHASHI
STEPHEN J. SANSWEET
JOSH LING

Photographers
YOSHIHIRO HATTORI
AKI KUSUDOH
MITSUAKI MORISHITA
STEVE ESSIG

For Lucasfilm
LUCY AUTREY WILSON
LOUISE RILEY
ALLAN KAUSCH
TINA MILLS
CARA EVANGELISTA
HALINA KRUKOWSKI

Supercollectors
GUS LOPEZ
CHRIS GEORGOULIAS